IEG WORLD BANK IFC MIGA
INDEPENDENT EVALUATION GROUP

Poverty Reduction Support Credits

An Evaluation of World Bank Support

2010
The World Bank
Washington, D.C.

1818 H Street, N.W.
Washington, D.C. 20433
Telephone: 202-473-1000
Internet: www.worldbank.org
E-mail: feedback@worldbank.org

1 2 3 4 13 12 11 10

Cover: Landscape at the beginning of a rice harvest; northern Vietnam. Photo by Tran Thi Hoa, courtesy of the World Bank Photo Library.

ISBN-13: 978-0-8213-8305-6
e-ISBN-13: 978-0-8213-8306-3
DOI: 10.1596/978-0-8213-8305-6

Library of Congress Cataloging-in-Publication Data have been applied for.

World Bank InfoShop
E-mail: pic@worldbank.org
Telephone: 202-458-5454
Facsimile: 202-522-1500

Independent Evaluation Group
Communications, Learning, and Strategy
E-mail: ieg@worldbank.org
Telephone: 202-458-4497
Facsimile: 202-522-3125

Printed on Recycled Paper

Contents

Figures

Tables

Abbreviations

ALCID	Adjustment Lending Conditionality and Implementation Database
CAS	Country Assistance Strategy
CFAA	Country Financial Accountability Assessment
CPAR	Country Procurement Assessment Report
CPIA	Country Policy and Institutional Assessment
DAC	Development Assistance Committee (OECD)
DPL	Development Policy Loan
DPO	Development Policy Operation
EU	European Union
FY	Fiscal year
GBS	General budget support
GDP	Gross domestic product
HIPC	Heavily Indebted Poor Country (Inititative)
HIPC AAP	Heavily Indebted Poor Country (Initiative) Assessment and Action Plan
HIV/AIDS	Human immunodeficiency virus/acquired immunodeficiency syndrome
IBRD	International Bank for Reconstruction and Development
ICR	Implementation Completion Report
IDA	International Development Association
IEG	Independent Evaluation Group
IMF	International Monetary Fund
M&E	Monitoring and evaluation
MDBS	Multi-donor budget support
OECD	Organization for Economic Co-operation and Development
PAF	Performance Assessment Framework
PEFA	Public Expenditure Financial Assessment
PFMP	Public financial management and procurement
PRS	Poverty Reduction Strategy
PRSC	Poverty Reduction Support Credit
PRSO	Poverty Reduction Support Operation
PRSP	Poverty Reduction Strategy Paper
TTL	Task team leader

Young African children. Photo by Curt Carnemark, courtesy of the World Bank Photo Library.

Acknowledgments

This report was conducted under the overall direction of Vinod Thomas, Cheryl Gray, and Mark Sundberg. Victoria Elliot, former manager of IEGCG, led the initiation of the report. The evaluation reflects contributions from a team of IEG staff and consultants who collected data in the field and undertook desk reviews, interviews, research, and analysis. Anjali Kumar, task manager of the evaluation, extends particular appreciation to Monika Huppi, who led the preparation of its Concept Note and many areas of the evaluative framework, and also to Andrew Waxman, who supported all areas of analysis.

The seven PRSC country case studies undertaken for the report were prepared by: Roger Grawe (Vietnam and Lao People's Democratic Republic), Arna Hartmann and Basil Kavalsky (Ghana), Norman Hicks (Armenia), Manuel Hinds (Nicaragua), and Brendan Horton (Benin and Mozambique), together with local consultants Mushegh Tumasyn in Armenia, Tran Thi Hanh in Vietnam, and Phongsavanh Phomkong and Saysanith Vongviengkham in Lao PDR. The team would like to thank all Bank field office staff, country managers, and country directors who facilitated country visits and took the time to talk to IEG during the field-based country case studies. The team would also like to thank the several officials and individuals in PRSC client countries, who agreed to meet with the IEG team, for their time and their perspectives.

Shalini Ahuja provided assistance on the approach paper, and Nara C. Meli provided research support on conditionality analysis. Andrew Waxman and Clay Westcott undertook the analysis of the role of public financial management and procurement in PRSCs, and Toneema Haq undertook a detailed review of PRSC outcomes in health and education services and water supply and sanitation, with inputs from Michael Lav. Norman Hicks provided further inputs to the analysis of growth and poverty outcomes under PRSCs, and Brendan Horton prepared sections on PRSC design and process. Anna Aghumian undertook PRSC portfolio reviews in several areas, including notably, the analysis of results frameworks and PRSC triggers. Brett Libresco contributed notably to the analysis of PRSC design and to staff surveys. Domenico Lombardi, Cheikh M'Backe Fall, and Mahin Tabrizian implemented the client surveys. Translation support for surveys was provided by Adelaide Barbey and Haydee Garraffo. Jesse Torrence supported the completion of the report, and together with Lisa Block, edited case study materials. The evaluation team greatly appreciates the thoughtful insights from many PRSC task team leaders as well as PRSC team members inside the Bank.

The team acknowledges, in particular, helpful discussions with Antonella Bassani, Rodrigo Chavez, Shantayan Devarajan, Manuela Ferro, Bernard Funck, Alan Gelb, Jaime Jaramillo-Vallejo, Orsalia Kalantsopoulos, Stefan Koeberle, Kathie Krumm, Homi Kharas, and Jan Walliser on the use of the PRSC. Valuable discussions were also held with Simon Mizrahi and Yasmin Ahmad at the OECD, Nick York at DfID, and Karen Christiansen, Stephen Lister, and Andrew Lawson, on aid flows and budget support. The team is also grateful for discussions with the European Commission's evaluation office on budget support, especially Catherine Pravin.

Valuable inputs were provided by peer reviewers Alan Gelb and David Goldsbrough, together with Stefan Koeberle and Jan Walliser, who also reviewed the report. Alison Evans (Overseas Development Institute), Louis Kasekende (African Development Bank), and Richard Manning (formerly of OECD–DAC) served as external expert reviewers of the final evaluation report; their extensive inputs are gratefully acknowledged. Comments on early drafts were also provided by John Eriksson and Martha Ainsworth, Hans-Martin Boehmer, Ken Chomitz, April Connelly, Ali Khadr, Nalini Kumar, J.P. Singh, Yoshine Uchimura, and Richard Worden.

Yvette Jarencio-Lukban processed the report, and William Hurlbut editorially reviewed an early version. Helen Chin edited the report for publication. Nik Harvey and Alex McKenzie provided support on making the report's materials available on the IEG website. Diana Hakobyan, Julia Ooro, and Yezena Yimer provided overall support.

The team acknowledges funding from the Swiss Development Corporation, which supported the preparation of the report, in particular the country reviews.

Vinod Thomas, Director-General, Evaluation
Cheryl Gray, Director, Independent Evaluation Group–World Bank
Mark Sundberg, Manager, Corporate and Global Evaluation Unit
Anjali Kumar, Task Manager

Foreword

This evaluation examines the relevance and effectiveness of one of the Bank's key tools to support IDA countries: the Poverty Reduction Support Credit (PRSC). Introduced in early 2001—in the context of global changes in aid architecture that recognized the importance of country ownership, government reform commitment, and multidimensional poverty reduction—PRSCs were intended to aid country-owned Poverty Reduction Strategies, support comprehensive growth, improve social conditions, and reduce poverty. Compared with previous adjustment lending, PRSCs were intended to ease conditionality, provide predictable annual support, and strengthen budget processes in results-based frameworks. Many of its principles were reflected in the Paris Declaration of Aid Effectiveness.

Within four years of their introduction, PRSCs came to account for almost 60 percent of IDA policy-based lending and a quarter of total Bank policy-based lending. During fiscal years 2001–08, the period of the present evaluation, the Bank approved 87 PRSC operations totaling US$6.6 billion. By end-September 2009, PRSC approvals increased to 99 operations, with another 20 in the pipeline.

Main Findings

- In terms of process, PRSCs worked well, serving in many respects as a prototype for Development Policy Loans (stronger country ownership, eased conditionality, more predictable resource flows, and greater emphasis on public sector management and pro-poor service delivery). PRSCs balanced tensions between predictability of financing and program credibility. They reflected commitment to aid harmonization and, in some countries, served as a donor focal point.
- PRSCs also stimulated dialogue between central and sectoral ministries in client countries, raising sector ministry accountability and complementing sector lending in budget or cross-cutting issues.
- Yet, significant issues remain. Conditionality can be further simplified and made more transparent. Extra-budgetary funds need to be curtailed as part of PRSC financial management goals. Moreover, despite attention to the Millenium Development Goals, only two-fifths of PRSC objectives in education, half in health, and less than a fifth in water supply and sanitation had an explicit pro-poor focus.

Recommendations

- The evaluation recommends further simplifying the language of conditionality, synchronizing the Bank's internal process with country and donor processes, underpinning PRSCs/Development Policy Loans (DPLs) with comprehensive pro-poor growth diagnostics, strengthening results frameworks, and limiting sector policy content in multisector policy-based loans to high-level or cross-cutting issues, complemented with parallel sector lending.

- PRSCs and other policy-based lending have converged over time toward a similar design, yet the PRSC label remains in use. Operational policies introduced in 2004 do not distinguish PRSCs from other DPLs, yet past practices linger. The evaluation recommends that PRSCs be phased out as a separate brand name—or that these differences be clearly spelled out.

Vinod Thomas
Director-General, Evaluation

Executive Summary

The goal of Poverty Reduction Support Credits (PRSCs), introduced in early 2001 under World Bank Interim Guidelines, was to help countries implement comprehensive, country-owned development strategies to promote growth, improve social conditions, and reduce poverty. PRSCs were intended to ease conditionality and to make annual flows to recipient countries predictable and integrated with their budgets. To reduce fiduciary risks associated with budget support, PRSCs were intended to strengthen domestic budget processes. They were seen as providing a framework for donor harmonization and were meant to focus on achieving clearly defined results.

In terms of process, PRSCs have worked well. Findings show that they incorporated many envisaged changes in design and implementation, including stronger country ownership, eased conditionality, and a shift of focus toward public sector management and pro-poor service delivery. PRSCs balanced tensions between predictability and program credibility. They reflected commitment to aid harmonization and in a small number of countries served as a donor focal point.

The outcomes of PRSCs are less clear. While PRSC countries have been somewhat superior performers in growth and poverty reduction, it is not possible to attribute this to the PRSC because PRSCs were generally offered to better performers and other better performers among International Development Association (IDA) countries that made comparable improvements in performance. PRSCs addressed some bottlenecks to growth but usually without a comprehensive growth strategy. Achievements in pro-poor service delivery are hard to measure due to weaknesses in results frameworks, but available data suggest, at best, modest translation of objectives into outcomes. Measurable improvement was made in some relatively straightforward areas of financial management, but it is not clear that more difficult public financial management or governance issues were tackled successfully. Moreover, as an instrument of sectoral lending, PRSCs are limited in their depth of technical dialogue, level of line ministry engagement, successful integration in the process of aid coordination, and outcomes achieved, although they have usefully raised cross-cutting issues and brought attention to sector budgets.

Although PRSCs differed from their predecessors at the time of their introduction, other policy-based lending has converged toward a similar design. Meanwhile, PRSC Interim Guidelines have been subsumed under new guidelines for Development Policy Loans (DPLs), issued in 2004. Today there are no clear criteria to distinguish PRSCs from other DPLs. Yet, in practice, differences linger from the past (such as the connection to Poverty Reduction Strategy Papers, scope, programmatic nature, and implicit country eligibility criteria). This evaluation recommends either that PRSCs be phased out as a separate brand name or that these differences be clearly spelled out.

The evaluation also recommends that the language of conditionality be simplified further, that the Bank's internal process be synchronized with country and donor processes, that PRSCs/ DPLs be underpinned by comprehensive pro-poor growth diagnostics, that results frameworks be strengthened, and that sector policy content be limited to high-level or cross-cutting issues, complemented with parallel sector lending. These lessons are particularly important in light of recent rapid growth in DPLs in response to crises.

PRSCs Today Are Regionally Concentrated

From fiscal 2001 to the first quarter of fiscal 2010 the Bank approved 99 PRSC operations totaling US$ 7.9 billion, and another 20 are in the pipeline. Within four years of their introduction, PRSCs came to account for almost 60 percent of IDA policy-based lending and a quarter of total Bank policy-based lending. The share of PRSCs in IDA disbursements to some individual countries (such as Benin, Burkina Faso, Ghana, Rwanda, and Uganda) exceeded half of total Bank disbursements. Even in those countries where the role of the PRSC was not prominent, for example, in Albania, Armenia, and Senegal, it accounted for 20–25 percent of IDA flows. Ten countries have embarked on their second or third PRSC series. Another nine countries have had a single series so far. In eight countries, PRSC operations did not mature into a programmatic series.

Africa has the largest portfolio of PRSCs among the Regions, with about half of all ongoing series, typically in the context of multidonor budget support. In the five Europe and Central Asia countries where the PRSC has been used (Albania, Armenia, Azerbaijan, Georgia, and Moldova), it has generally provided a relatively small share of country budget needs. Three PRSC countries in Europe and Central Asia have graduated from IDA or chosen other instruments. There are currently no ongoing PRSCs in South Asia or Latin America. Changes in political conditions rendered it impossible to continue with PRSCs in Nepal, Nicaragua, and Sri Lanka, and PRSCs in Guyana, Honduras, and Pakistan have also ceased. The PRSC has never been a part of the Middle East and North Africa lending portfolio.

PRSC Design Reflects Parallel Changes in Aid Architecture

Parallel trend changes in aid architecture recognized the importance of country ownership and government commitment to reform. A greater multidimensional emphasis on poverty reduction was introduced with the Millennium Development Goals, supporting pro-poor service delivery.

These changes were reflected in the World Bank's Comprehensive Development Framework in 1999, which emphasized a long-term, holistic vision of development. The Poverty Reduction Strategy (PRS) initiative was launched in tandem to put key principles of the Comprehensive Development Framework into practice. PRSCs were introduced under Interim Guidelines in 2001 to aid the operationalization of the Poverty Reduction Strategy Papers (PRSPs) and provide structural support for the International Monetary Fund's Poverty Reduction and Growth Facility. By fiscal 2005, new Bank guidelines for development policy lending reflected the same principles.

Other lenders also increased budget support aid. Alignment with country systems and harmonization among donors were central tenets of the Paris Declaration of Aid Effectiveness, which also focused on capacity building, transparency, and results based on better monitoring systems.

These changes render it more difficult to isolate the effects of the PRSC and its achievements because the character of all Bank development policy lending changed over the period of the PRSC. And for recipient countries, the PRSC paralleled increased budget support flows in a multidonor framework. Despite these issues, the analysis shows how lessons learned from the PRSC remain relevant for policy-based lending today.

Convergence in PRSCs and Other Policy-Based Lending

Convergence is evident in design—for example, eased conditionality and enhanced pro-poor focus—as well as in overall outcomes. PRSCs effectively served in many regards (for example, eased conditionality, sectoral focus, programmatic nature) as a prototype for DPLs introduced since September 2004, and the PRSC Interim Guidelines were subsumed under their framework. The PRSC label still carries connotations of criteria used since the time of their introduction, but today there is no distinct set of guidelines for the PRSC, despite the use of the brand name.

Increased Flexibility in PRSC and All Policy Lending

Stronger Country Ownership

PRSC program ownership was usually strong, especially compared with previous adjustment lending. In Armenia, for example, all counterparts agreed that the PRSC, derived from the participatory PRSP, led to strong country ownership and leadership of the PRSC program. Whereas the Bank had largely determined programs of adjustment credits, the government determined overall strategy in the PRSP, and the PRSCs supported the PRSP program. PRSC ownership has been particularly high at the level of central ministries such as finance and planning, though less so with sectoral ministries such as health or education. PRSCs stimulated dialogue between the center and sectors and raised their accountability. By contrast, recipient governments' engagement with legislative bodies and civil society was low.

PRSCs aligned reasonably well with national development strategies, especially where the PRS was merged with the national development strategy. Alignment improved over time. In Vietnam, the PRSP merged with the National Development Strategy. Uganda's national Poverty Eradication Action Plan now serves as its PRSP. PRSCs occasionally included policies outside the national plan, reflecting evolving country circumstances.

Shift in Focus toward Public Management and Pro-Poor Service Delivery

The sectoral focus of the PRSC showed a marked shift away from macroeconomic adjustment toward public sector management and key social service delivery. In Lao PDR, the first PRSC series covered virtually all sectors, but in the second series a more selective focus on health and education was adopted. Indeed, all Bank adjustment lending began to reflect a reorientation toward areas emphasized by the PRSC.

Eased Conditionality

PRSCs responded to concerns about the extensive and overly rigid nature of conditionality with fewer legally binding conditions than earlier adjustment loans and a gradual decline in program benchmarks. Armenia provides an example of this pattern. Its Structural Adjustment Credits had a peak of 66 conditions, in multitranche operations, while its first, second, and third PRSCs each had about 10–12 legally binding conditions in the form of prior actions. Armenia's fourth PRSC included only 7 such conditions. Following the introduction of new guidelines for adjustment lending in late 2004, other policy-based lending showed a similar trend, and today there is little difference in the numbers or nature of conditions of PRSCs and other policy-based lending.

Yet some country clients continue to believe that there are too many conditions, reflecting unclear perceptions of the differences among prior actions, triggers, and program benchmarks, especially in large multidonor programs.

PRSCs have been markedly more flexible than earlier adjustment lending, as demonstrated by the high number of trigger modifications, or actions for subsequent operations. In Ghana, for example, an agreed measure to complete the rollout of a budget management system in five ministries was deemed met when achieved in only two, and a significant unmet trigger in the energy sector was waived and made a requirement for the following PRSC. Yet, flexibility does not seem to be at the expense of program adherence because PRSC managers often delayed the loan or adjusted their amounts downward in cases of program slippage.

The Bank has clearly been prepared to exit a PRSC series when the reform program goes off track, as happened in Nicaragua following a change of government. However, following the termination of PRSCs, the Bank has often remained substantially engaged, sometimes though other policy-based loans. This underscores the question of the brand value of the PRSC label.

Somewhat More Predictable Financing

PRSCs have led to some increase in the dependability of obtaining financing from year to year, as well as increased stability in the volume of financing. And PRSCs have tended to disburse in a more timely manner than previous lending. In Burkina Faso, for example, whereas 60 percent of budget support disbursements through the end of PRSCs 1–3 took place during the last quarter of the budget year, the approval of PRSC 4 was accelerated to May 2004 to permit a vote by the National Assembly before its June recess.

Limited Donor Harmonization

While PRSCs made effective contributions to donor harmonization under a variety of arrangements, they rarely served as a focal point for donor coordination (Vietnam being an exception). In many large, budget support groups, the Bank had limited influence in shaping the overall agenda. There has been progress in achieving joint Performance Assessment Frameworks, which are the overall donor matrixes of policy frameworks, but upstream harmonization of the PRS process and its integration in the policy matrix has been limited. More also remains to be achieved in the harmonization of results indicators, capacity building, and especially in reporting arrangements.

The Bank's effectiveness is also curbed by limited synchronization of its internal processing calendar with the donor cycle. Agreement on the substantive agenda can be unduly influenced by individual donors. Recipient countries sometimes seek to leave major items off the agenda. The Bank has sometimes reverted to means outside the joint matrix to achieve its objectives. Furthermore, harmonization involves intensive transaction costs, which team leaders feel are not adequately recognized and sometimes crowd out substantive issues.

From a wider perspective, clients value harmonization for its reduced transaction costs, but face difficulties with initial increases in conditionality as individual positions are aggregated. In some circumstances clients prefer separate arrangements to spread risks. Donors, especially small ones, face high transaction costs but value having a voice at the table. Further synchronization will be more difficult due to legitimate differences in donor priorities.

Outcomes Are Less Clear

Weak Results Frameworks

PRSC results frameworks were initially weak in many operations, although there is some evidence of improvement over time. In Mozambique, for example, the first PRSC had no explicit results framework. PRSC 2 had a results framework but it omitted key areas, and the subsequent series for the first time contained a results framework for the series as a whole. Many shortfalls in PRSC results frameworks can be attributed to shortcomings in underlying country monitoring systems. Upstream shortcomings in results frameworks for PRSPs also contribute. Weaknesses remain in terms of clearly defined and consistent outcome indicators, intermediate milestones, and baseline data. Indicators for poverty outcomes are also lacking.

Unclear Achievements in Pro-Poor Service Delivery

The ultimate objective of PRSCs has been to support national development plans for achieving poverty-reducing economic growth. Assessing the contribution of PRSC operations to growth and poverty outcomes is difficult due to the fundamental problem of attribution. The PRSC is only one, typically small, element in a range of contributing factors.

PRSC countries performed well on growth and macro indicators, but so did relevant comparators. Differences in creating a growth-enabling institutional environment are small. Most PRSCs did not have a comprehensive overall growth strategy, focusing in many cases on reforms related to the investment climate (Benin, Ghana, Lao PDR, and Mozambique) and select other issues. It is difficult to trace a direct link from PRSC growth-related measures to country growth outcomes. In some successful countries (Vietnam, for example), a growth-oriented reform momentum was already under way.

PRSC countries have a good record on income poverty reduction as well as on the achievement of the Millennium Development Goals—better than comparable high-performing IDA countries despite broadly similar initial conditions. Yet establishing a clear link between the PRSC and propoor service delivery is difficult. A portfolio review shows that most PRSCs had program objectives in these areas, though such program components usually ran in parallel to sector projects, and social sector development objectives were usually ancillary to core objectives. Only about two-fifths of PRSC objectives in education, and half in health, had an explicit pro-poor focus. Proportions for water supply and sanitation were lower, at less than a fifth.

PRSC program components in health and education focused particularly on budgetary aspects, with an emphasis on increasing resources and improving the efficiency of resource allocation. In Vietnam and Lao PDR, for example, the introduction of a medium-term expenditure framework was a priority in the education sector. But countries lagged in their ability to link budgetary inputs with results and outputs. In most countries the PRSC was not able to make the budget the vehicle for most sectoral policy interventions, even in pro-poor areas. Large proportions of country sectoral resources remain off-budget.

Limitations in the monitoring framework make it difficult to track outcomes, especially poverty outcomes. To the extent that indicators are available, targets have been fully met one-third to one-half of the time, across the three sectors of health, education, and water supply and sanitation.

Improved Public Financial Management, Largely in Areas That Are Easier to Tackle

PRSCs have helped to advance public financial management and procurement (PFMP) reform in most borrowing countries. PFMP reform programs in PRSCs have been well grounded in recent diagnostics and have generally conformed to Bank guidelines on fiduciary risk analysis. Many PRSCs have integrated two or more diagnostic tools, helping to sequence their recommendations. Countries performed moderately well in developing an appropriately sequenced and donor-supported PFMP strategy, although implementation has sometimes been slower than expected.

Areas of successful reform in PRSCs, such as budget classification systems, have arguably been the easier ones to tackle. Remaining weaknesses reflect tougher challenges, including the inability of most PRSC series to reduce the proportions of extra-budgetary funds or to include all donor funds on-budget, also pointing to limits in progress by donors on the use of country systems under the Paris Declaration. A prominent area of weakness has been the public financial management results framework, which was complete or largely complete in only about half of the countries reviewed. Finally, the impact of PRSCs—and of donor budget support more generally—on overall governance and levels of corruption is a debated issue with little meaningful evidence to support claims either way.

Partial Support to Sectors

In many respects, the PRSC is an imperfect vehicle for sector support. PRSC engagement focuses on central ministries. While dialogue between central ministries and sectoral agencies has been strengthened, surveys suggest the depth of their engagement may have been limited. Efforts to streamline conditionality imply that some areas of importance are not highlighted. Sector staff acknowledge the PRSC's usefulness for high-level dialogue but express reservations about its effectiveness for tackling details. Few support having PRSCs be the sole vehicle for sector engagement, as envisioned by some Bank managers in the early years of PRSCs. When attempted, the Bank usually reverted to parallel sector financing. In Benin, Burkina Faso, and Mozambique, Country Assistance Strategies for early PRSC series expressed intent to subsume health lending in the PRSCs, but sector projects were subsequently resumed. And outcomes of sector components of PRSCs in health appear weaker than in health-sector investment lending.

There are also tensions in sector working groups within the harmonization process. In many countries they reflect financing arrangements that may be earmarked or even off-budget, which is counter to the philosophy of joint budget support. Also, counterparts sometimes prefer separate arrangements.

Sector staff point out that the Bank's incentive framework introduces resource variability and limited recognition for sectoral team participation, as compared with delivery of freestanding sectoral projects. Incentives affect sector managers as well.

Recommendations

1. Phase out the PRSC as a separate brand name for development policy lending or clarify when it is appropriate to use

Convergence in the design and content of PRSCs and other development policy lending, in terms of conditionality and sector focus, suggests that there is limited rationale for the separate existence of the PRSC today. However, there are also implicit criteria backing the PRSC brand name. If the PRSC brand name is still important, clear guidelines (which are currently lacking) and criteria for eligibility should be spelled out and applied.

2. Simplify the language of conditionality for PRSCs/DPLs by eliminating the term "triggers" and by transferring program benchmarks to the monitoring framework

In line with its use of the term "prior actions," the Bank could further simplify its lending framework by dispensing with the term "triggers" and substituting the term "indicative prior actions for future lending." Lending would then be based simply on prior actions already achieved and indicative prior actions for future lending. This would exhibit greater flexibility and improve understanding.

To clearly delineate legally binding conditions from program benchmarks, which are still referred to as binding and nonbinding conditions by clients and others in the aid community, program benchmarks should be removed from the policy matrix/Performance Assessment Framework and, instead, combined with the program monitoring framework.

3. Enable more effective participation of the Bank in a multidonor budget support lending framework by better synchronizing Bank internal process with donor processes

At present, Bank financial commitments in a multidonor framework must sometimes be made before the Bank's internal review of the PRSC. This can limit the Bank's substantive contributions and comments on program content. Synchronizing the Bank's internal processing schedule with country and donor processes would ensure Bank input in PRSC/DPL formulation.

4. Underpin operations with comprehensive diagnostics

PRSCs (and DPLs) should reflect country-specific growth diagnostics, which are undertaken based on analytic underpinnings that identify an overall growth strategy reflecting the linkages among growth, poverty reduction, and broader social development.

5. Strengthen PRSC/DPL results frameworks, link them with the underlying PRS/national development strategy, and increase their poverty focus

Results frameworks of PRSCs should be consistently linked to those in the PRS or national development strategy, and its annual reviews and should be simplified to a small set of core outcomes. Adequate baseline and intermediate indicators and pro-poor results indicators should be required and built on country monitoring systems to the extent feasible.

6. Focus sector content in policy loans on high-level or cross-cutting issues

PRSC/DPL sector content should focus on areas where it has been consistently effective—on cross-sectoral or central ministry issues critical to facilitating key sectoral reforms and strengthening sector budget processes. Complementary parallel sector lending, linked to PRSCs/DPLs, remains important to address detailed technical issues and facilitate program ownership by line ministries.

Management Response

Management welcomes the Independent Evaluation Group (IEG) evaluation of Poverty Reduction Support Credits (PSRCs), covering the period from fiscal years 2001 through 2008. Management appreciates the fact that many of the conclusions from its 2009 Development Policy Loan (DPL) Retrospective are independently confirmed by the evaluation.

Introduction

In addition, there is agreement on some of the elements where DPLs can be strengthened. Management does have a set of observations on areas in which it has differences with the analysis in the IEG evaluation. Some are around understandings on what is a PRSC, where Management notes that this is not a separate brand name. Others have to do with measurement of outcomes, the relationship of Development Policy Operations (DPOs) to other types of lending, and alignment and donor harmonization.

Elements of Agreement

The IEG evaluation contains a number of important findings about the Bank's PRSC support that are consistent with the positive trends identified in the recently completed DPL Retrospective, which examined all DPOs approved between April 1, 2006 and March 31, 2009:

- DPOs reflect stronger country ownership with good alignment with national development strategies;
- The Bank has made substantive progress in streamlining conditionality in its development policy lending;
- DPOs have been markedly more flexible in the interpretation of conditions and that over time this flexibility has been used selectively and appropriately;
- The predictability of DPO disbursement has improved over time in IDA countries;
- The focus of DPOs and their conditionality have shifted from macroeconomic adjustment, trade liberalization, and private sector development toward public sector management and social service delivery;
- DPOs have become increasingly focused on results, although the quality of results frameworks has varied; and
- DPOs prepared jointly with other development partners in the context of multidonor budget support frameworks have effectively contributed to donor harmonization.

Support for Strengthening DPOs

Management also agrees with IEG's observations on where DPOs could be improved. The report's recommendations in the following areas are especially welcome: the need to support operations with analytical underpinnings; the need to strengthen results frameworks; and the need to focus sector content on high-level and cross-cutting issues. Although progress has been made on many of these critical areas, as noted in the 2009 DPL Retrospective, IEG's observations are useful to support Management's ongoing efforts to strengthen DPO support to countries in achieving development results.

Observations on Differences

PRSCs Are Not a Separate Brand Name

Management notes that, at their origin, PRSCs were introduced to "support IDA-eligible country's policy and institutional reforms to help implement a country's poverty reduction strategy," and they were governed by interim guidelines for a period of three years (2001 to 2004) and by the Bank's OD 8.60. In August 2004 the new OP/BP 8.60 (Development Policy Lending) replaced OD 8.60 and updated and replaced the interim guidelines, as indicated in the preamble to the operational policy. Hence, since 2004, before this evaluation was initiated, there has been no difference, either in processing, design, or implementation between an operation that carries the title "Poverty Reduction Support Credit" (or Grant) and any other Development Policy Operation with a different title. PRSCs and Poverty Reduction Support Grants are guided by OP/BP 8.60 and since its introduction there have been no explicit or implicit criteria for the use of the PRSC title in a development policy operation. Unlike DPLs with Deferred Drawdown Options, and Special DPLs, for instance, PRCSs are not formally designated as a separate "DPL Option" in OP/BP 8.60. Their only distinguishing feature is one of content—they are aligned with the country's PRSP and help implement its development priorities and goals. It is this content and alignment that the title reflects.

IEG Ratings of PRSC Outcomes Based on IEG Evaluations of Implementation Completion Reports, FY01–08

	Number of PRSCs rated by IEG	Percentage of PRSCs rated by IEG
Operations with Implementation Support Credits rated by IEG	51	
Of which are rated:		
Satisfactory	25	49%
Moderately satisfactory	18	35%
Moderately unsatisfactory	8	16%
Unsatisfactory	0	0

Outcomes of PRSCs

Despite recognizing difficulties with issues of attribution, the IEG evaluation concludes that growth outcomes of PRSCs have been weak. Management notes that IEG made only limited use of its own validations of PRSC Implementation Completion Reviews (ICRs) in making this assertion. Management is of the view that it is not possible to attribute growth outcomes (positive or negative) to a single operation used by the Bank to support a country's national development strategy. This is because the achievement of the broad objectives of growth and poverty reduction are the result of many different factors, including the support by the Bank through a variety of instruments. If the evaluation had made more use of IEG validations of PRSC outcomes, which focus on the specific objectives of each PRSC series, it would have revealed compelling evidence of the good performance of PRSCs. Between 2001 and 2009, the Board approved 99 PRSCs. Out of this total, there are 33 ICRs available covering a total of 64 PRSCs. IEG validations of these ICRs are available for a total of 51 operations (as of September 22, 2009). Within the universe of PRSCs that have ICRs validated by IEG, there were only eight operations with outcomes rated *moderately unsatisfactory*, representing about 16 percent of the total. In none of the 51 PRSCs for which an IEG validation is available were outcomes rated as *unsatisfactory*. In 84 percent of the cases, therefore, PRSC outcomes were rated as *moderately satisfactory* or higher by IEG (see table).

The favorable performance for DPOs overall is also corroborated by the analysis presented in IEG's Annual Review of Development Effectiveness (ARDE) for 2008 and 2009, which show that PRSCs have consistently been rated as *satisfactory* in achievement of development outcomes during the past few years. The 2008 ARDE, for example, found that PRSC outcome ratings had increased steadily since FY03, with 100 percent of them rated *satisfactory* in FY06. The 2009 ARDE found that project performance was strong in FY08, with 81 percent of all Bank-supported projects rated *satisfactory* and with DPOs receiving, on average, higher ratings than investment operations.

Support to Sector Reforms

The report emphasizes in several places (especially in chapter 2) that, at the time of its introduction,

PRSCs were expected to replace sectoral lending. Management would like to reiterate that PRSCs were not designed with the intention to replace sector lending and that such an objective was never part of the operational policy guiding development policy lending. Quite the opposite—over time, Management has been expanding the range of financial and knowledge products it offers to its members, to meet an increasingly diverse range of client needs. Oftentimes, DPOs are accompanied and complemented by analytical work, by sectoral DPOs, and investment lending. Between FY05 and FY06, for example, DPOs titled as PRSCs represented only 15–16 percent of all IDA lending, and this share fell to 12 percent in FY07 and then further to 8–9 percent in FY08–09. In addition, PRSCs as a share of all DPO commitments in IDA countries topped 27 percent in FY05 and now represent 21 percent of all DPO commitments for IDA countries.

Replacement of Freestanding Sector Lending

Management questions the report's finding that the replacement of sector lending was explicitly discussed as part of the Country Assistance Strategy in 10 out of 27 countries that had a PRSC operation (chapter 2). Management notes that in a few CASs, there are references to the fact that development policy lending is the preferred aid modality for specific governments, among other reasons, because of lower transaction costs to governments, but even when this is the case, the Bank's program includes sectoral investment lending, which complements (not substitutes for) development policy lending.

Flexibility in Joint Budget Support Groups

The 2009 DPL Retrospective highlights that development policy operations prepared jointly with other development partners, including PRSCs, have contributed toward reducing transaction costs for governments and enhancing synergies in policy-based aid. Management has also observed that (i) in the context of joint budget support groups, there is a tendency for donors to cluster around the "lowest common denominator" in terms of policy content; and (ii) that in highly harmonized contexts, the harmonization process can also imply loss of flexibility for governments to include new areas of importance in the joint agenda. Management is of the view that these factors could reduce the effectiveness of the Bank's support to IDA clients, and introduce rigidity in the response to changing conditions and government priorities. In addition, they may undermine the ownership of the program. The report could have recognized that some flexibility needs to be retained to adjust the results framework of DPOs (including Performance Assessment Frameworks) to situations in which country circumstances and government priorities have changed or new information became available and may have deviated from what was originally outlined in the Performance Assessment Framework (PAF). Moreover, the results frameworks of these PAFs tend to include expected results that are of a much higher order than a DPO or any other form of budget support can realistically influence.

Contribution to Donor Harmonization

Management questions the statement in the Executive Summary that PRSCs rarely served as a focal point for donor harmonization. When first introduced, PRSCs supported a country's PRSP, which provided the basis for donor coordination and harmonization around a government's strategic objectives. This message contradicts the report's own conclusions in chapter 7 that PRSCs did usually serve as a catalyst for attracting donors to general budget support. For the same reason, Management also questions the view expressed in the Executive Summary that upstream harmonization of the PRS process and its integration in the policy matrix is limited. In all countries where a joint budget support group has been established and a joint PAF is in place, donors agree on a common framework to support the implementation of the country's PRS. The joint PAFs actually reflect the policies and outcomes of the government's development plans and strategies, and Management is of the view that this harmonized framework leverages donor assistance to achieve the country's poverty reduction objectives as it provides an opportunity for parallel financing of a government's budget. It is not clear, therefore, why IEG claims that upstream harmonization of the PRSP process and its integration in the policy matrix is limited.

Outcomes in the Health Sector

Management questions the report's finding that the "outcomes of sector components of PRSCs in health appear weaker than in health sector investment lending." Management notes that health outcomes of Bank operations in general have been weak and this evaluation does not present evidence to show that these outcomes are weaker for DPOs (or DPOs titled PRSCs) as compared with investment lending.

Caveats

Although Management agrees with the thrust of the findings of the IEG evaluation, it would like to point out that the report contains a few examples of statements—specifically, regarding the interpretation of some of the findings—that would have benefited from further elaboration and qualification. Overall, Management agrees with most of the IEG findings and, with the exceptions noted above regarding the assumption that the PRSC remains a separate brand name and that the use of the term "trigger" should be eliminated, accepts its recommendations. Detailed responses to the recommendations are outlined in the attached Management Action Record.

Management Action Record

Recommendations	Management response
1. Phase out the PRSC as a separate brand name for development policy lending or clarify when it is appropriate to use it. Convergence in the design and content of PRSCs and other development policy lending suggests that there is no rationale for the separate existence of the PRSC today. However, there are also implicit criteria backing the PRSC brand name. If the PRSC brand name is seen to still be important, clear guidelines (which are currently lacking) and criteria for eligibility should be spelled out and applied.	**Agreed.** All operational policy and guidance on development policy lending were unified with the introduction of OP/BP 8.60 in 2004. OP/BP 8.60 and operational guidance do not list PRSCs as a separate option. Since 2004, therefore, PRSCs have not had a separate existence. Poverty Reduction Support Credit (or Grant) is simply a title given to operations, usually programmatic, to signal their alignment with a PRSP. Management will emphasize this in training activities and guidance to staff to eliminate any remaining **misunderstandings** on this matter. Management is not prepared to object, however, if a government wants to call the development policy operation that it receives from the World Bank a PRSC. Management considers this action complete, as subsequent to the evaluation we have clarified this in DPO guidance.
2. Simplify the language of conditionality for PRSCs/DPLs by eliminating the term "triggers" and by transferring program benchmarks to the monitoring framework In line with its use of the term "prior actions," the Bank could further simplify its lending framework by dispensing with the term "triggers" and substituting the term "indicative prior actions for future lending." Lending would then be based simply on prior actions already achieved and indicative prior actions for future lending. This would exhibit greater flexibility and improve understanding. To clearly delineate legally binding conditions from program benchmarks, which are still referred to as binding and nonbinding conditions by clients and others in the aid community, program benchmarks should be removed from the policy matrix/Performance Assessment Framework and, instead, combined with the program monitoring framework.	**Disagreed.** Management is of the view that the thrust of this recommendation is embedded in the framework for the provision of programmatic development policy lending. Triggers—as described in Board approved OP/BP 8.60—are "indicative prior actions for future lending." As evidenced in the evaluation, the use of triggers for future operations has been flexibly applied. Legally binding conditions in DPOs are only prior actions and tranche release conditions. These are clearly identified in program documents and in legal agreements. Both are documents of the World Bank and are made public. However, Performance Assessment Frameworks are not Bank documents, but are developed jointly by governments and our development partners. Therefore, Management cannot commit to undertake the actions suggested by this recommendation.
3. Enable more effective participation of the Bank in a multidonor budget support lending framework by better synchronizing Bank internal process with donor processes. At present, Bank financial commitment to support, in a multidonor framework, must sometimes be made before the Bank's internal review of the PRSC. This can limit the Bank's substantive contributions and comments on program content. Synchronizing the Bank's internal processing schedule with country and donor processes would ensure Bank input in PRSC/DPL formulation.	**Agreed in principle.** More effective participation of the Bank in multidonor budget support (MDBS) groups would be valuable in helping countries achieve their development goals. Management agrees that it would be optimal to achieve such synchronization. However, MDBS lending frameworks are prepared and implemented in tandem with other development partners, and there can be tradeoffs and limits to Management's ability to commit to a particular operation in the absence of Senior Management and Board approval. As indicated in the 2009 DPL Retrospective, Management agrees to review its experience with MDBS frameworks and derive lessons from these collaborative engagements and to use these lessons to identify ways to do better in the future. This action will be completed when the proposed review of experience with MDBS frameworks agreed to in the DPL Retrospective has been concluded and lessons disseminated.
4. Underpin operations with comprehensive diagnostics PRSCs (and DPLs) should reflect country-specific growth diagnostics, which are undertaken based on analytic underpinnings that identify an overall growth strategy reflecting the linkages among growth, poverty-reduction, and broader social development.	**Agreed.** As discussed in the 2009 DPL Retrospective, Management fully agrees that the policy and institutional actions supported by a DPO should be underpinned by comprehensive analytic work. However, Management would like to note that diagnostic work needs to be related to the content of the operation. For example, a DPO that focuses on the health sector should be underpinned by comprehensive analytic work on health. Management will monitor and report on progress in strengthening the diagnostic underpinning of DPLs in the context of its periodic DPL Retrospectives.

Management Action Record *(continued)*

Recommendations	Management response
5. Strengthen PRSC/ DPL results frameworks and link them with the underlying PRS / national development strategy and increase their poverty focus. Results frameworks of PRSCs should be consistently linked to those in the PRS or national development strategy and its annual reviews, and simplified to a small set of core outcomes. Adequate baseline and intermediate indicators and pro-poor results indicators should be required and built on country monitoring systems to the extent feasible.	**Agreed.** As discussed in the 2009 DPL Retrospective, DPOs have become increasingly results focused, but there is scope for further improvement in their results frameworks. Management agrees with the recommendation to strengthen DPL results frameworks with the adequate use of baseline and results indicators that are linked to the actions supported by the operation. Management notes, however, that the results frameworks of DPOs need to be more specific than those prepared for a PRSP or a national development strategy. In the context of its 2009 DPL Retrospective, Management has agreed to update guidance to staff on how to design results frameworks. This action will be considered completed when the revised guidance to staff agreed to in the DPL Retrospective has been completed and disseminated.
6. Focus sector content in policy loans on high level or cross-cutting issues. PRSC/DPL sector content should focus on areas where it has been consistently effective: cross-sectoral or central ministry issues critical to facilitating key sectoral reforms and strengthening sector budget processes. Complementary parallel sector lending, linked to PRSC/DPL, remains necessary to address detailed technical issues and facilitate program ownership by line ministries.	**Agreed.** Management agrees with this recommendation to focus sector content of DPOs on areas that can enhance the effectiveness of the reforms supported by the Bank and with the provision of parallel sector lending necessary to address specific sector issues that cannot be addressed by the DPL instrument in isolation. Management will continue to monitor the content of DPOs in the context of its periodic DPL Retrospectives.

Chairperson's Summary: Committee on Development Effectiveness (CODE)

On November 4, 2009, the Committee on Development Effectiveness (CODE) considered the report *Poverty Reduction Support Credits: An Evaluation of World Bank Support*, prepared by the Independent Evaluation Group (IEG), together with the draft Management Response.

Summary

The Committee felt that the IEG evaluation was positive overall and a good complement to the recently discussed Development Policy Lending (DPL) Retrospective. The Committee welcomed the agreement between Management and IEG on the importance for PRSCs to incorporate analytical underpinnings and to strengthen their results framework. However, it also noted some disagreements on key issues, including the need to clarify the use and meaning of the PRSC "brand name" as a specific instrument supporting country-owned development strategies, the contributions of PRSCs to growth and poverty reduction, and the role PRSCs have had in facilitating donor harmonization.

Members raised diverse views on the use of "PRSC" as a separate brand name for DPL support for IDA. In this regard, the Legal Counsel confirmed that the unified framework adopted by the Bank in 2004 for all policy-based lending through OP 8.60 covers operations entitled PRSC, while leaving room for customization. Members agreed on the difficulties of measuring the impact of PRSCs on growth and poverty reduction given the issue of attribution, and the need for more work by IEG and Management on attributing poverty outcomes to particular operations. Related to this, members underscored the importance of having a communication strategy for the general public about the evaluation findings and recommendations, including Management Response, in order to avoid misperceptions. Members raised several comments on IEG's recommendation for the Bank to have a greater voice in the multidonor budget support lending framework, through better synchronization of Bank and country processes. They felt that the Bank's leading role should be adapted to countries' specific conditions.

Next Steps

The Committee noted the following next steps:

- For Management to review its response in light of the CODE discussions.
- For IEG to disclose this evaluation report in accordance with the IEG disclosure policy.

The following main issues were discussed during the meeting:

Brand Name

Members and speakers raised questions on whether PRSCs are instruments with distinguishing characteristics or are identical to other DPOs.

They expressed diverse views, pointing out that having a brand name may help to identify the instrument's objectives and to assess quality, and that a brand name helps to differentiate PRSCs' specific alignment to Poverty Reduction Strategies (PRSs) from other DPLs. They noted that further information was needed to clarify the relevance of distinguishing PRSCs from DPLs. Management clarified that PRSCs were processed under interim guidelines prior to 2004. However, since OP/BP 8.60 was approved in 2004, PRSCs are not subject to separate policy or guidelines and should not be identified as a different instrument. Today, PRSC or PRSG is a title given to a DPO, usually programmatic, to signal its alignment with a PRSP. IEG pointed out that although, *de jure*, there is no distinction, *de facto*, many Bank task team leaders, managers, and client countries still view the PRSC as having some characteristics distinct from other DPLs.

In response to a specific request for a legal clarification, the Legal Counsel explained that, under the unified policy framework for all policy-based loans (PBL) adopted in 2004 through the introduction of OP 8.60, the Bank discontinued the use of special names and acronyms previously used for PBL, such as SECALs and PSALs. The policy framework uniformly applies to all DPL as a single lending instrument, while leaving room for customization. However, the Board agreed to retain the use of the term PRSCs for development policy support to IDA countries with a PRSP, to maintain continuity with the well-established approach of using PRSPs as a basis for IDA support.

PRSC

Members felt that more emphasis should be given to tracking growth and poverty reduction in PRSCs, although recognizing that there is a difficult attribution problem. They noted that IEG did not find performance differences between PRSC countries and better performing non-PRSC IDA countries. Noting the differences between IEG and Management on measuring the attribution to growth and poverty reduction, some speakers encouraged early discussions on this matter. One member stressed the need to focus on the quality of conditionalities as well as simplifying or reducing their number, and the need to avoid misinterpretations regarding legally binding conditions, including triggers and program benchmarks.

Speakers raised comments and questions on the use of PRSCs in fragile countries; the relation between large budget support and country debt management; the complementarity of PRSCs, sectoral DPLs, and investment lending (for specific sectors); and technical and capacity-building support.

Results Framework

Members broadly agreed on the importance of strengthening the results framework and maintaining consistent outcomes indicators and baseline data but taking into account countries' capacity constraints. One member felt that the evaluation of CASs against the core objectives of poverty reduction may be more appropriate than trying to measure PRSCs' contributions to poverty reduction.

Harmonization

Members expressed diverse views on IEG's recommendation to enable more effective participation of the Bank in a multidonor budget support lending framework. Their comments underlined the different models of donor harmonization, based on each country's situation or sector-specific support; that the Bank is just one of many participants, and that it is not in a position to ensure a leading role in a multidonor partnership framework. In addition, there was a suggestion to undertake further work on the impact of harmonization on transaction costs to the Bank. The need for greater flexibility in adjusting multidonor budget support group's Performance Assessment Frameworks (PAFs) to changing country circumstances was also cited.

Carolina Renteria, Acting Chairperson

Synthesis of Comments from External Expert Panel Review

General Comments

The external experts who reviewed this evaluation commended it as comprehensive and competent in its analysis, with soundly based judgments supported by a well-triangulated range of quantitative and qualitative data. The lessons learned were deemed quite rich and a good guide in redesigning the PRSC instrument or considering similar instruments at the World Bank or sister multilateral development banks. Many findings echoed those of other, similar studies outside the Bank, and the evaluation would benefit from more cross-references to such studies.

The main finding of the evaluation—that PRSCs have made important contributions but largely in the arena of budget/public financial management, rather than observable sector outcomes, along with some important changes in the design and implementation of development policy lending, was not considered a surprising finding. Other evaluations of budget support point to similar changes in process. However, the net impact of the PRSC was also the outcome of a number of parallel programs by other donors, and a deeper exercise of the relationship between development lending by all donors and development outcomes would be needed to better appreciate the impact of budget support to country-owned development strategies.

Detailed Comments

PRSC Design: Differences Relative to Past Structural Adjustment Lending and Other DPLs

One of the main achievements of the PRSCs was in processes and design. At inception, PRSCs really were a substantially different way of doing business for the Bank. They helped strengthen country ownership and supported a shift in focus to public sector management and pro-poor service delivery. The report makes a convincing case that, although there were important design differences between PRSCs and past structural adjustment/balance of payments-style lending, now there are few discernible differences between PRSCs and DPLs as currently constituted. The PRSC design has thus in a sense been validated within the Bank by the creation of the DPL instrument.

PRSC Conditionality

The discussion about conditionality could be more hard-hitting. The use of language around core conditions (benchmarks, triggers, waivers, milestones, etc.) is nontrivial and has to be radically simplified if trust and transparency with county partners is to grow. There is some skepticism in the wider development community about whether the Bank has in fact reduced the number of conditions, with some arguing that the proliferation of benchmarks is simply conditionality by another name. It is important that the evaluation is very clear on the value, or otherwise, of core conditions and what can be done to continue to simplify while supporting ownership and better performance.

PRSC Sector Focus

The evaluative evidence points unequivocally to the limited reach of PRSCs at the sector level. This would seem to support the case for complementary instruments working at systemwide and sector levels. There is a lot of evidence, including in this report, that general budget support instruments are very useful for dialogue on governmentwide policy issues and on some high-level sectoral ones, but not useful for any more detailed sector policy dialogue. However, there is no mention of the new breed of Sector Budget Support instruments and their place in the Bank's instrument mix. Some cross-referencing to what is happening at the sector level, and what might be appropriate in the way of policy-based lending at the sector level, would be very helpful. There is more work to be done on assisting countries to build constructive relationships between finance and sectoral ministries.

PRSC Predictability and Regularity

The report's conclusions on predictability ring true and seem soundly based—that is, that there was some increase in both the proportion of commitments disbursed and the regularity of disbursement, and that better alignment with the preparatory process is harder (though arguably at least as important) as other aspects of aid and budget alignment. However, the evaluation does not investigate the optimum cycle for PRSC-type lending. This could feed into the debate about the time needed to deliver on results, the importance of medium-term commitments, and how to create/support recipient country policy space. Finally, although PRSCs may have improved the predictability of resources from the World Bank, it could be argued that overall resource predictability did not necessarily improve. There is a risk that in case of a disagreement, donors could jointly withdraw their support and the recipient country would be confronted with a large gap in its budget. It is for this reason that some African countries prefer to have project-based support.

The PRSC Process—Alignment with Country Systems, Operationalization of PRS, Results

The general picture of gradually increasing alignment from a weakly aligned beginning seems clear and well-supported by evidence. The comment that, in practice, alignment is much closer with the ministry of finance/planning, that there is little contact with legislatures, and that links to sectoral ministries and civil society are highly variable, all ring true. The report could be strengthened by highlighting more the internal political economy of recipient countries (for example, the PRSC tends to strengthen the ministry of finance and, therefore, create tensions with line ministries such as those for health and education).

On the operationalization of a country-driven PRS, the report may miss the significance of policy dialogue and good advice on operationalization (for example, development of key institutions and improved monitoring by civil society of service delivery). The report could have better addressed the extent to which the PRSCs have helped shape the dialogue around core policy issues within the government and among the government, the Bank, and other development partners.

The report's cautious conclusions regarding results and monitoring are well supported and seem entirely plausible. Reflection on how to move this discussion from accountability to the donors toward accountability of PRSC host governments to their electorate would have been welcome. Homegrown results frameworks will be far more significant than box-ticking the often complex requirements of donors, including the Bank.

PRSC Contribution to Donor Harmonization around a Country-Owned, Medium-Term PRS

The report asserts that, despite their contributions to donor harmonization, PRSCs rarely served as focal points for donor coordination, and the Bank had limited influence in shaping the overall agenda. This judgment seems soundly based. There is no doubt that the effective management of large donor groups providing general budget support financing is a major current issue. The report is consistent with other surveys in pointing out that such groups can cause overly complex conditionality and results matrixes. The fact that the Bank's influence is limited is not, however, an undesirable outcome. The Bank's influence, like that of every individual donor should be limited if country ownership is to mean anything. Without doubt, the Bank had a major role in harmonizing and aligning donors around the PRSC, but this should not be presented as a determinant of success.

The issue of transaction costs is correctly raised. It is encouraging that some recipient government officials feel that harmonization has cut transaction costs to them. On the donor side, the complaints of Bank staff would be echoed by many of their counterparts in other donor agencies. The analysis of aid channeled though national systems for PFMP could be framed in a more challenging way by looking at how far non-general budget support flows use such systems.

PRSC Outcomes—Effectiveness in Strengthening Public Financial Management

This issue is addressed in a single chapter, using a clear methodology and drawing on a large number of sources for its findings. The conclusion, that PRSCs were reasonably effective in design, helping address recipients' needs in PFMP systems, harmonizing such programs among donors, and generally implementing them in a timely manner, seems well-based. It is also very consistent with the findings of the OECD–DAC's 2006 evaluation of budget support.

PRSC Outcomes—Setting Conditions for Sustained Growth and Supporting Service Delivery to the Poor

A common critique among the expert panelists was the need for more discussion of the "spend/absorb" debate in the report so as to better understand exactly how PRSC resources were used by client governments and its macro and micro effects. For example, were the additional resources provided through the PRSC used to sustain key aspects of government spending or to pay down domestic debt and cut government borrowing? Were they used to facilitate additional imports or to boost net reserves? To the extent that some client countries decided to regulate absorption of aid disbursements and build up their reserves to avoid the effects of "Dutch disease"; could this explain the relatively weak development outcomes in PRSC countries?

Despite the report's lack of analysis on the extent to which financial resources were spent/absorbed, its conclusion that the PRSC instrument was probably not particularly influential in boosting growth rates is probably accurate. However, the report also takes a rather limited view of pro-poor growth in several of its judgments, in its reference that "In some countries, an early poverty focus shifted toward growth-oriented educational strategies emphasizing technical and vocational training in an effort to address growing skilled labor shortages." Surely, countries are right to expand technical and vocational education as labor market demand increases, to sustain growth and employment.

Further discussion would also be welcome on how effectively the PRSCs have helped introduce a growth focus into the PRS agenda—that is, did PRSC policy dialogue help rebalance donor efforts and national action toward growth, while maintaining a focus on the distribution of the benefits of growth to the poor?

The analysis of how well PRSCs have supported service delivery to the poor was generally sound and addresses the heart of the issue—the complementarity between what one should expect of a general budget support-type instrument and what one should expect from sector-based instruments. The findings that "a high proportion of measures incorporated in individual PRSCs to support the achievement of sectoral objectives in the areas of health, education, and water supply and sanitation focused on budget and public finance. . ." seem plausible and indeed logical. However, the question about whether PRSCs are more or less effective than other interventions, for example, in health, may be somewhat misplaced given the necessarily different focus of a general budget support-type instrument and a sector-specific instrument.

The report should also do more to highlight its finding that PRSC countries were associated with greater progress on the Millennium Development Goals. The suggestion that PRSCs have been associated with, if not contributed to, generalized progress toward the Millenium Development Goals is not trivial.

Conclusion and Recommendations

There is no conclusion that states that PRSCs have delivered and that budget support works in some fundamental ways. This could be stated more clearly, with all the appropriate caveats about the scale and type of achievements.

While the PRSC has probably lost its distinctiveness, and the evidence in the evaluation is pretty persuasive on this, the "poverty reduction" element of the Poverty Reduction Support Credit was terribly important as a signaling device. Instead of dropping the PRSC label, the report could consider renaming it something slightly different, as such branding may be useful as a signaling device, and there may be some unfinished business that a PRSC-type instrument should still be addressing, especially in light of the financial crisis and the need to build systemwide resilience in low-income economies. It is accepted that PRSPs are now morphing increasingly into national development strategies and hence the poverty reduction element of the PRSC has less of an obvious anchor. But an alternative view would be to reflect better the changing landscape and rename the PRSC as the Poverty Reduction and Growth Support Credit.

Notwithstanding these points, the recommendations seem sensible but incremental. Perhaps this is the best way forward, but the financial crisis and long arm of the food-price crisis in low-income countries adds a sense of urgency to what needs to be done on everything from domestic resource mobilization to climate-resilient growth, to social protection. Urgent answers are needed to the question of how future Bank DPLs will support low-income countries and the place of the PRSC within this context.

Alison Evans, Director, Overseas Development Institute
Louis Kasekende, Chief Economist, African Development Bank
Richard Manning, former Director, OECD–DAC

Chapter 1

Evaluation Highlights

- This evaluation assesses the relevance and effectiveness of PRSCs and their contribution to poverty-reducing growth.
- PRSCs were introduced to operationalize countries' development strategies.
- PRSCs embodied differences in focus and design compared with previous adjustment lending.
- PRSCs were based on Interim Guidelines that were never formalized.
- Later guidelines for development policy lending subsumed PRSCs, which today have no formal underpinning.
- Parallel with changes in Bank lending, the character of aid flows from other donors also changed.

Mule-drawn cart; Mali. Photo by Curt Carnemark, courtesy of the World Bank Photo Library.

Introduction

At the time of its introduction in early 2001, the Poverty Reduction Support Credit (PRSC) signaled a new modality for adjustment lending to low-income International Development Association (IDA) countries, anchored in a country-owned, comprehensive, partnership-oriented, and poverty-focused development strategy. PRSCs were introduced to help implement countries' development strategies, embodied in Poverty Reduction Strategy Papers (PRSPs), introduced in tandem with the World Bank's Comprehensive Development Framework.

Adjustment Lending and Poverty Reduction Support Credits

Poverty Reduction Strategies (PRSs) provided the basis for Bank and International Monetary Fund (IMF) concessional lending and debt relief under the joint Heavily Indebted Poor Countries (HIPC) Initiative. PRSCs were intended to parallel the IMF's Poverty Reduction and Growth Facility, with a focus on long-term and poverty-focused institutional strengthening.

While PRSCs were subject to prevailing provisions for Bank-supported adjustment lending, they were heralded by new Interim Guidelines that specified the underlying principles (annex 1).[1] Country ownership was the first principle. Whereas traditional adjustment operations were held to be based on the Bank's vision of development, the PRSC would be based on the country-owned PRSP, developed with the participation of all segments of government and civil society. PRSCs were intended to be based on a comprehensive and holistic view of development, covering a range of medium-term structural, social, and institutional issues (such as social services delivery, public sector management, regulatory framework, and governance), in contrast to the focus of traditional adjustment lending on stabilization, market liberalization, and private sector development. The poverty–reducing focus of the PRSC was intended to increase attention on social services, in line with expectations under the Millennium Development Goals. And the PRSC program was also intended to serve as a vehicle for donor harmonization and alignment around a set of development objectives.

PRSCs differed from previous adjustment lending in having greater country ownership, less onerous conditionality, greater predictability, and a strong focus on reinforcing budgetary processes.

The PRSC design was intended to provide programmatic support framed by a series of annual single-tranche operations, in contrast to preceding multi-tranche adjustment operations. The PRSC was also expected to reduce the burden of conditionality, based on actions already achieved, prior to the submission of an operation to the Bank's Board for approval.[2] PRSCs introduced the concept of adaptable triggers for subsequent operations, which could be modified, substituted, or waived, in place of binding ex-ante legal conditions. The programmatic nature of annual lending was intended to increase the predictability of support and to complement countries' budget resources; greater attention would also be paid to alignment with countries' domestic budget cycles.

Finally, PRSCs were intended to explicitly recognize the role of institutions and governance in achieving success in development, and strong

Box 1.1. Is the PRSC a Distinct Instrument?

Many Characteristics of PRSCs Have Been Subsumed under Development Policy Loans

The Bank's new policy for Development Policy Loans, issued in August 2004 under OP 8.60, do not distinguish between PRSCs and other DPLs. In practice, DPLs adopted many features of the PRSC Interim Guidelines of May 2001, including a broad-based consultative process underpinning a program of structural reform that focused on achieving poverty-reducing growth, a sustainable macro and institutional framework, enhanced donor harmonization, the use of a results-based approach, and a monitoring and evaluation framework. Moreover, the analysis here shows that many of the characteristics of PRSCs have been subsumed under DPLs, as the new OP 8.60 intended. There was a clear shift in the structural focus as well as the character of conditionality in policy-based lending.

But the PRSC Label Still Retains Some Distinguishing Features

In practice, the PRSC aims to be a distinctive brand name and retains distinguishing features, including:

- Providing broad-based reform support, based on the country's medium-term national development strategy and/or country-owned PRS;
- Policy-based lending as part of a programmatic series, based on Country Assistance Strategy and Poverty Reduction Strategy Paper (CAS/PRSP) cycles;
- A policy reform program oriented toward poverty-reducing growth;
- A well-performing macro policy and institutional environment, with adequate capacity in financial management and sufficient control of corruption; and
- A demonstrated record of sustained reform commitment.

Many IDA CASs considered the adoption of PRSCs, but rejected their use because conditions were not deemed adequate, due to doubts about sustained reform commitment or limited depth of dialogue. In other countries, PRSCs have been rejected as the operation of choice by managers because they are perceived to be broad-based, while narrower, more focused operations have been considered more strategically useful (and in some cases, easier to supervise). In some Europe and Central Asia countries approaching middle-income status there has been hesitation to use the PRSC due to its implied poverty focus, which is felt to be associated with low-income countries. In sum, it appears that there are generally accepted, implicit criteria guiding the selection of operations that can earn the PRSC label.

The Africa Region department drew up its own guidelines.

reform commitment was a prerequisite. PRSC programs emphasized reinforcing public financial management systems to enable aid to be channeled through country systems with manageable levels of fiduciary risk. Some of the features described were not new, although PRSCs embodied a marked change in their emphasis and practice.

Although not explicitly stated in the Interim Guidelines, PRSCs came to be offered, usually, to better-performing IDA countries with a demonstrated record of reform and sustained commitment to a medium-term national development strategy aimed at poverty reduction. PRSCs became a signal of dependable Bank support to countries capable of sound fiduciary management, where aid could be fungible and disbursed into a country's budget, to be efficiently allocated in accordance with country priorities. These principles came to be clearly articulated in the Africa Region, which became the most intensive user of the PRSC instrument.

Later, PRSCs were subject to guidelines for all Bank development policy lending.

The Interim Guidelines of the PRSC were never formalized. New Bank guidelines for adjustment lending were introduced in late 2004, subsuming the PRSC Interim Guidelines and bearing many of its characteristics.[3] Today, PRSCs are a part of Development Policy Loans (DPLs)/Credits and there are no guidelines for the PRSC as a distinct lending instrument. Nevertheless the PRSC label remains, albeit as a subset of programmatic development policy operations, traditionally reserved for well-performing IDA countries, for broad-based support toward national strategies focused on poverty-reducing growth.[4]

The PRSC remains popular, especially in Africa, where new PRSC countries continue to be added each year, and it remains the Bank's most important form of policy-based lending in many IDA countries.[5] This evaluation aims not only to examine the extent to which PRSCs were able to operationalize countries' Poverty Reduction Strategies but also, in view of their continued prominence, to examine their relevance and effectiveness today as an instrument of Bank lending for poverty alleviation.

PRSC Growth and Regional Distribution

Within four years of its introduction, by fiscal 2005, PRSCs had rapidly come to account for almost 60 percent of IDA policy-based lending, which amounted to almost a quarter of total Bank policy-based lending at that time.[6] The share of the PRSC in total IDA disbursements, including investment lending, grew from 5 percent in fiscal 2002 to a peak of 17 percent in fiscal 2005, and declining to 11.3 percent in fiscal 2008 (figure 1.1 and appendix table A1.1).[7]

The share of the PRSC in IDA disbursements to individual countries was sometimes considerably higher, often attaining or exceeding half of total Bank disbursements in countries such as Benin, Burkina Faso, Ghana, Rwanda, and Uganda. In some years PRSC flows exceeded 60 percent of IDA flows to Burkina Faso and over 80 percent of IDA flows to Uganda. PRSC disbursements averaged a third of total disbursements to PRSC countries in the years in which they had a PRSC operation (appendix table A1.2).

PRSC operations initially grew rapidly in number and importance.

For all recipient countries, the share of PRSCs in total World Bank disbursements has averaged 30 to 40 percent over the past five years, with perhaps some trend decline within this band. PRSCs have never made up a large part of government budget needs—from 7 percent for countries receiving PRSCs in 2001 and 5.4 percent in 2004, the share declined steadily thereafter to 1.5 percent in 2008. PRSCs also appear to have declined relative to total aid and to total budget support aid that PRSC countries have received from all sources (figure 1.2 and appendix table A1.4). This is despite some pro-

PRSCs accounted for over half of IDA disbursements in many countries.

Figure 1.1. PRSCs: Shares in Policy-Based and Total Lending (FY01–08)

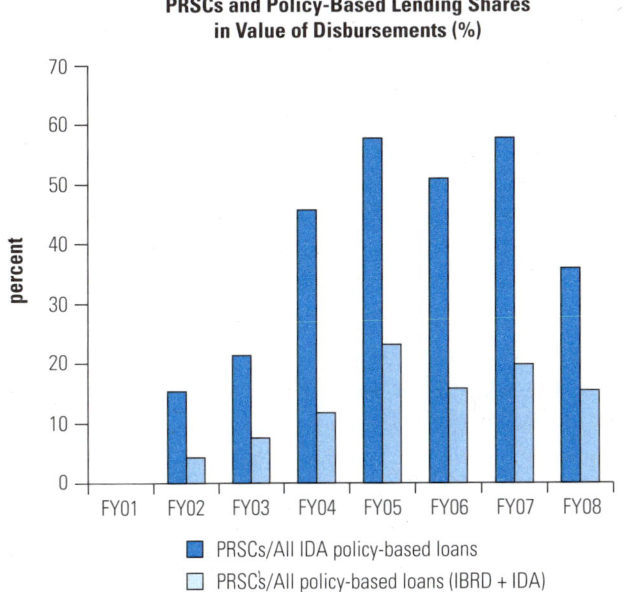

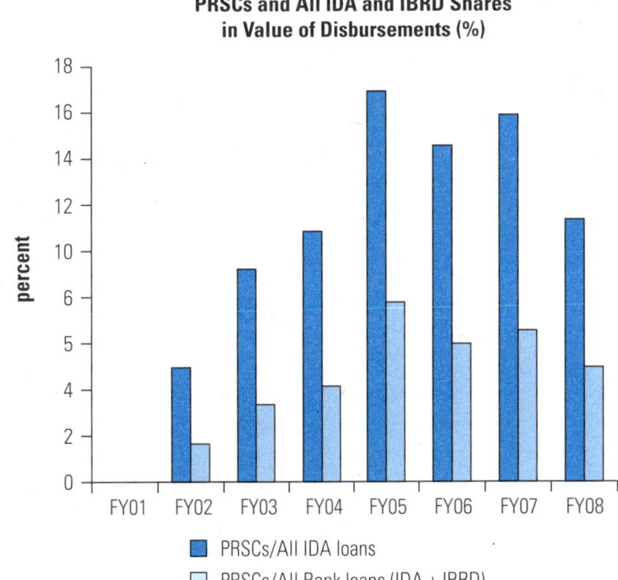

Source: World Bank data.

Figure 1.2. PRSC Lending in Proportion to Country Income, Budget, and Aid Flows (1995–2008)

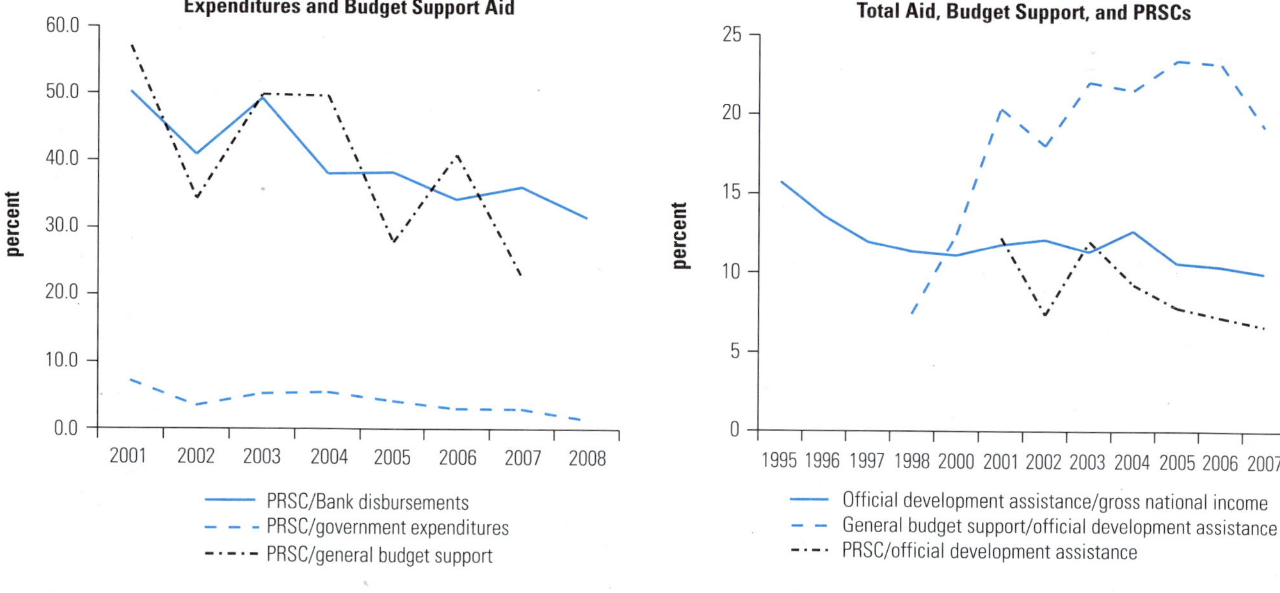

Sources: Appendix table A1.4, based on World Bank data (for government expenditures); OECD-DAC aid aggregates (for total official development assistance); joint budget support evaluations of the Overseas Development Institute, and OECD Paris Declaration monitoring survey (for budget support data); and World Bank data.

More recently, PRSC shares in Bank disbursements have declined, as have their contributions to budget support in recipient countries.

portional decline in aid flows to PRSC countries, relative to their national income, from somewhat over 15 percent to about 10 percent, and reflects an overall increase in budget support aid as a proportion of total aid, at least until 2006.

PRSCs expanded from 21 operations in fiscal 2001–04 to 66 operations in fiscal 2005–08 (figure 1.3, appendix table A1.3). Over this period the Bank approved 87 PRSC operations. Total approvals by end-fiscal 2008 amounted to $6.6 billion. Further approvals of $1.3 billion brought the total to 99 operations by end-September 2009. Another 20 operations amounting to $1.7 billion are under preparation. New PRSCs approved each year rose from 2 per year in fiscal 2001–02 to 10 per year in fiscal 2004, and between 15–19 per year in fiscal 2005–08 (figure 1.3). The number of countries engaged in ongoing PRSC operations increased to 20 by fiscal 2005, and fluctuated around this level thereafter.

Some Bank operations have PRSC characteristics but are not labeled PRSCs.

Of the 27 countries that have received PRSC funding through fiscal 2008, 10 have embarked on their second or even third PRSC series (table 1.1). Another 9 countries have had a single PRSC series so far. But in 8 countries, PRSC operations were abandoned and did not mature into a full programmatic series. Some early PRSCs began preparation as Structural Adjustment Credits—in Vietnam, Lao People's Democratic Republic, and Nicaragua.[8] The Bank also had poverty-focused programmatic loans that did not bear the PRSC label—for example, Bangladesh Development Credits (four in 2003–08) and Tajikistan Programmatic Development Policy Grants (three from 2006 to the present). Especially between 2002 and 2005, several other IDA countries considered, or even began, the preparation of PRSCs but did not proceed with them.[9] PRSCs had other implicit criteria—providing broad-based support

Figure 1.3. PRSCs: Ongoing Programs, New Operations Approved, and Regional Distribution (FY01–08)

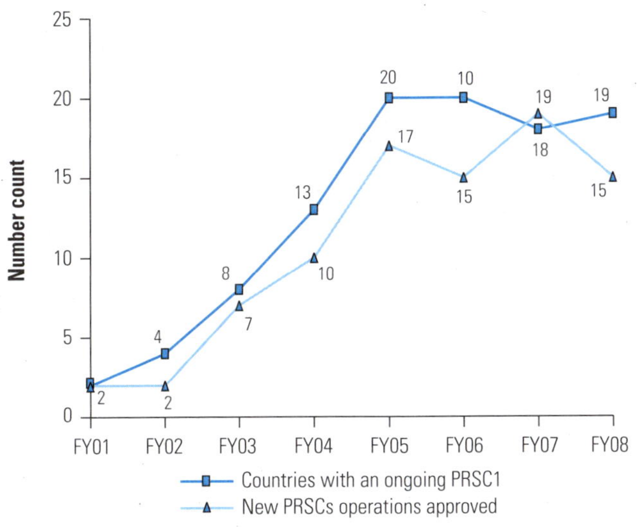

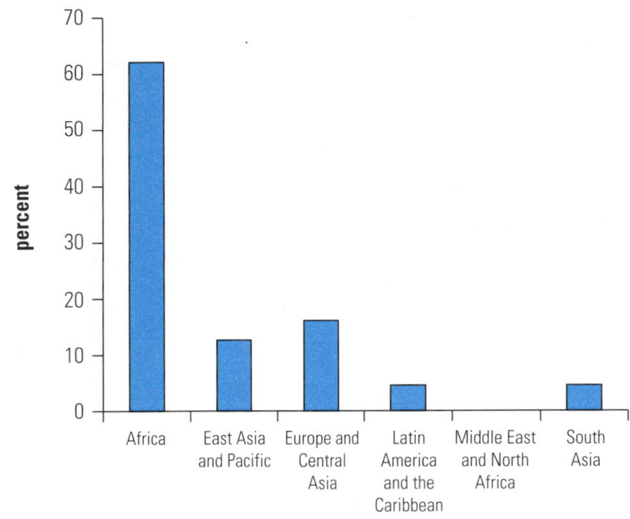

Source: Appendix table A1.1 and appendix table A1.2, based on World Bank data.
Note: Ongoing programs are ones between approval date and closure date.

Table 1.1. PRSCs: Countries, Series, and Operations (FY01–08)

Long (2 or 3 series begun)				Medium (1 completed series or ongoing operations)				Early terminations (incomplete series; 1–2 operations)			
Country	**No. of PRSCs**	**No. of series**	**Dates**	**Country**	**No. of PRSCs**	**No. of series**	**Dates**	**Country**	**No. of PRSCs**	**No. of series**	**Dates**
Burkina Faso	7	3	FY02–present	Albania	3	1	FY02–05	Azerbaijan	1	1	FY05
Benin	4	2	FY04–present	Armenia	4	1	FY05–08	Ethiopia	2	1	FY02–05
Ghana	6	2	FY03–present	Cape Verde	3	1	FY05–present	Guyana	1	1	FY03
Lao PDR	4	2	FY05–present	Georgia	4	1	FY06–present	Honduras	1	1	FY04
Madagascar	5	2	FY05–present	Lesotho	1	1	FY08–present	Nepal	1	1	FY04
Mozambique	4	2	FY05–present	Malawi	1	1	FY08–present	Nicaragua	1	1	FY04–07
Rwanda	4	2	FY05–present	Mali	2	1	FY07–present	Pakistan	2	1	FY05–07
Tanzania	5	2	FY03–present	Moldova	2	1	FY07–present	Sri Lanka	1	1	FY03
Uganda	7	2	FY01–present	Senegal	3	1	FY05–present				
Vietnam	7	2	FY01–present								
Totals	*PRSCs*	*Countries*			*PRSCs*	*Countries*			*PRSCs*	*Countries*	
	53	10			23	9			10	8	

Source: World Bank data.

to countries with strong reform commitment. The group of PRSC look-alikes is small.[10] This evaluation therefore does not adjust, through omission or inclusion, for those operations that have PRSC characteristics but do not bear the label.

Parallel Changes in the Lending Environment and Aid Architecture

Changes in lending policies introduced with the PRSC reflected larger trend changes in the global aid architecture, affecting the Bank as well as other donors (box 1.2). Critics found limited links between structural adjustment programs and economic growth in the absence of country ownership. The Bank's emphasis on country-driven aid and strengthened budget processes was reflected in aid programs of other lenders that also increased their budget support aid. And calls for donor harmonization and alignment with country systems were central tenets of the 2005 Paris Declaration of Aid Effectiveness, to which the Bank was a signatory. New Bank guidelines for development policy lending, introduced in late 2004, reflected all of these principles.

Policies toward other adjustment lending changed over the PRSC period, so did the nature of aid flows from other sources.

These factors increase the difficulty of isolating the effects of the PRSC. First, development policy lending was changing Bank-wide, and its comparators were therefore shifting. Second, changes in thinking toward aid and the development agenda affected not only the Bank but also other partners in development. In recipient countries, therefore, changes in the character of aid flows with the PRSC occurred in tandem with changes

Box 1.2. PRSCs in the Bank's Regions—Diverse Patterns

Africa—The Africa region began using PRSCs early (Uganda in fiscal 2001, Burkina Faso in fiscal 2002) and has always had the largest portfolio of PRSCs among the regions (13 countries by fiscal 2008). The region has stood has out in having a clear vision for the PRSC since 2003, as a reward for high performers with trustworthy public financial management systems. Africa's PRSCs have strongly emphasized building and using country systems and donor harmonization around a common medium-term reform framework.

East Asia and Pacific—In Vietnam, the first PRSC was largely a continuation of Bank lending in the 1990s. In Lao PDR, budget support, provided via the PRSC, served to leverage government reform efforts, which accompanied support to its large-scale hydroelectric projects and planned Bank investment. PRSC public financial management reform incorporated benchmarks for revenue management in accompanying projects.

Europe and Central Asia—In the five Europe and Central Asia countries where the PRSC has been used (Albania, Armenia, Azerbaijan, Georgia, and Moldova), it has generally provided a relatively small share of country budget needs. PRSC policy measures are less focused on building country systems (as in Africa) and more on transitioning toward market-led growth. Donor harmonization has not been a major element due to limited other budget support. Overall, the PRSC's regional role is small. In fiscal 2009, Georgia is the only country with an active PRSC program. Three Europe and Central Asia PRSC countries have graduated from IDA or chosen other instruments.

Latin America and Caribbean—Three countries had embarked on PRSCs (Guyana, Honduras, and Nicaragua), but currently there are no ongoing operations. PRSCs were discontinued largely due to political changes limiting reform sustainability.

Middle East and North Africa—The PRSC has never been a part of the region's lending portfolio. There are only three IDA-eligible countries in the region (Djibouti, Sudan, and Yemen). Yet, it is interesting that two, Djibouti and Yemen, had relatively high Country Policy and Institutional Assessment (CPIA) scores and a history of adjustment lending/development policy lending and may have been PRSC eligible. Yemen's Institutional Reform Credit, approved in December 2007, focuses on growth and governance, and did not use the PRSC label.

South Asia—Although Nepal, Pakistan, and Sri Lanka initiated PRSCs over the period 2003–05, there are currently no ongoing operations. Nepal and Sri Lanka's PRSCs were terminated after the first operation because political instability jeopardized the ability to commit to a medium-term reform strategy. Pakistan's PRSC also lost relevance when it was overtaken by domestic events. PRSCs in South Asia supported ongoing reform efforts, though the longer-term capacity development approach of Africa was less evident.

Box 1.3. The Debate over Aid and Budget Support

The effectiveness of aid in supporting growth—and of budget support aid, as compared with project aid—has long been debated. Shortly before the introduction of the PRSC, aid literature emphasized the critical role of country ownership of reform programs supported by aid in order to achieve sustained progress (Killick 1996, Collier and others 1997, Killick and others 1998), and that conditionality on its own could hamper the reform agenda (Gilbert, Powell, Vines 1999). The literature also emphasized that domestic governance and institutions lie at the heart of the success or failure of structural reforms (Barro and Sala-i-Martin 1997; Barro 1998) and research demonstrated the negative implications for growth of weak institutions and corruption (Mauro 1995). Budget support or program aid was advocated for those countries that had sound fiduciary systems for the management of public funds. This approach was motivated by a greater appreciation for the fungibility of aid (Devarajan, Swaroop, and Zou 1999), from a realization of the importance of building and using country systems, and by an appreciation of the role of priority sector spending in reducing poverty via improved service delivery (Koeberle 2003, White and Dijkstra 2003, Morrisey 2004). The central tenets of country ownership and good fiduciary management were reflected in the design of the PRSC, which was based on the belief that aid supports growth-enhancing economic reforms when the government is willing and able to put into place the appropriate policy environment (Dollar and Pritchard 1998, Dollar and Svensson 2000).

Yet today, broad-based concerns about aid remain, as well as specific concerns about the impact of budget support. Some recent research has found, for example, that aid may not have any observable association with growth and casts doubt on the aid-growth relationship, even in environments with sound policies (Rajan and Subramanian 2005 and 2008). Concerns have also been voiced that large resource flows through aid can lead to adverse macroeconomic consequences, weaken economic management, and create dependency. Instances are pointed out where aid may also crowd out local industry or initiatives (Moyo 2009) or simply be wasted (Calderisi 2006). More specific concerns have been voiced about budget support-based aid, particularly with regard to the fiduciary aspects of recipient budget systems (Alexander 2008) and potential for leakage into unintended areas such as patronage or military expenditure (Collier 2007, 2009). Such concerns are acknowledged, although not examined, in this evaluation, as they may be less pronounced in PRSC countries, which typically have more robust fiduciary environments.

in other aid flows. And third, these changes evolved during the period of implementation.

Objectives and Scope of the Evaluation

The overarching goal of PRSCs was to support the implementation of country-owned, medium-term development strategies that promote growth, improve social conditions, and reduce poverty. The instrument was used for a series of objectives:

- Help strong-performing IDA countries to implement their medium-term PRSs;
- Strengthen the use of domestic planning and budgeting systems by making predictable medium-term commitments, disbursed in line with countries' budget cycle requirements;
- Provide a framework for aid harmonization;
- Strengthen the institutional framework for budget and public financial management; and
- Focus on the achievement of results, in the context of a clearly articulated framework for results measurement.

The objective of this evaluation is to assess whether Poverty Reduction Support Credits today are a relevant and effective mechanism to support a process of structural development that promotes growth, improves social conditions, and, important in the context of the present global crisis, helps alleviate poverty in low-income countries. The evaluation will assess the extent to which the PRSC's core objectives, described above, have been met.

This evaluation assesses the relevance and effectiveness of PRSCs and their contribution to poverty-reducing growth.

The analysis in this report builds upon IEG's evaluation of the Poverty Reduction Strategy (PRS) initiative (IEG 2000, 2004) and previous analyses of the PRSC instrument (World Bank 2005c). The results chain guiding the evaluation (figure 1.4) describes the sequence, from inputs (resource flows, policy dialogue or technical assistance, design and processes) to outputs in the form of implementation of an identified subset of PRS objectives, better alignment and predictability, and better

Figure 1.4. Poverty Reduction Support Credit Evaluation: Results Chain

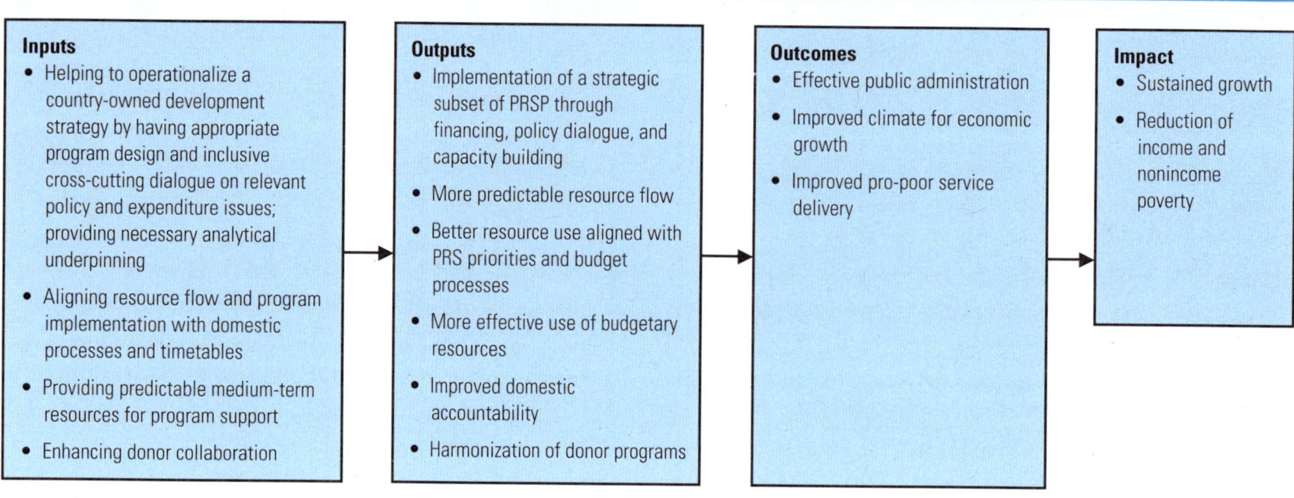

Note: The above results chain draws on the PRSP results chain developed for the IEG evaluation of the PRS process, as well as methodology developed for recent non-Bank general budget support evaluations (IDD and Associates 2006a).

donor coordination. The evaluation then explores outcomes for building a better growth-enabling environment, strengthening public financial management, and improving the delivery of pro-poor services, using the health and education sectors as examples.

Methodology and Data Sources

A detailed discussion of the methodology and data sources used is available in annex 3 of this report. The evaluation seeks to (i) compare the performance of PRSC beneficiaries before and after engagement in the program, as well as (ii) relative to eligible IDA countries that have not benefited from PRSCs. A further filter used is to compare PRSC countries with other better-performing IDA countries.

The evaluation compares pre- and post-PRSC performance, and compares PRSC to non-PRSC countries, including better performers.

This evaluation is based on five major sources of information: (i) a comprehensive desk review of the PRSC portfolio, including country documents, analytic work, and associated IEG evaluative material; (ii) seven case studies of countries, which cover 31 PRSC operations, 8 completed PRSC series, another 4 ongoing series, and 33 percent of total disbursements for PRSCs over the period fiscal 2001–08; (iii) three IEG surveys (annexes 5–7)—the first focusing on task team leaders (with responses from 40 team leaders in all 27 PRSC countries), the second including 76 sector specialists from six sectors who served as PRSC team members, and the third covering senior government officials, in 24 out of 27 PRSC countries, who were engaged with PRSCs as key counterparts; (iv) relevant internal and external databases; and (v) an extensive review of the literature.

Chapter 2 evaluates PRSC design features and the extent to which they met expectations. Chapter 3 evaluates PRSC alignment with client countries' national development strategies, contribution to the operationalization of the PRS, and PRSC results orientation. Chapter 4 focuses on the PRSC as an instrument of donor harmonization, especially in a multidonor budget support environment. Chapters 5 and 6 focus on PRSC outcomes in strengthening public financial management and contributions to creating a pro-poor, growth-enabling environment. Chapter 7 summarizes findings and proposes recommendations.

Chapter 2

Evaluation Highlights

- PRSCs typically went to better performers.
- Screening of countries for limited reform commitments improved.
- PRSCs had fewer legally binding conditions than preceding adjustment loans, but conditionality is similar to other policy-based lending today.
- Conditionality for subsequent operations in a PRSC series was more flexible, and financing was more predictable and better aligned with domestic budget cycles.
- Perceptions of differences between legally binding conditions and benchmarks have blurred.
- Tensions between predictability and program adherence were balanced using downward adjustment or termination of the series.
- PRSCs emphasized public sector management and pro-poor social service delivery, as did later Development Policy Loans.
- PRSCs were rarely able to fully incorporate sectoral lending.

Primary-school student. Photo by Trevor Samson, courtesy of the World Bank Photo Library.

PRSC Design

Poverty Reduction Support Credits, by design, were intended to embody new characteristics to help them realize objectives that distinguished them from other World Bank policy-based lending.[1] We evaluate the extent to which PRSC operations were awarded to countries with strong reform commitment and whether they embodied eased and more flexible conditionality, greater predictability, and better alignment with national budget cycles. PRSC sector focus is reviewed to see whether there was increased emphasis on improving pro-poor service delivery in areas such as health or education, and the extent to which the PRSC instrument offered a new vehicle for sector lending that subsumed parallel sectoral investment operations.

Country Selection

How Have Countries Been Selected for a PRSC?

PRSC Interim Guidelines' eligibility criteria included an adequate PRSP (which virtually all IDA countries have today), commitment to a program of structural and social reforms in support of poverty reduction, and adequate fiduciary and public financial management arrangements or a readiness to improve them. Later, a high level of fiduciary capability and overall good performance became an explicit part of PRSC selection strategy in the Africa region, where PRSCs became a reward for sustained reform.[2]

Analysis of factors associated with the selection of an eligible IDA country for a PRSC shows that strong institutional and public management performance, using the Bank's Country Policy and Institutional Assessment (CPIA) as a proxy, explains a substantial part of PRSC country selection. Over 2001–04, a movement in average overall CPIA scores, from 2.5 to 3.0, increased the likelihood of selection by one-fourth.[3] Using CPIA subcomponents for public financial management, lower corruption, and better public sector performance yields results that are highly similar to overall CPIA scores.[4] And PRSC countries have higher average CPIA scores, even compared with other well-performing IDA countries with CPIA scores of 3 and above (appendix table A2.1).[5]

Surprisingly, the success of previous policy-based lending, as evaluated by IEG, had no significant effect on PRSC country selection. By contrast, having a PRSC in the early period is related to selection for a PRSC in the second period, suggesting that continuation of the program may have been a consideration for a new operation.

Country institutional scores predict much of the likelihood of getting a PRSC.

For the 2005–08 period, greater government stability moderately increased the likelihood of PRSC selection.[6] This finding corroborates desk reviews of terminated PRSC series, which show six aborted PRSC series in fiscal 2001–04 out of 13 countries, compared with only one among 14 countries where the PRSC was initiated over fiscal 2005–08.

The Interim Guidelines emphasize reform commitment as a criterion for PRSC selection, suggesting that PRSCs could include countries that are not presently high performers, provided com-

Past performance and government stability had a lesser role in country selection.

mitment is strong. One PRSC country, Lao PDR, was selected despite a CPIA score below 3.0, and had outcomes similar to other PRSC countries. But there were no later examples.

Sector Focus

PRSC sector focus is shown to be markedly different from earlier adjustment lending. These changes were sustained. Later development policy lending, following the guidelines of late 2004, evolved in the same direction as the PRSC. Differences in sectoral orientation are negligible today.

PRSCs had a lesser focus on macro adjustment, and a greater focus on public financial management and pro-poor lending, as compared with previous adjustment lending.

The sector orientation of a policy-based lending operation is assessed here by its policy framework of conditions, with the caveat that this approach may not reflect changes in the nature of conditions over time. The Bank's Adjustment Lending and Conditionality Implementation Database has distinguished between "legally binding" conditions and "desired actions but not legally binding," which are benchmarks of program performance.[7] While overall successful performance of a program is required for its continuation, the achievement of specific program benchmarks is not a requirement.[8]

PRSCs Compared with Pre-PRSC Policy-Based Lending

Compared with pre-PRSC policy-based loans, PRSCs increased the focus on sectors associated with pro-poor service delivery (figure 2.1). This is most notable in the health sector, which accounted for 13 percent of all sectoral conditions among the 87 PRSC operations that took place from fiscal 2001 to fiscal 2008, compared with only 5.7 percent of conditions among the 92 IDA adjustment operations in the preceding six years (fiscal 1995–2000). PRSCs also exhibited a considerably greater sectoral emphasis in water supply and sanitation (4.0 percent compared with 0.6 percent) and in education (8.1 percent compared with 3.6 percent). In many poor countries where PRSC loans are made, agriculture is often the most important source of livelihood and therefore has strong potential for alleviating poverty. However, PRSCs focused slightly less on agriculture (including natural resources, environment, and rural development) than previous IDA adjustment lending (5.8 percent compared with 7.4 percent in former adjustment loans).[9]

Emphasis on health, education, and water supply and sanitation increased, while agriculture declined in emphasis.

PRSCs clearly focused less on sectors oriented toward macro adjustment, such as finance (5.2 percent, compared with 16.8 percent in prior adjustment lending), energy and mining (3.1 percent, compared with 7.1 percent), and industry and trade (4.4 percent, compared with 25.2 percent).[10] PRSCs also have a markedly greater public sector focus than prior adjustment lending, with 53.3 percent versus 27.9 percent of total conditions.[11]

Differences between PRSCs and previous adjustment loans are more marked relative to all countries (IDA+IBRD; figure 2.1). For example, between fiscal 1995 and fiscal 2000, the financial sector had a share of 24.6 percent of sectoral conditions in all structural lending, compared with 16.8 percent for IDA alone, and 5.2 percent for PRSCs. Conversely, education had a share of only 2.3 percent in all lending, compared with 3.6 percent for IDA and 8.1 percent for PRSCs.[12]

Over time, the sectoral composition of PRSC operations became, if anything, more like PRSCs and less like former adjustment loans and credits, focusing even more on health (13.8 percent in fiscal 2005–08, compared with 10.8 percent in fiscal 2001–04) and more on education (8.1 percent in the latter period, compared with 7.8 percent in the former period). However, there was a slight fall-off in focus on water supply and sanitation (3.2 percent in the later period versus 6.5 percent in the earlier period). PRSCs also continued to focus progressively less on finance (4.9 percent in fiscal 2005–08, compared with 6.0 percent in fiscal 2001–04), and less on industry and trade (2.8 percent versus 8.9 percent earlier). However, there was also a reduced focus on agriculture, rural development, and the environment (5.4 percent in fiscal 2005–08 versus 7.2 percent).

PRSCs over fiscal 2001–04 looked very different from other policy-based IDA credits over the period fiscal 1995–2004. There was greater public sec-

Figure 2.1. PRSC Sector Focus Compared with Earlier Policy-Based Lending (FY1995–2000)

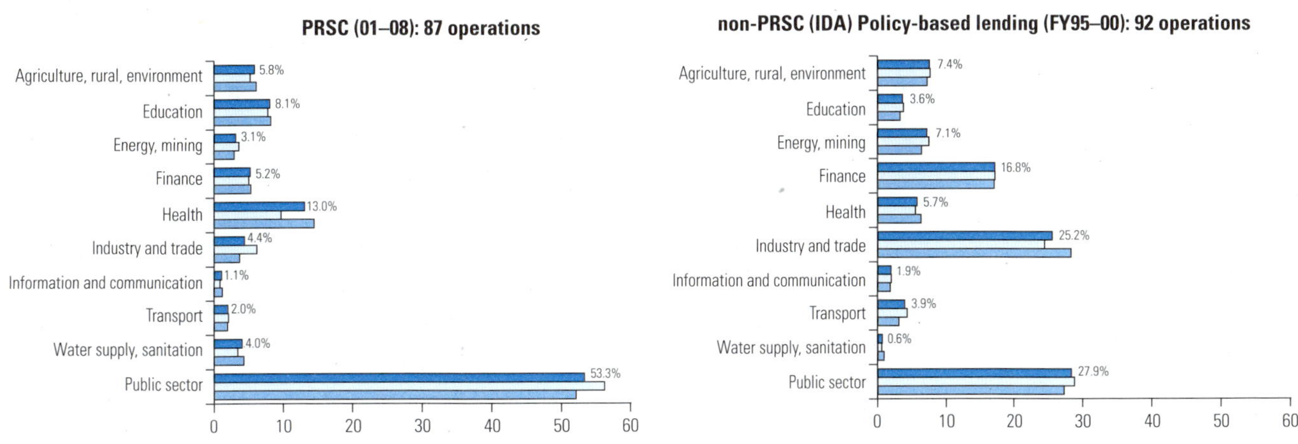

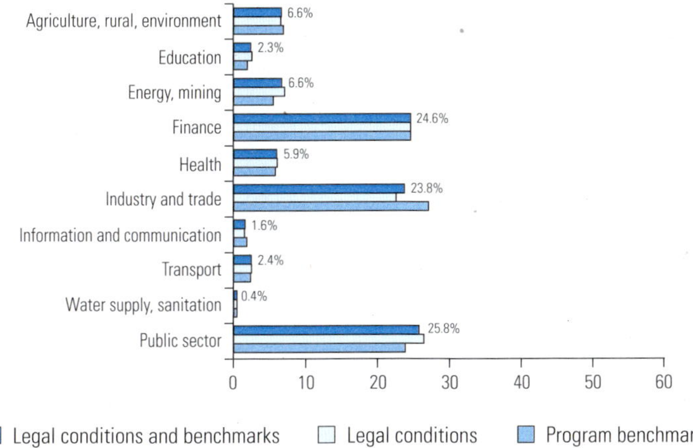

Source: World Bank database. Thematic group and sector data are reclassified on the basis of the 10 sectors above, to clarify database classifications, reflect sectors of PRSC interest, and to more accurately represent the sectoral content of loans.

tor focus on PRSCs (47 percent, compared with 35 percent in other IDA policy-based loans) and less of a focus on finance, industry, and trade in the PRSCs (6 percent, compared with 13.9 percent in IDA policy-based loans). PRSCs also exhibited a greater focus on health, education, and water supply and sanitation. These differences are even more pronounced when International Bank for Reconstruction and Development (IBRD) countries are added to the comparison group.

In the subsequent fiscal 2005–08 period, however, together with the continued and heightened pro-poor orientation of the PRSC discussed above, a parallel change is observed in the character of other policy-based loans, which also began to adopt the governance and service delivery characteristics of the PRSC. All policy-based lending operations, taken together, increased their focus on governance and public sector management (from 31.2 percent to 55.4 percent). In the education sector, at 8.1 percent, the PRSCs had fewer policy conditions than other policy-based lending operations to IDA countries (14.2 percent) and even to all IDA+IBRD countries (9.5 percent).[13] And while the share of the financial sector in PRSC operations was as low as 4.9 percent, its share in all IDA policy-

Sector focus on pro-poor service delivery and public sector management increased in PRSCs over time.

After 2005, the focus of all adjustment lending evolved in the same direction as the PRSC.

PRSCs had wider sectoral coverage than previous adjustment lending, especially in program benchmarks.

based loans other than PRSCs had also declined to 5.8 percent, as compared with 13.9 percent in the earlier period. By the end of the period, significant changes in the character of non-PRSC operations implied that there was little difference in their sectoral orientation compared with the PRSCs. The PRSC may thus be regarded as the precursor for the new style of development policy lending.[14]

PRSC task team leaders agreed that PRSC operations were very different from previous adjustment lending, though not from later DPLs.

PRSC task team leaders corroborated these findings (annex 5). Seventy percent of respondents considered PRSC operations very different from earlier Structural Adjustment Loans, but only 19 percent thought there was a slight difference compared with other Development Policy Loans, and 11 percent thought there was no difference.

Sectoral Lending through PRSCs—A Wider Focus?

Especially at the outset, PRSC operations were wider in scope and coverage than previous adjustment operations. Over time, PRSCs generally became more specifically focused.[15]

As table 2.1 shows, PRSCs did have a wider sectoral coverage than pre-PRSC policy-based loans over fiscal 1995–2000 (6.4 sectors, on average, as compared with 5.3 sectors for IDA as a whole). Wider sectoral coverage is seen as well when compared with parallel policy-based loans over fiscal 2001–04. PRSC sectoral coverage, especially in terms of legally binding conditions, declined somewhat over time. But sectoral coverage for other policy-based lending also declined, more so than PRSCs. Wider sectoral coverage of PRSCs can be traced, particularly, to program benchmarks.[16]

Did PRSCs Replace Some Freestanding Sector Lending?

At the time of its introduction, there was some expectation, although not explicit in guidelines, that the PRSC would gradually become the primary vehicle for some areas of sectoral lending.[17] Fiscally responsible countries would make their own allocation decisions through the budget mechanism, reducing parallel sector projects.[18] The replacement of sector lending in at least one sector was explicitly discussed as a part of the Country Assistance Strategy in 10 out of 27 PRSC countries (table 2.2), 9 of which were in the Africa region.[19] Replacement was expected to happen in one or more of six sectors: health, education, nutrition, water, agriculture, and environment and natural resources. The most frequently mentioned sectors are health (nine cases) and education (six cases).

Initially, there was some expectation that PRSCs would gradually fold into sectoral lending.

However, only four countries (Benin, Cape Verde, Rwanda, and Senegal) replaced sectoral operations, up until fiscal 2008, in even one sector. In another five countries, PRSCs temporarily replaced sectoral investment projects in at least one sector (Benin, Burkina Faso, Madagascar, Mozambique, and Uganda). New sectoral projects began about three to nine years after the previous sector-related project had closed.[20] And the intention to begin replacement has not been pursued further in Tanzania and Mali and has been dropped for certain sectors in Madagascar and Mozambique.

Box 2.1. PRSC Sector Coverage—Narrowing over Time

In Vietnam, the government was keen to make the reform matrix as comprehensive as possible. The PRSC covered has roughly 17 policy areas across the four pillars of the reform agenda: business development, social inclusion, natural resource management, and improved governance. Limited subsequent engagement has been noted in areas such as water supply and sanitation.

In Lao PDR, the first three PRS operations included policy areas in health, education, transport, rural electrification, water supply, and forestry management, but all areas (except health and education) were dropped for the second programmatic series, to focus the reform effort.

In Nicaragua, the sectoral focus was narrower, with no legally binding conditions in health (a decision due to other donors' involvement). There was some involvement in education and water and sanitation, but the much of the reform effort focused on public sector management.

Table 2.1. PRSCs and Other Policy-Based Lending: Average Number of Sectors (FY1995–2008)

		FY1995–2000		FY01–04		FY05–08	
		n	Average	n	Average	n	Average
No. of sectors:	PRSC			21	6.4	66	6.1
All conditions	IDA	92	5.3	63	4.7	57	3.8
	IDA+IBRD	192	4.7	138	4.3	140	3.4
No. of sectors:	PRSC			21	4.8	66	4.2
Legally binding conditions	IDA	91	4.8	63	4.1	57	3.0
	IDA+IBRD	191	4.4	138	3.8	140	2.8
No. of sectors:	PRSC			18	6.0	52	6.3
Program benchmarks	IDA	55	4.1	33	4.6	40	3.8
	IDA+IBRD	110	3.7	60	4.5	87	3.3

Source: World Bank database.
Notes: Based on the 10-sector classification of conditions as mapped by IEG.

Table 2.2. PRSC Operations: Intended and Actual Replacement of Sectoral Lending (FY01–08)

Sector		Intention to replace		Replaced permanently		Replaced temporarily		Not replaced
Health	9	Benin, Burkina Faso, Madagascar, Mali, Mozambique, Rwanda, Senegal, Tanzania, Uganda	2	Rwanda, Senegal[a]	3	Benin, Burkina Faso, Mozambique, Uganda	3	Madagascar, Mali, Tanzania
Education	6	Benin, Cape Verde, Madagascar, Mozambique, Tanzania, Uganda	1	Cape Verde	3	Benin, Madagascar, Uganda	2	Mozambique, Tanzania
Nutrition	1	Madagascar					1	Madagascar
Water	3	Benin, Madagascar, Mali	1	Benin	1	Madagascar	1	Mali
Agriculture	1	Mozambique					1	Mozambique
Environment and natural resources	1	Benin	2	Benin				
Total number of countries	10		4		5		4	

Sources: Country Assistance Strategy (CAS) and Country Partnership Strategy reports and CAS completion reports of PRSC countries, relevant program documents, and Country Assistance Evaluation reports from the World Bank and IEG.
a. Rwanda and Senegal have AIDs projects that are not counted here.

In sum, although attempted in many countries, instances of successful replacement were rare. While some countries experimented with the new modalities for sectoral lending, in most such cases project-specific lending resumed within a few years.[21]

Ten countries planned in their CASs that the PRSC would absorb freestanding lending in at least one sector.

In the health sector, where PRSCs were expected to replace sector-specific lending most frequently (appendix tables A2.4 and A2.5), replacement occurred in two countries (Rwanda and Senegal), not counting AIDS projects,

In most countries where replacement of sectoral investment was tried, the attempt was temporary.

and in another four countries it was replaced on a temporary basis (Benin, Burkina Faso, Mozambique, and Uganda).[22] In three countries (Madagascar, Mali, and Tanzania), replacement never materialized. In education, the PRSC replaced sectoral operations temporarily in three cases (Benin, Madagascar, and Uganda), and permanently or until fiscal 2008 in one case (Cape Verde). Envisaged replacements never materialized in another two (Mozambique and Tanzania). Five joined or are planning to join the Education-for-All Fast Track initiative. Other sector projects cover secondary education (Uganda and Tanzania) and higher education and vocational training (Madagascar, Mozambique, and Tanzania).

Yet, the PRSC was, by design, intended to replace sectoral investment operations only where the right preconditions existed: a costed sector strategy, ownership of reform process by relevant ministries, and sufficient capacity to carry out the reform effort using country systems. In Benin, case study findings suggest that the intention to replace sector lending in health and education was likely premature. In countries where preconditions were really present, there was relative success (as in the Cape Verde education sector).

Preconditions to replace sectoral lending were rarely mature.

PRSCs and Support to Sector Projects

Conversely, the PRSC continued to play a strong supporting role in sectoral operations through reinforcing conditionality, without attempting to bring the sectors wholly under the umbrella of the PRSC. In Vietnam, for example, in key social sectors (health, education, water supply and sanitation) ongoing sector operations continued, with no intention to replace them with the PRSC. An IEG review shows that about 60 percent of PRSCs have core policy actions in sectors with ongoing investment operations. For example, there were corresponding sector projects in 58 out of 61 PRSCs with legally binding conditions in the health sector, and 41 out of 43 PRSCs in the agriculture and rural development sectors (appendix tables A2.2 and A2.3). By contrast, the PRSC was more frequently the sole vehicle for lending in public sector and economic management, where there were rarely corresponding projects.

The PRSC contributed to sectoral objectives by reinforcing crosscutting and overarching issues.

There are wide differences in views on PRSCs among sectoral staff, but most endorse its potential to add value on crosscutting themes.

Bank Staff Views on Sectoral Lending through PRSCs—Team Leaders

PRSC team leaders are divided in their views on the sectoral role of the PRSC instrument. Only 54 percent consider it could be the main instrument for dialogue and engagement in all sectors.[23] And more than half among those who expected the PRSC to replace sector-specific lending noted that transition to the PRSC was only selectively effective and worked best when the right preconditions were fulfilled (for example, government commitment, a clear sector strategy, and detailed budget costing; see annex 5).[24]

Team leaders do not attribute shortcomings in sectoral outcomes to the quality of sector staff, but rather to inadequate resource incentives and managerial acknowledgement. Ninety percent fully or partly agreed that team staff had the right skills in budgeting and strategic planning to effectively develop sector dialogue, strategy, and budgeting practices via the PRSC in their sectors. Moreover, 93 percent of team leaders fully or partly agreed that there was strong ownership among all Bank PRSC team members, and 87 percent expressed the belief that the PRSC was strengthening cross-sectoral collaboration within the Bank team.

Bank Staff Views on Sectoral Lending through PRSCs—Sector Specialists

A separate survey of sector specialists who served as members of PRSC teams suggests equally divergent views (annex 6).[25] A quarter of respondents believed that the PRSC had not been able to open up new opportunities in the sector. But at the other end of the spectrum, 42 percent felt it to be significantly or entirely true. However, staff did not support the inverse question of whether the PRSC closed off opportunities for sectoral engagement—89 percent of all respondents felt that this is not true or only partly true. Generally, a majority of staff (56 to 72 percent) believed that the PRSC had accomplishments beyond a freestanding operation, aided macro-level constraints, and included relevant conditionality. However, a similar majority also believed that the PRSC encountered policy or capacity issues that could not fit within the PRSC framework (58 percent). About a third (32 percent) believed that the PRSC led to a loss in depth of technical dialogue. Less than a third believed that the PRSCs helped with the timeliness and predictability of budget allocations to line agencies (29 percent). It was strongly felt that there was there was little or no overall increase in sectoral resource allocation (89 percent).

In virtually all areas, the PRSC as an instrument is viewed more favorably by Poverty Reduction and Economic Management staff.[26] However, the difference is usually not large—between two and five percentage points for most questions.

Conditionality

PRSCs Compared with Other Policy-Based Lending: 1980–2008

A key aim of the PRSC was to reduce the burden of conditionality. This was to be achieved by focusing on (i) a limited set of legally binding conditions, which would be undertaken before presentation to the Bank's Board—that is, *prior actions*, and (ii) indicative prior actions, which were not legally binding, for subsequent operations within a medium-term framework. These were described as *triggers* for the next operation in a programmatic series. Prior actions of subsequent operations, however, would be expected to be based primarily upon triggers defined in the previous operation. Previous adjustment loans had legally binding conditions for *Board presentation* or loan *effectiveness*, which were also conditions prior to loan approval, similar to prior actions, and subsequent legally binding conditions for *tranche release*, for multitranche operations. In structural adjustment lending these were defined at the outset of a series. The present evaluation uses the term "legally binding conditions" to refer to such conditions in previous adjustment lending, and to prior actions under new policies for DPLs. Previous adjustment lending also indicated desirable actions that were not legally binding for program implementation. PRSCs and subsequent DPLs refer to progress markers of overall program implementation, which are not legally binding, as program *benchmarks*.

Some staff believe the PRSC leads to a loss of depth in sector dialogue and has not helped resource predictability to the line agencies.

For purposes of comparison, PRSC prior actions effectively replace the legally binding Board presentation and effectiveness conditions of prior adjustment lending. All conditions in PRSC loans have to be met prior to Board presentation. PRSC *program benchmarks* may be compared to the "desired actions which are not legally binding" of previous adjustment lending.[27]

Over the 19-year period, fiscal 1980–2008, there were almost 900 adjustment lending operations Bank-wide, including the 88 PRSCs of fiscal 2001–08 (table 2.3). PRSC have a lower average number of legally binding conditions (12.1) as compared with all non-PRSC policy-based operations over this period (24.7). Looking at the PRSC subperiod, 2001–08, the number of legally binding conditions in other policy-based loans was lower (16.2 per operation) but still higher than the PRSC average (12.1). Conversely, program benchmarks in PRSCs were higher than other policy-based adjustment operations (29.3 compared with 14.4).

Legally binding conditionality in all adjustment lending saw a trend decline, but non-PRSC conditionality declined faster than PRSCs.

However, legally binding conditions or prior actions in all policy-based loans underwent a major trend decline, from an average of 46 per loan in 1992, to an average of 9 in fiscal 2008 (figure 2.2 and appendix table A2.7). And in non-PRSC policy-based loans such conditions declined faster than in PRSCs, at 1 per year from 1991 to 2001, accelerating to 2.5 per year from fiscal 2001 to fiscal 2008.[28] The decline was more pronounced, for non-PRSC operations compared with PRSCs, after the introduction of new guidelines for DPLs in fiscal 2005. For PRSCs, the average number of legally binding conditions declines from 12.0 to 11.1 per year from fiscal 2005 to fiscal 2008, while for non-PRSCs, the average declines from 19.4 to 11.4 per year.[29]

Conditionality declined gradually in all policy-based lending, which had begun before the PRSC.

Table 2.3. PRSCs and Other Policy-Based Loans: Average Number of Conditions (FY1980–2008)

		Average number of conditions per operation		
	Number of operations	Total	Legally binding conditions[a]	Program benchmarks[b]
All policy-based operations	888	39.4	23.5	15.9
Non-PRSC	800	39.1	24.7	14.4
PRSC	88	41.4	12.1	29.3

Source: World Bank database.
a. Prior actions.
b. Nonbinding conditions.

Figure 2.2. PRSCs and Other Policy-Based Lending—Trends in Conditionality (FY1980–2008)

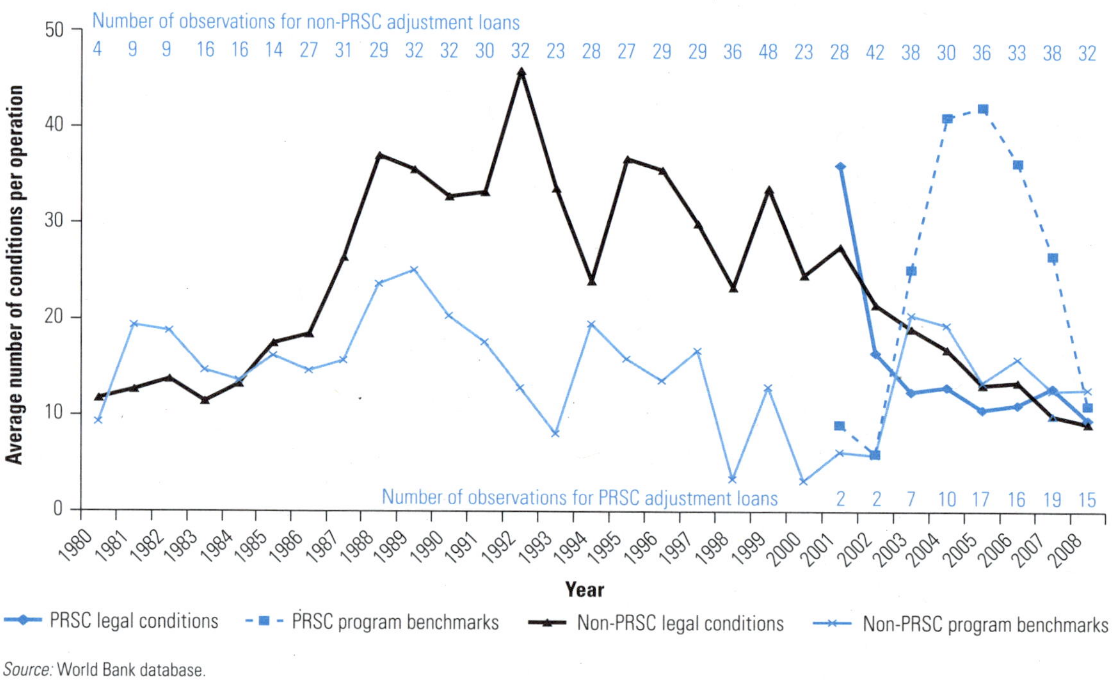

Source: World Bank database.

Some observers believe that total conditionality in PRSCs did not decrease because program benchmarks, which are not legally binding, increased in parallel to the decline in legally binding conditions.[30] But while PRSC program benchmarks rose steeply initially, from 6 in fiscal 2002 to 41.8 in fiscal 2005, they sharply declined thereafter to 11 in fiscal 2008. This sharp decline was not mirrored in non-PRSC adjustment operations, where program benchmarks rose less in the earlier period.

By the end of fiscal 2008, there was significant convergence in the numbers of conditions of PRSC and non-PRSC loans.

By the end of fiscal 2008, there was significant convergence in the numbers of conditions of PRSC and non-PRSC loans. Program benchmarks averaged, respectively, 11 and 12.7, while legally binding conditions averaged 9.5 and 9.2 in fiscal 2008.

Table 2.4. PRSC Countries—Number of Conditions in Pre-PRSC Policy Loans (72 operations)

		50–75 conditions		25–50 conditions		Less than 25 conditions	
	Number of loans	Number of loans	%	Number of loans	%	Number of loans	%
First policy loan	26	4	16	12	46	10	38
Second policy loan	26	2	8	10	38	14	54
Third policy loan	20	1	5	6	30	13	65

Source: World Bank database.

Legally Binding Conditionality: Pre-PRSC and PRSC Series

An examination of trends in specific series of adjustment operations for PRSC countries, compared with prior adjustment lending in these countries, confirms a trend decline in conditionality that began prior to introduction of the PRSC (appendix table A2.7). All 27 PRSC countries, except Lesotho, had received policy-based lending prior to receiving their first PRSC. From an average of 27 legally binding conditions in the three prior adjustment loans (1987–2005), there was a decline to 11.1 per PRSC operation.[31] At the time of their first adjustment operation, 4 PRSC countries had 50–75 conditions (Albania, Benin, Honduras, and Lao PDR). Another 12 countries had between 25 and 50 conditions, and another 10 countries had fewer than 25 conditions (table 2.4).

By the third pre-PRSC adjustment operation, only one country (Georgia) had more than 50 conditions. Six had between 25 and 50 conditions and 13 countries had less than 25. Armenia is one example; its Structural Adjustment Credits had a peak of 66 conditions, while PRSC 1, PRSC 2, and PRSC 3, respectively, had 7, 13, and 11 legally binding prior actions each (and 26, 21, and 24 program benchmarks each). PRSC 4 included only 7 prior actions.

Conditionality—Prior Actions and Triggers

Looking at PRSC series as a whole, a similarly limited decline in the number of prior actions and triggers is observed, of less than a half per year (–0.39; omitting one outlying early operation in Vietnam).[32] A review of six countries with five or more PRSC operations (omitting Vietnam, these are Burkina Faso, Ghana, Madagascar, Mozambique, Tanzania, and Uganda) shows that none have significant declines in the number of triggers and only one, Burkina Faso, has a statistically significant decline of one or two prior actions or triggers per year (appendix table A2.8). This confirms the observation that conditionality in PRSCs was low from the outset, and that subsequent reductions occurred largely in program benchmarks.

Client Perceptions of PRSC Conditionality

Over 70 percent of country respondents believe that PRSC programs recognized internal constraints, dynamically adjusting prior actions to country realities. Yet, about 60 percent of clients believe that the PRSC matrix still has too many conditions. One factor may be blurred perceptions regarding the differences between prior actions, which are legally binding conditions, and triggers, which are indicative prior actions for future operations but not legally binding, and program benchmarks, which are also nonbinding. Large donor dynamics are another factor. About a quarter of country clients surveyed feel that there is inadequate recognition of implementation constraints (annex 7 and box 2.2).

Flexibility—Modification of Conditions

Adjustments in Conditionality—Triggers and Subsequent Prior Actions

It was envisaged that PRSCs would be more flexible than adjustment operations in responding to changing country conditions, incomplete information, or less-than-satisfactory implementation. PRSCs would adapt to reality through adjustments to triggers by modifying their content

Box 2.2. PRSCs: Client Perceptions of Conditionality

Numbers of Conditions. There remained a belief that conditionality was somewhat excessive. One respondent believed that the large number of conditions was driven by donor dynamics, where each donor wanted their particular sectors of interest covered by the PRSC matrix. But another stated that increased conditions in PRSC series reflected their own ambitious reform agenda.

Character of Conditionality. Compared with adjustment lending, PRSC conditionality was felt to be better because of: (i) greater use of measurable indicators; (ii) less intrusive nature because it is drawn from a country's own strategy; (iii) focus on development, as opposed to the correction of imbalances; and (iv) output-based policy lending under the PRSC, compared with input-based conditionality under sector adjustment credits. Yet, one respondent thought that there is still a "zero or one approach," where the failure to meet a trigger may jeopardize the whole program. This was contrasted with the more flexible approach of the European Union (EU), where missing a trigger undermined only a part of a tranche, not the entire program.

Program Implementation and Political Change. In some countries, the PRSC counteracted political uncertainty by pacing reform implementation to sustain momentum. But others pointed to a lack of flexibility shown by Bank teams in responding to pervasive political challenges. One official pointed out the hesitation of Bank teams to renegotiate programs agreed to by a previous government. Another suggested PRSC alignment with the country's political cycle.

Limits to Recognition of Implementation Constraints. One stakeholder from an emerging European country recalled that the Bank had wanted to push for certain liberalization measures that the government was not prepared to adopt. Another stakeholder, in Latin America, reported the unsuccessful struggle faced by his country authorities in conveying to the Bank that a reform of the civil service would never be supported by the government or the parliament. A stakeholder from Sub-Saharan Africa talked about Bank intrusiveness, in the context of a dispute over maize prices, although the maize sector was not part of the national strategy. A respondent from West Africa maintained that the Bank had shown limited understanding of some major sectors (cotton, in this case), which led to difficulties in program implementation. Others (Europe and Central Asia, South Asia) reported that the Bank expected the government to take actions for which it had no direct control. They suggested instead that the Bank should highlight potential implementation difficulties to countries.

Sources: IEG country case studies and IEG client survey.

or timing or dropping them if they proved unrealistic. Findings show that the Bank exhibited a radically different level of flexibility with regard to the interpretation of conditions, compared with prior adjustment lending, with modifications in about a quarter of envisaged triggers per country, or modifications in some triggers in almost all operations, taking account of the evolution of country conditions and technical and political difficulties of implementation.[33]

The Bank adopted a very different level of flexibility for PRSCs, compared with former adjustment loans.

By contrast, conditionality in adjustment lending previous to the PRSCs was implemented with rigor and little flexibility. A review of subsequent tranche conditionalities, across 72 pre-PRSC adjustment operations in reviewed PRSC countries, revealed an average number of waivers granted of only 0.4, compared with an average number of 27 conditions. Only 1.5 percent of conditions were waived.[34]

Especially in the early years, potential risks to a PRSC program were not always envisaged, as suggested by the foregoing analysis, which shows that having a PRSC already can be a predictor of embarking on a subsequent operation.[35] Yet, by and large, the Bank was able to balance the inherent tensions between the goal of predictable flows of funds and the maintenance of program content by also using downward adjustments of volumes, or exiting PRSC series if the overall reform program could not remain on track. Where terminated, however, the Bank has remained engaged through a combination of policy-based or investment loans, sometimes with disbursements as large as under the PRSCs, raising the question of the perceived value added of the PRSC label.

Table 2.5. PRSC Countries—Trigger Flexibility in PRSC Operations (FY01–08)

		FY 01–08		FY 01–06		FY 07–08		FY 01–05		FY 06–08	
Number of operations[a]		60		34		26		19		41	
	No.	Avg	%	Avg	%	Avg	%	Avg	%	Avg	%
Triggers: avg. no. per loan	671	11.2		11.0		11.0		10.9		11.4	
1. Triggers fulfilled/unchanged	393	6.6	59	6.5	60	6.3	57	6.1	56	6.8	59
2. Triggers amended	61	1.0	9	1.0	9	1.0	9	0.9	9	1.1	9
3. Triggers downgraded	100	1.7	15	1.5	14	1.8	16	1.5	13	1.8	16
4. Triggers upgraded	33	0.5	5	0.5	4	0.5	5	0.7	7	0.5	4
5. Triggers dropped[b]	33	0.5	5	0.7	6	0.5	5	1.1	10	0.4	3
6. Triggers dropped to limit no. of conditions[c]	21	0.4	3	0.3	3	0.3	3	0	0	0.5	5
7. Triggers replaced	11	0.2	1	0.2	2	0.1	1	0.3	3	0.1	1
8. Triggers postponed	19	0.3	3	0.2	2	0.4	4	0.2	2	0.4	3
Prior actions not included in previous operation[d]	60	1.4		1.9		0.5		3.2		0.5	

Sources: PRSC project documents, PRSC development credit agreements, and World Bank database.

a. Sixty PRSC operations had triggers (that is, omitting those with only prior actions).

b. These triggers were omitted without further explanation.

c. These triggers were sometimes fulfilled, but omitted from the list of prior actions (core conditions) and instead regarded as benchmarks (desired actions that are not legally binding).

d. These prior actions were implemented but not included in the project document of the previous operation.

By contrast, PRSCs had a very large number of triggers modified during program implementation (table 2.5 and appendix table A2.10). Of the 60 PRSC follow-up operations over fiscal 2001–08, with a total of 671 triggers, only 59 percent (393) were satisfied without any modification. Modifications were made to at least one trigger in 57 operations (93 percent). On average, for those countries that had more than one PRSC, net modifications to triggers (subtracting new prior actions introduced) amounted to 16.8 percent of all triggers. If new prior actions are not netted out, the average is 26 percent—that is, a quarter of triggers envisaged for new operations are subsequently adjusted in some fashion. On average, per operation, only 6.6 triggers out of 11.2 remained unchanged.

Overall, it is evident that there was an extremely high level of flexibility in terms of adjustments in conditionality. In a few individual operations, adjustments appeared to be the norm instead of the exception. In Ghana, one agreed measure was to complete the rollout of a budget management system in five ministries. When it was achieved in only two ministries, the Bank judged the trigger to have been met on the basis that progress was substantial. Essentially the Bank attitude was that substantial compliance and a good faith effort to achieve the agreed goals was equivalent to full compliance.

Indicative triggers in PRSC operations may be compared with legally binding tranche-release conditions in previous adjustment lending.

Waivers for tranche-release conditions were rare, but most PRSCs had modifications in some triggers.

Task team leaders surveyed in 9 out of 27 countries (6 in Africa and 3 in other regions) suggest that there was some pressure within the Bank to move ahead with PRSCs in some circumstances of less than satisfactory reform. Such pressure may provide an explanation for the large numbers of adjustments observed.

Over time, there appears to have been some reduction in such flexibility. The number of triggers satisfied without modification of any description rose from 6.1 in fiscal 2001–05 to 6.8 in fiscal 2006–08 (table 2.5). And there was some decline in the number of prior actions, introduced ex-post, which recognized unanticipated achievements, even

Some PRSCs included new "prior actions," which had not been anticipated as triggers earlier.

Over time there was some reduction in the number of triggers modified.

if outside the scope of the agreed matrix. In fiscal 2001–05, there were, on average, about 3.2 prior actions per operation without corresponding triggers; their number reduced to only 0.5 per operation in fiscal 2006–08. Their decline suggests a more rigorous adherence to the agreed matrix and clearer ex-ante design of operations and prior consultations. However, it could also be interpreted as some loss of flexibility in recognizing achievements and bringing them into the scope of dialogue.

Predictability and Regularity

One reason for greater flexibility was to achieve more dependable aid flows on a regular basis. The analysis below shows that on a year-to-year basis, PRSCs were able to achieve somewhat more predictable aid flows than previous adjustment lending.[36]

Predictability of Policy-Based Lending Before and After the PRSC

A first measure of predictability is simply the likelihood, in any given year, for a PRSC recipient country of getting a PRSC, compared with prior years. A somewhat wider measure considers the likelihood of a PRSC country receiving *any* form of policy-based budget support after embarking on a PRSC program, as compared with previous adjustment lending. The third measure considers volumes of budget support flows received via PRSCs, compared with previous adjustment lending. The fourth is the relative stability of PRSC resource flow, as a proportion of total IDA/IBRD flows.

On the whole, there was some increase in predictability of funding, though there were gainers and losers.

To a limited extent, the volume of annual funds flows also stabilized.

On average, adjustment assistance was received in 54.8 percent of the five years preceding the advent of PRSCs, compared with 68.9 for all active PRSC years up to the present (appendix table A2.12). The ratio increases further to 70 percent when account is taken of non-PRSC policy-based loans made in parallel to or subsequent to terminated PRSC series up to the present. This suggests a slight improvement in predictability of obtaining fast-disbursing loans in a given year, once a country had a PRSC program, although there were both gainers and losers.[37] PRSCs were also able to reduce variations in volume of funding provided, compared with the previous adjustment period (appendix table A2.13).

On average, across all PRSC countries, the coefficient of variation in annual aid volumes declined from 1.10 to 0.91 (appendix table A2.14). And the predictability of the share of budget support loans in total Bank flows to each recipient country also improved somewhat. The average coefficient of variation declined from 1.02 (pre-PRSC) to 0.86 (PRSC period). The reduction is somewhat greater, from 1.02 to 0.81, comparing PRSCs with prior adjustment lending, for the five-year period before PRSCs and the entire PRSC period up to the present.[38]

Quite a different overall measure of predictability was also undertaken, comparing PRSC lending projections, as envisaged in country strategy documents, with actual disbursements. Of 63 PRSC operations laid out in relevant Country Assistance Strategies,[39] most (34) disbursed within $5 million of the amount predicted in the Country Assistance Strategy/Country Partnership Strategy. Nineteen operations saw an increase of between $5–70 million and 10 decreased by $8–100 million. These data indicate fairly good predictability and corroborate findings of the gap between commitments and disbursements for all budget support to 11 PRSC countries, which also suggests some decline in the gap between commitments and disbursements. Greater PRSC predictability mirrored overall greater predictability in budget support aid from all sources (appendix table A2.15).[40]

Adjustment of PRSC Loan Volumes

How did PRSCs balance the need for more predictable annual resource flows with tensions that could arise if the program could not be kept on track? A review of programs facing difficulties shows that a number of measures were used—reducing the loan amount, delaying or discontinuing a series if a program went off track.[41]

Nine out of 27 PRSC countries terminated their PRSC series, not only for performance reasons (table 2.6). Albania graduated from IDA and chose

Table 2.6. PRSC Countries: Adjustment in Loan Amounts or Termination of Series (FY01–08)

PRSC series discontinued early	Albania, Azerbaijan, Ethiopia, Guyana, Honduras, Nepal, Nicaragua, Pakistan, Sri Lanka
PRSC amounts adjusted downward (IDA resource issues/reform commitment)	Benin, Ethiopia, Ghana, Lao PDR, Madagascar, Pakistan, Rwanda, Tanzania, and Uganda
PRSC amounts with significant upward trends	Benin, Burkina Faso, Tanzania, Vietnam

Source: PRSC program documents, interviews, and World Bank data.

to discontinue support under the PRSC title, usually associated with IDA countries. Yet, fast-disbursing Bank assistance continued, albeit with a lapse of two years. Azerbaijan, an oil exporter, terminated after PRSC 1, following a rise in its oil production and exports linked to rising oil prices. Nonetheless, the Country Partnership Strategy (2007–10) reflects continued government reforms.

Other countries terminated (Ethiopia, Honduras, Nicaragua, Guyana, Nepal, and Sri Lanka) largely due to the political environment, with a loss in reform commitment, or change in national priorities. In four countries (Guyana, Honduras, Nepal, and Sri Lanka) PRSCs were terminated after a first operation and, therefore, noncompliance with triggers was not a factor. In the remaining two countries, Ethiopia and Nicaragua, compliance with triggers was reasonable. Only 2 out of 9 triggers were reduced in scope in Ethiopia, and 2 out of 27 in Nicaragua. Indeed, in Nicaragua, 7 new prior actions were introduced without previous

Box 2.3. Post-PRSC Bank Assistance Usually Continued, Often as DPLs

Some countries that terminated their PRSCs later received policy-based loans via sectoral support. Others received aid via investment lending. While resource flows did not always attain the levels or predictability planned under the PRSC, the magnitude was often large.

Ethiopia: Aid resumed after the PRSC, replaced by the Protection of Basic Services Project. Although formally an investment project, it was in fact a one-tranche social sector budget-support project (SWAp). Another non-PRSC Development Policy Loan is being explored (IEG PPAR on Ethiopia, 2008).

Guyana: After its single PRSC operation, a single-tranche IDA DPL (Poverty Reduction and Public Management grant) of $9.7 million was approved in April 2006, followed by several small investment projects. However, total disbursements are now well below the levels prevailing prior to PRSC approval.

Honduras: Following the closure of its first operation, the new PRSC series planned for 2007–10 was abandoned because of the election cycle and the country's inability to commit to a medium-term reform program. Preparation began on a single-operation Development Policy Credit which was not implemented. However, a supplement to a previous Financial Sector Development Credit was approved in 2008, following the food price crisis.

Nepal: When the PRSC series stalled, after a disbursement of $75 million, IDA support continued via an Education for All (EFA) credit, a Poverty Alleviation Fund, and a Health Sector Project. Total IDA lending in the PRSC year (fiscal 2004) was $101 million. Subsequent annual lending was about $80 million, somewhat lower than in fiscal 2004.

Nicaragua: PRSCs were not replaced by any fast-disbursing assistance until fiscal 2009, when a single-tranche DPC was approved. Investment projects continued through this period.

Sri Lanka: IDA returned to traditional investment projects after the end of the PRSC. However, disbursements in the period fiscal 2004–08 averaged $125 million per year; roughly the same order of magnitude as PRSC 1. Despite the PRSC failure, IDA disbursements were about $50 million per year more than the pre-PRSC period.

Box 2.4. Factors Leading to Downward Adjustments of PRSC Amounts—Examples

In Ethiopia, volumes of PRSC 1 and 2 were reduced because of disagreement over the telecommunications reform and delays in implementing actions to spur rural sector growth.

In Ghana, there was a decision in the fiscal 2008–11 CAS to reduce the share of budget support to 28 percent of overall Bank lending, compared with 40 percent in the preceding CAS (fiscal 2004–07). While the primary reason was to counterbalance increased Bank contributions to the Multilateral Debt Relief Initiative, there was also signaling of failures to meet triggers, with three modifications in six operations.

In Madagascar, reduction in the size of the PRSCs followed a decision to reduce the share of PRSCs in the overall lending program following a reduction in Madagascar's IDA allocation. Madagascar had seven modifications to triggers in four operations.

In Uganda, PRSCs have been trending downward since PRSC 2 ($170 million) and are currently about $100 million, due to overall program issues, although Uganda has had few modifications of triggers.

Source: IEG desk reviews of CASs, ICRs, CASCR Reviews, IEG ICR Reviews, and interviews.

Downward adjustments of loan amounts also occurred.

triggers. In Guyana, some prior actions turned out not to have been fully implemented in a timely manner, leading to a delay in loan effectiveness of nine months. In Honduras, political developments led to a change in the reform agenda and the need for support declined following the attainment of HIPC completion.

Resource transfers usually continued, which raises questions about the real effect of terminating PRSC support.

Downward adjustments of loan amounts sometimes occurred due to slow PRSC progress, as reported by task team leaders in Ethiopia, Ghana, Lao PDR, Pakistan, and Tanzania. Overall IDA resources were also, in some cases, diminished (Benin, Madagascar, and Rwanda). Frequently, reductions in PRSC volumes were compensated by increases elsewhere or restored in later operations—for example, in Pakistan, where the level of PRSC 1 was reduced by $50 million owing to nonfulfillment of two prior actions, but an equivalent amount was restored in PRSC 2 when the actions had been taken.

PRSCs tended to disburse about the same time in each annual budget cycle, though not always early in the cycle.

In at least four countries, PRSC amounts trended upward over time: Benin (21 percent), Burkina Faso (16 percent), Tanzania (8 percent), and Vietnam (2 percent). It is reassuring that Tanzania and Vietnam were the second and third best performers with the lowest number and percentage of triggers relaxed. Benin was the fifth best. Only two of its 39 triggers were relaxed. Burkina Faso however performed less well, with 9 net triggers relaxed. Adjustments in PRSC amounts, however, also reflect the IDA performance-based allocation mechanism, where country institutional change is an important factor dependent on overall program considerations beyond the PRSC.

Regularity and Timing of Disbursements Relative to the Budget Cycle

PRSCs were also expected to improve the regularity of Bank disbursements and align them with countries' budget cycles, to ensure their inclusion in budget revenues. Appendix table A2.16 shows that in 15 out of 28 countries, more than 50 percent of operations disbursed in the same quarter. In an even greater proportion of cases, disbursement of successive operations occurred in contiguous quarters (the quarter preceding or following the quarter of the previous year's disbursement. In only 4 out of 90 operations—Rwanda (Poverty Reduction Support Grants 2 and 3); Senegal (PRSCs 1 and 2)—were successive disbursements more than 15 months apart. Overall, PRSCs maintained considerable regularity in disbursements.[42]

A related issue concerns the timing of disbursements relative to the fiscal year of the country being financed, ideally by the last quarter of the preceding fiscal year or in the first quarter of the fiscal year that is being supported. Table 2.7 shows that, in aggregate, about 33 percent of Bank disbursements were in the fourth quarter and another 18 percent in the first quarter. There was evidence of improvement of alignment over time. In Burkina Faso, 60 percent of disbursements of budget support took place during the last quarter of the budget year, hampering budget management. Accordingly, PRSC 4 was approved by the Bank in May 2004, to permit a vote by the National Assembly before its June recess (figure 2.3).

Table 2.7. PRSCs: Indicators of Disbursement Regularity Relative to Recipient Fiscal Year

Quarter	No. of PRSC disbursements	Percent
Q1	17	18.3
Q2	21	22.6
Q3	24	25.8
Q4	31	33.3
Total	93	100.0

Source: Disbursement data, World Bank, and information on country fiscal years from task team leaders.

Stakeholders indicate that budget support provided through the PRSCs has been fairly or very predictable. Shortfalls were not a major issue. Yet other donors achieved a higher proportion of first quarter disbursements than the Bank did. Data from the Strategic Partnership with Africa Budget Support Working Group, which compares commitment and disbursement data for 11 African PRSC countries, show that close to half of total budget support aid was committed for the first quarter (49 percent). Most of this (42 percent) was disbursed. By the last quarter, disbursement proportions exceeded commitments.[43]

Disbursement delays may also be due to lags in country actions for loan effectiveness. In Benin, the delay between Board approval and disbursement varied from 3 months (PRSC 3) to 10 months for PRSC 4. Funds initially allocated to support one Beninese fiscal year were in fact included as part of the subsequent year, although resources were mobilized to cover the gap.

However, good alignment requires not only matching disbursement with the expenditure cycle but, ideally, matching the annual budget preparation and review cycle with PRSC preparation and follow up. This is much more difficult to achieve. In Mozambique, the donor memorandum of understanding requires the Bank to commit to financial support for a given budget year by a certain time

Figure 2.3. Burkina Faso: Quarterly Disbursement Data for PRSCs and Former Policy-Based Loans (1991–2008)

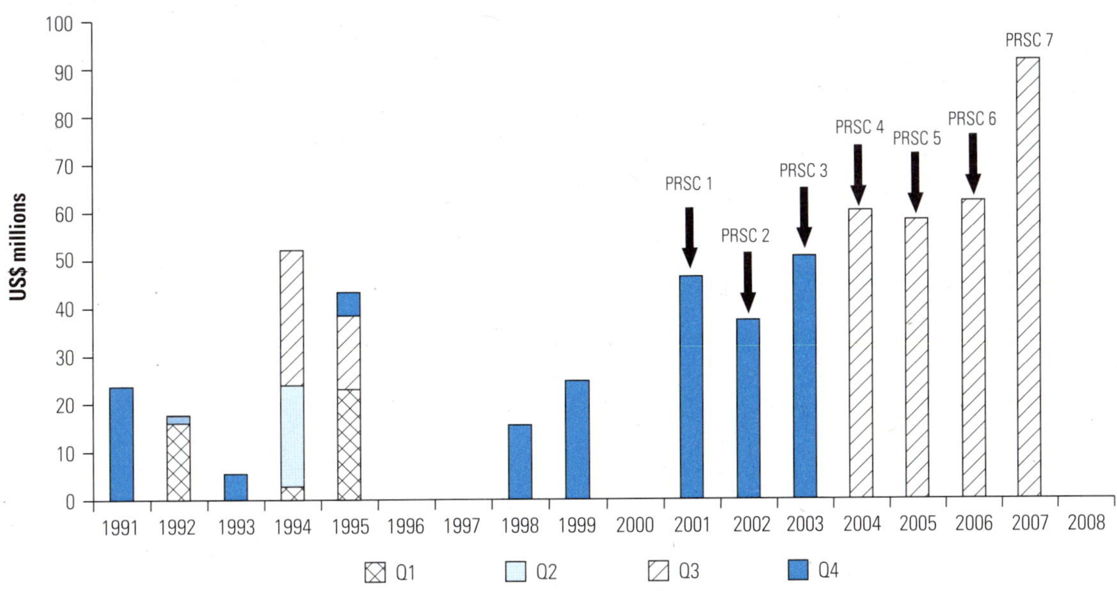

Source: Based on World Bank data.
Note: A fiscal year is from January to December; quarterly numbers refer to calendar quarters.

Box 2.5. PRSC Predictability and Regularity—Achievements and Limitations

In Vietnam, the PRSCs were disbursed on schedule just before the beginning of the country's fiscal year (January). This is in contrast to the relatively uneven disbursement over the structural adjustment period of the 1990s, and the gap between the last Structural Adjustment Credit and the PRSC.

By contrast, the IEG country case study for Armenia found little evidence of more regular disbursements for PRSCs than preceding Structural Adjustment Credits. But since PRSC disbursements were a small share of budget resources, timing was largely irrelevant. The government was able to offset variations in PRSC timing with short-term borrowings and cash reserves.

Source: IEG country case studies.

Country alignment ideally requires matching the entire cycle of PRSC preparation with the country's budget preparation and annual review process.

in the preceding year. But this requires commitment prior to budget approval by parliament or review within the Bank. In Armenia, the PRSC preparation was aligned with budget preparation, so that the budget fully reflected the fiscal and policy implications of the PRSCs.

To summarize, PRSC countries did benefit, though not dramatically, from greater stability in year-to-year aid flows, perceptibly increased stability in volume, and a more stable share of fast-disbursing funds in total Bank resources. These conclusions change little if non-PRSC policy-based lending is included with PRSCs. Quarterly regularity was good although not optimal for budget planning. And aid flows from all sources also improved in predictability.

Wider aspects of country alignment are explored in the next chapter, which reviews the extent to which governments have expressed ownership of the PRSC program, its contribution to the budgetary process, and the extent to which it is embedded in a realistic and well-articulated results framework.

Chapter 3

Evaluation Highlights

- PRSCs have good alignment with national development strategies and enjoy greater ownership than preceding adjustment lending, at least in the core ministries.
- PRSC countries have been more successful at operationalizing national development strategies, but the gap is closing.
- The PRSC has been effective in raising the importance of the budget as a tool for policy formulation.
- PRSC results frameworks were initially weak but have improved, though shortcomings remain in defining baselines, intermediate milestones, and indicators for tracking pro-poor outcomes.
- Weak results frameworks for PRSCs partly reflect upstream shortcomings in results frameworks for the PRSPs/CASs.
- The multidonor process can sometimes make it difficult to establish results frameworks.
- Weak monitoring and evaluation frameworks reflect limited country statistical capacity.

Girl stands to respond to teacher's question in crowded high school. Photo by Scott Wallace, courtesy of the World Bank Photo Library.

PRSC Process

With the introduction of the Bank's Comprehensive Development Framework, countries were encouraged to articulate their own approach toward poverty-reducing growth. Some countries already had national development plans; others were encouraged by the Bank to prepare such plans in the form of Poverty Reduction Strategy Papers (PRSPs). Implementing the national development strategy, or PRSP—in particular its prioritization, budgeting, and execution—was soon perceived to be a complex task.[1] The Poverty Reduction Support Credit was introduced to operationalize these development strategies by providing expertise as well as budgetary resources.

This chapter examines the extent to which PRSCs were aligned with countries' visions of development and whether they served as vehicles for the operationalization of the development plan by strengthening domestic budget processes. It examines the extent to which the PRSC process gained the ownership of recipient countries, at core and line ministries, in recipient governments, and with parliamentarians and civil society. Finally, it examines the extent to which operationalization was assisted by clear PRSC results frameworks to track development processes and outcomes, and contribute to the improvement of associated monitoring and evaluation (M&E) systems.

Alignment with National Development Strategies

Alignment—Alternative Models

Modes of alignment of PRSs to national strategies varied, and consequently there were different models of alignment of the PRSC and PRS/national strategy. In some countries where a national development strategy already existed, as in Vietnam, the PRSC process gradually aligned itself to this strategy despite an initially separate PRSP. In some cases, such as Mali and Cape Verde, there was limited initial ownership of PRSP-based PRSC conditionality because the government already had its own national development strategy (box 3.1). Yet, over time the two documents have converged. In other cases, such as Albania, the PRSC has been based entirely on the government's own National Strategy for Social and Economic Development (NSSED), which acts as the government's PRSP. An alternative model is that of Benin and Burkina Faso, where there was no preexisting national development strategy. Over time, the PRSP evolved into such a national strategy, taking on its own identity in the national context.

Some countries had a development strategy before the PRSP but over time these usually merged.

Country clients strongly concur that the PRSC is well aligned with countries' development strategies (annex 7) and overwhelmingly note that alignment had improved over time, as government teams gain knowledge of the PRSC and work with Bank counterparts (90 percent to 100 percent strongly agree).[2] Task team leaders concur that alignment of broad directions has been very good (95 percent agreement) and a majority (56 per-

Box 3.1. PRSC: Alignment with National Development Strategies

National Development Plans Evolving into the PRSP

In Uganda, the 1997 *Poverty Eradication Action Plan* (PEAP), the country's first comprehensive national development strategy, served as a national plan to focus budget support. It has influenced priorities for spending across sectors while sectors have separately developed more detailed strategies. The second and third generations of this document (2000 and 2004) served as Uganda's PRSP.

In Vietnam, PRSC 1 was developed based on an Interim PRSP; subsequent PRSCs were closely aligned with the national development strategies: the Comprehensive Poverty Reduction and Growth Strategy and, later, the Socio-Economic Development Plan. Both development strategies effectively served as the PRSP for deriving policy measures for the PRSC.

PRSP Replacing National Development Plans

The Mali PRSP of 2002 was initially viewed as imposed by donors, because the government already had its own national poverty strategy, the *Strategie Nationale pour la Lutte contre la Pauvreté*, adopted in 1998. The second-generation PRSP, adopted in late 2006, had more ownership as it was crafted with wider government and civil society participation. In Cape Verde, the PRSP initially seemed to be perceived as Bank-IMF imposed, especially since the government already had a five-year plan. While the task team leader believed that the PRSC was relatively well aligned with the PRSP, country clients took time to endorse this position as country ownership of the reform program developed.

PRSPs Evolving into National Development Plans

Benin adopted two PRSPs, the first in 2003 and the second in 2006. The second is referred to as the Strategy for Growth and Poverty Reduction (SGPR) rather than PRSP 2. It is the key strategy document for the government. PRSC conditionalities are believed to pertain to the implementation of the government's own program document. In Burkina Faso, as in Benin, the PRSP has been adopted as the government's own strategic planning document, although additional sectoral strategies also exist. In 1999, Burkina Faso prepared its first Poverty Reduction Strategy Paper (*Cadre Stratégique de Lutte contre la Pauvreté*—CSLP) for the period 2000–2003. This was the government's unifying framework for national policy, although separate long-term sectoral strategies existed for health, education, rural development, budget management capacity, and governance. The revised PRSP of 2004 is accompanied by a Priority Action Program, which incorporates poverty-targeted sector strategies.

Source: IEG desk reviews, discussions with country clients and task team leaders.

Box 3.2. PRSCs: Adopting Measures Outside the PRSP in Armenia

Following careful preparation of a PRSP that was used to shape the Medium-Term Expenditure Framework and annual budgets, the PRSC adopted a subset of its issues—focused on public sector reforms—including expenditure management and tax policies, as well as reform programs for health, education, and social protection.

However, it also included themes not highlighted in the PRSP related to private sector development and competition: improvements in civil aviation, enactment of a telecommunications regulatory framework, creation of an electricity market, and improvements in the regulatory framework for banking and insurance. At the same time, the PRSC did not touch on issues raised in the PRSP, such as the development of small and medium enterprises, improvements in antimonopoly regulation, or the extension of micro credit.

Source: IEG desk reviews, discussions with country clients and task team leaders.

cent) affirm that alignment has improved over time. PRSCs have been selective about the areas of the PRSPs that they emphasize, sometimes including themes beyond the scope of PRSPs. About half of surveyed clients (54 percent) believe that the PRSC introduced new elements, outside the national development strategy. Yet, an overwhelming number (91 percent) believe that such contributions have generally been a positive contribution.

Ownership and Policy Dialogue

Country Clients and Bank Task Team Leaders

Client country stakeholders affirm ownership of the PRSC program in core ministries (finance, planning, economy).[3] Only 3 respondents out of 38 disagreed. There is also strong, if somewhat lower, support from priority sector min-

Box 3.3. Ownership of the PRSP/PRSC—Reform Process

In Benin, strong ownership was indicated by the government's unprompted decision to update its public financial management reform program, based on the most recent Public Expenditure Financial Assessment (PEFA). In Lao PDR, the PRSC process has become increasingly country-led over the PRSC 1–3 period as government officials came to appreciate its benefits. On the other hand, in Nicaragua, there was limited ownership and the PRSC was perceived to have been Bank-designed. Moreover, it included activities that were not supported by the government (such as titling of properties in the Atlantic Territories).

Box 3.4. Ownership of the PRSC Process—Legislative Bodies

In Mozambique, the *Assembleia da Republica* does not vote on the PRSC, but rather on the *Plano Económico e Social* (PES), which contains the agreed upon measures from the Performance Assessment Framework (*Matriz Reduzida De Acções Prioritárias*). In Guyana, Nicaragua, and other countries, there was no or close to no oversight or ownership of the PRSC and its reform program by parliament (or the national assembly).

By contrast in Benin, Burkina Faso, Madagascar, Mali, Rwanda, and Senegal, that is, PRSC countries with French public finance systems, the judicial branch of government has explicit accountability over the PRSC reform process via its role in overseeing public expenditures, from the national audit office (*Cour des Comptes*). Legislative involvement in the PRSC is therefore higher.

Sources: World Bank, BMZ, and GTZ 2007; IEG team leader survey, and country case studies.

istries, such as health, education, and water supply, at 82 percent of responses. The sense of ownership declines progressively from groups further removed from the core PRSC process. Support from legislative bodies declines to some 60 percent of responses; and there is a sharp decline from civil society, to only 53 percent—with almost as many persons (47 percent) disagreeing or strongly disagreeing that there was buy-in at this level.[4] The sense of ownership, attributed to the PRSC's foundation in the government's plans, has been reinforced by the flexibility shown by the Bank with respect to interpretation of conditionalities.

Country clients and task team leaders affirm strong ownership of the PRSC process.

Reactions from Bank task team leaders are very similar; 95 percent believe that counterparts in the ministry of finance have very strong or strong ownership of PRSC programs. Opinions regarding councils of ministers and line agencies are split between strong or limited country ownership. Parliament and civil society are believed to have limited or no ownership of the PRSC process, partly because the principal vehicle for engagement of civil society and other stakeholders outside the central government has been the formulation (and in some cases annual review) of the PRS or national development strategy, rather than its implementing vehicle, the PRSC.

A few countries, such as Nicaragua, believed the PRSC to have been Bank-designed.

Close alignment of the PRSP and its annual review with the PRSC led to better inclusion of civil society participation (for example, in Uganda). However, in other countries, team leaders expressed concern that government may handpick civil society organizations (CSOs) to be included in the process, based partly on political loyalties. And according to some sources, participation by legislative bodies appears to depend on the nature of the challenge function of the legislature over the executive bodies of government, that is, whether the legislature votes on the adoption of the PRSC or otherwise.

Task team leaders believe that the PRSC has made a clear contribution to the importance given to budget discussions and to interministerial dialogue. Seventy-seven percent believe the PRSC increased the comprehensiveness of the budget and raised its importance (82 percent). Ninety-three percent indicated that the PRSC was effective or very effective in enhancing dialogue between the ministry of finance and line agencies, while 78 percent rated the Bank as effective or very effective in enhancing cross-sectoral dialogue.[5]

Interministerial Dialogue—Country Case Study Evidence

Country case studies suggest a positive but variable contribution to enhanced interministerial dialogue (table 3.1).[6] In some cases, the quality of sectoral dialogue has been driven by the multidonor process, and in cases such as Ghana, weakened by donors who put greater emphasis on sector-specific tools in lieu of budget support. And it appears that sometimes the joint dialogue has reduced the depth of technical discussions at the sectoral level (Mozambique).

Table 3.1. PRSC Process: Impact on Government Policy Dialogue

Question: Has the PRSC process contributed to an enhanced dialogue within government on policy and performance?

Country	Score	Comments
Armenia	5.0	The PRSC has been useful in raising operational ministry concerns with the prime minister and ministry of finance, and has provided for coordination among ministries on key reforms. For instance, reforms in regulation involved improved coordination between trade, transport/communication ministries, and the independent regulator. However, there is no evidence that it provided for continuous overall dialogue on the general poverty or development strategy among ministries.
Benin	4.0	Counterparts believe the PRSC has been a useful instrument for dialogue on policy reform, reinforced by the annual review process undertaken jointly with other donors. In sectors such as water, the PRSC helped elevate pending issues that require action from other parts of government, adding the weight of donor support. The PRSC process has also helped to focus internal government discussion on important policy issues, but progress has been slow and, when attained, not always sustained.
Ghana	3.0	While the PRSC/multidonor budget support process has had important impact on aligning donors around a common agenda, it is less evident that the process has enhanced dialogue within government on policy and performance. The ministry of finance is the key partner in the process, and dialogue with other ministries has been assisted by the process, but this has not been a crucial element. The PRSC process has been useful for agencies not typically on the critical paths of government policy discussions, such as the procurement agency and the internal audit agency. If the budget process had been used more proactively for integrating donor support into the general budget, rather than continuing to support sector-specific pools, program dialogue might have been strengthened further. Aside from the linkage between the ministry of finance and the line ministries, there is limited evidence that the PRSC contributed to a cross-ministerial dialogue on cross-cutting issues that require more than one ministry's involvement in their achievement, such as child nutrition programs.
Lao PDR	5.0	The Poverty Reduction Support Operation (PRSO) effectively promoted policy dialogue within government around priority sectors in poverty reduction and the role of the budget as a key instrument in achieving PRS objectives.
Mozambique	4.0	Line ministries indicated that the PRSCs had helped foster dialogue with the ministry of planning and development as well as with the ministry of finance. The PRSC approach also enabled the Bank to consolidate and enhance dialogue with the government, at both macro and sectoral levels, through coordination with the Group of 19 general budget support (GBS) donors. But sector ministries thought that the PRSC dialogue was not enough and must be accompanied by a sector-specific dialogue, because G-19 discussions do not focus on technical aspects of policy implementation. Therefore, the PRSC has not proven to be an adequate vehicle for in-depth sector dialogue on its own.
Nicaragua	4.0	There is no doubt that the PRSCs contributed significantly to enhance policy and performance dialogue.
Vietnam	5.0	Stakeholders agree that the PRSC has provided a platform for enhanced dialogue with government agencies on pro-poor policies. Both line ministries and core ministries cite the PRSC process as contributing to a dialogue around the budget and other mechanisms as tools to promote pro-poor policy objectives.

Source: IEG country case studies.

Operationalization of the Development Plan

Translating the broad principles of a strategy document into an effective blueprint for implementation requires the preparation of a coherent and unified strategy that is effectively prioritized and costed.[7] An effective budget process requires a regular calendar, with clear roles and challenge functions of the government as well as political players. Budget execution over a multiyear period requires the integration of the budget into a medium-term expenditure framework, which spells out phased execution required for program realization. And to track achievement of budget targets, mechanisms of budget reporting are required, integrated into an annual review.[8]

Over 80 percent of task team leaders believe that the PRSC was effective in raising the importance of the budget as a tool for policy formulation and accountability. Almost as many believe that the PRSC has effectively increased the comprehensiveness of the budget—presumably by bringing on budget areas of expenditure that were previously off budget. Country clients concur—90 percent agree or strongly agree.

Operationalizing Budgets—Monitoring Results

PRSC countries have been able to improve the operationalization of their national development strategies better than other IDA-eligible countries, although the latter have also improved their performance and appear to be closing the gap compared with PRSC countries. Table 3.2 presents a comparison, based on data collected for 2005 and 2007 from 62 IDA-eligible countries that have been implementing a PRS since March 2006.[9]

Interministerial dialogue improved, but the quality of sector dialogue may have lost some depth.

Task team leaders believe that the PRSC raised the importance of the budget as a tool of policy implementation.

Data are reported separately for three elements of operationalization: the degree to which government action has a unified strategic framework, reflecting overall medium-term strategy as well as sector strategies; the extent to which there is pri-

Box 3.5. PRSCs' Contribution to Operationalizing the National Development Plan

In Benin, the achievement of sectoral objectives has been improved through the use of program budgeting, with budget preparation and budget execution increasingly undertaken by sector ministries. The government has adopted a comprehensive strategy for implementing results-based budgeting and is progressing toward finalizing a budget classification that would permit systematic evolution of pro-poor budget expenditures, with more program budgeting execution reports and public expenditure tracking surveys. In Lao PDR, the first series of PRSOs (1–3) largely achieved objectives in translating the National Growth and Poverty Eradication Strategy into an actionable program, through their strong focus on public financial management. The recent Budget Law (2006) was key to ensuring that public resources are directed toward national priorities.

Source: IEG country case studies.

Table 3.2. PRSC and Non-PRSC Countries: Operationalization of Development Strategies

	Composite rating		Unified strategic framework		Prioritization		Strategic link to the budget	
	2005	2007	2005	2007	2005	2007	2005	2007
PRSC countries average (27)	2.0	2.2	2.1	2.3	2.0	2.3	1.9	2.0
Non-PRSC IDA countries (CPIA 3+) average (23)	1.6	1.9	1.7	2.0	1.8	2.2	1.3	1.5
Difference from PRSC	*–0.4*	*–0.3*	*–0.4*	*–0.3*	*–0.2*	*–0.1*	*–0.6*	*–0.5*
Non-PRSC IDA countries (CPIA <3) average (10)	1.1	1.2	1.1	1.4	1.4	1.3	0.9	1.1
Difference from PRSC	*–0.8*	*–0.9*	*–1.0*	*–0.9*	*–0.6*	*–1.0*	*–1.0*	*–0.9*
Non-PRSC IBRD country (1 country: Serbia and Montenegro)	1.3	1.7	1.0	2.0	2.0	2.0	1.0	1.0
Difference from PRSC	*–0.6*	*–0.5*	*–1.1*	*–0.3*	*0.0*	*–0.3*	*–0.9*	*–1.0*

Source: Analysis of World Bank data, December 2007.

oritization of short, medium, and long-term objectives and targets; and the strategic link to the budget, specifically the degree to which the strategy has been costed in a medium-term expenditure framework.

All indicators for PRSC countries are higher than those for non-PRSC countries, even if compared with better-performing IDA countries, and they improved between 2005 and 2007. But such an improvement also took place for non-PRSC IDA countries, even those that scored lower than 3.0 on composite CPIAs. Moreover, the difference in scores between PRSC countries and other groups, in most areas, has somewhat diminished.

While there is anecdotal evidence from country case studies and team leaders on instances where a PRSC has helped leverage improvements in operationalization, it appears that improvements were being introduced in many countries and may have occurred, to some degree, in the absence of PRSC support.

Another Bank study, with information on the operationalization of the PRS/national development strategy for a select group of IDA PRSC countries, suggests variety in the degree to which operationalization has been achieved across PRSC countries and across different aspects of the operationalization process.[10] This study examines the degree of linkage of the PRS to the budget process on such criteria as whether there is a budget calendar, whether the functions of administrative and political players in the budget approval process are well specified, and whether there is a medium-term expenditure framework to help translate program needs into expenditure planning. Finally, it investigates the extent to which the Annual Progress Review of the national development plan/poverty reduction strategy, is integrated with budget implementation reporting.

PRSC countries' progress in linking the PRS to budget implementation varies by budget area and does not appear to be linked to the length of the PRSC series.

IEG applied standardized scoring to these descriptions, summarized in appendix table A3.3. There is no consistent pattern across individual PRSC countries. Some with long PRSC series, such as Tanzania and Uganda, score well in some areas (links of PRS to budget, having a medium-term expenditure framework, and for Uganda, a clear budget process), but less well in others (integrated budget reporting). Burkina Faso, a country with a long PRSC presence, has relatively low scores on operationalization, except for the clarity of the budget process.[11]

Results Frameworks, Monitoring, and Evaluation

An integral element of the PRSC (and all IDA lending) was an increase in emphasis on managing for results.[12] To what extent did PRSCs impart a results focus to the development process? The following specific questions are examined: (i) Was the PRSC results framework well adapted to the implementation of the PRSC? (ii) How well defined were PRSC results frameworks, in particular regarding the definition of measurable end-of-series, intermediate, and baseline targets and indicators? (iii) How consistent was the reporting of results? The quality of results frameworks depends on the quality of underlying M&E systems, therefore, (iv) To what extent did the PRSC draw on national M&E systems used for domestic accountability outside the framework of aid flows?; and (v) Was capacity building for developing national M&E addressed?

Evaluation of the Results Framework for All PRSCs (2001–08)

A comprehensive IEG desk review of results frameworks covered all 87 PRSCs undertaken during this period, based on questions derived from Bank guidelines for good practice in results frameworks.[13] Questions were grouped around the following themes: (i) the overall evolution of policy and monitoring matrixes; (ii) the existence of end-of-series outcome indicators and quality; (iii) the existence and quality of intermediate (annual indicators); and (iv) reporting on the results framework.[14] Operations were grouped in series to enable the examination of results from baselines to end-of-series outcomes, within a series of operations. The resulting group of 38 series of operations comprises 27 sets of first series, 10 sets of second series, and 1 set of third series.

Overall Policy and Monitoring Matrixes. The desk review shows that PRSC policy matrixes evolved over the life of the credits, reducing the number of objectives, reformulating objectives to better reflect the essence of the PRSP programs, and improving the causal chain from action to desired outcomes. Lessons learned from first-series operations were incorporated into the design and content of the policy matrixes of the second series. Results indicators became more precise over time. Thus in first-series PRSCs, only 48 percent of operations had clearly defined indicators in all sectors, but this rose to about 80 percent in the second series. As an example, in Mozambique, the first PRSC had no explicit results framework.[15] PRSC 2 had a results framework but omitted key areas of public sector management and investment climate improvement. The second series, for the first time, contained a results framework for the whole series.[16] The number of operations with universally vague indicators fell from 15 percent in the first series to zero in the second. However, desired end-of-series outcomes have always been and remain numerous, arguably excessively so (between 1 and 15 in 20 percent of operations, and 16 or more in the remaining 80 percent). There has been no reduction over time in the number of indicators.

End-of-Series Outcome Indicators and Their Monitoring (appendix table A3.1). Specific findings on end-of-series indicators show that by the end of the period reviewed about three-quarters (76 percent) of all PRSCs reviewed included monitoring indicators for most end-of-series outcomes, though not all were measurable (68 percent), and less than half of end-of-series indicators had targets. Moreover, targets were only well defined 42 percent of the time and are clearly quantified only about a quarter of the time (29 percent).

However, there is clear evidence of improvement between PRSCs in the first and second series. Most PRSCs had end-of-series outcome indicators in 70 percent of first-series operations, rising to 90 percent of second-series operations. There was a dramatic increase in the proportion of measurable end-of-series indicators, from 56 percent to 100 percent. Targets for such indicators grew more frequent (41 percent to 60 percent) and were better defined (37 percent to 50 percent), and targets were more clearly quantified, improving from 22 percent of operations to 40 percent. Nevertheless, these findings illustrate that as the nature and specificity of targets is made clearer, the proportion of PRSCs that satisfy the requirements remains less than half.

Many early PRSCs did not have well-formulated indicators, though there was improvement over time.

Baselines and Intermediate Indicators. Both types of indicators are required to steadily measure progress toward end-of-series indicators. In both areas, weaknesses remain, although the situation has been improving over time. Thus, baselines are well defined for all indicators only about 50 percent of the time, although it is somewhat higher (60 percent) in cases where there have been two series. On average, across all PRSCs, three-fifths (60 percent) had no intermediate (annual) indicators. In the second series, this declined somewhat and about half of all operations have some intermediate outcome indicators. Looking at targets for intermediate indicators, there has also been improvement—from 33 percent in the first series to almost twice as many, 60 percent, in the second series (appendix table A3.2). One caveat on the interpretation of improvements over time, however, is that there are only 10 second series, compared with 27 first series.

Reporting: Results Frameworks and Progress against Targets. On average, PRSC program documents have only commented on progress in developing results frameworks a quarter of the time (26 percent), and in this important area there is no significant difference between first and second series. At best, the documents comment on the weakness of the results framework in preceding operations and the need to improve it. Program documents report sparingly on progress in developing results frameworks, although this subject receives most attention in Implementation Completion Reviews.

Baseline, intermediate, and end-of-series indicators have improved, but all have scope for further improvement.

Performance has been much better as regards reporting progress against targets. In countries with only one PRSC series, progress occurred in about 70

Only 46 percent of PRSC series had complete end-of-series indicators.

percent of eligible cases. There was a significant improvement during second series (eight cases, or 80 percent). This suggests that an improvement in the quality of reporting was enabled by the existence of well-defined intermediate outcome indicators. For end-of-series reporting, complete information is provided in this regard in only 46 percent of eligible cases, either in the final program document of the series or its Implementation Completion Review.

These findings broadly suggest that results frameworks are increasingly in compliance with development policy lending guidelines. Yet shortcomings remain, especially in the progression from some form of indicator to an indicator that is targeted, well specified, and quantifiable, with annually defined intermediate milestones.

Core conditionality in all adjustment declined, but non-PRSCs declined faster than PRSCs.

PRSC Results Frameworks: Case Studies and Team Leaders' Survey

Results frameworks in seven PRSC countries were evaluated and scored on a six-point scale by IEG, based on the overall question: Is the PRSC embedded in a clear, medium-term results framework, which links policy actions to outcomes with specific monitoring milestones? Results suggest average or below average achievements, with two scores of 2 (Armenia and Nicaragua) and four scores of 3 (Benin, Ghana, Lao PDR, and Vietnam).[17] Only one country (Mozambique) scored above the mid-point, at 4. Details of individual countries' experiences are given in annex 6.

Case studies corroborate shortcomings in results frameworks at all levels.

First of all, numerous deficiencies are observed, in virtually all these countries' PRSC Results Frameworks, at the level of definition, consistency, and quality. Examples include: (i) lack of specific milestones; (ii) lack of a consistent set of milestones from one operation to the next (Armenia); (iii) indicators that could not be measured or evaluated; (iv) outcomes with no specified indicators and the lack of a clear results chain from actions to outcomes (Nicaragua), and vague time horizons or sequencing (Lao PDR); (v) limited ex-post monitoring of results (Armenia); and (vi) the finding of implausible results from monitoring on some occasions, in terms of consistency or variability.

Case studies also illustrate difficulties in framing results (in some areas), country capacities, and limited statistical data.

Case studies also illustrate, from the client perspective, difficulties faced by country officials in defining targets and milestones, especially in countries with no prior experience of PRSCs, where previous custom was limited to the setting and monitoring of macro targets and indicators (Nicaragua). Furthermore, monitoring the impact of certain public expenditures is difficult as they are based on an administrative rather than a functional classification (Benin). Additionally, statistical capacity for data gathering is limited and the necessary infrastructure for data collection is limited.

Another set of issues can be traced to upstream shortcomings in associated results frameworks for the parallel PRSPs or CASs, which the PRSCs were intended to mirror. Problems of being ill defined, inconsistent, or difficult to measure are often observed at this level. Some results frameworks for PRSPs were unwieldy, with too many indicators and targets (Armenia). Limited monitoring of upstream PRSP indicators and limited incentives on the part of government officials to undertake systematic reporting of such indicators have also been shortcomings.

Finally, some difficulties are associated with the multidonor framework under which some PRSC countries operate. While long-term Performance Assessment Frameworks (PAFs) have disadvantages of rigidities, the annual renegotiations of targets and milestones, in conjunction with the annual review of the multidonor matrix or PAF (Ghana), can also lead to a loss in strategic direction because government incentives focus on setting easily attainable targets.[18] Yet other case studies indicate that a common donor position is possible, as was the case in Mozambique, where the three-year forward-looking results framework has been linked to a three-year PAF and, thereby, to the national development plan and related review mechanisms. In this case the need for a satisfactory conclusion of the joint review for ob-

Box 3.6. PRSC Shortfalls in Results Frameworks—Armenia

In Armenia, each PRSC had specific milestones and expected results, but they did not refer to past achievements and did not use a consistent set of milestones. Most PRSCs produced a new table with slightly different indicators, reflecting the focus of the new PRSC. For instance, PRSC 1 set a target for tax revenue-to-GDP to rise from 14.1 percent in 2003 to 16.2 percent in 2006, and to 17 percent by 2007. The actual figure for 2006 turned out to be 14.4 percent, as reported in PRSC 4. The program document discusses the reasons for limited growth but does not mention the shortfall in the target. Instead, it sets a new target of 15.2 percent for 2007.

Shortfalls in the results focus and monitoring of the PRSC parallel deficiencies of the PRSP results focus. While the government established a PRSP monitoring and evaluation framework in 2004, it did not function effectively. Results have not been measured against consistent milestones. The framework identified 177 indicators, of which 36 were targets and 141 were intermediate indicators. No information was available on 44 indicators, and many others were incomplete. Ministries lack incentives to report or improve upon indicators. There was little or no ex-post monitoring of results, of either the PRSC or the PRSP, and no evidence that the government uses the results indicators to access progress or modify policies.

Source: IEG country case studies.

Box 3.7. PRSC Results Frameworks: Task Team Leaders' Views

One task team leader (TTL) stated that one of the greatest benefits of the PRSC approach was the move toward a results approach. TTLs for two countries in Africa felt that the PRSCs were having considerable success in improving coordination among government officials to generate and report results, and in addressing the core weaknesses in budgeting and reporting for results.

TTLs for several other countries in Asia and Africa pointed to a series of challenges, for example, differences in views on results frameworks among donors and consequent difficulties in coordination; the difficulty of developing the PRSC framework when the underlying PRSP framework was not framed in an operational manner; the need to change incentives for TTLs so as to encourage results over delivery; and the need for better support to task managers for the development of results frameworks. TTLs also pointed out the need to maintain supervision of measures already taken to avoid backtracking but to balance this to avoid a scorecard approach to PRSC supervision. In sum, TTLs are aware of the need to improve results frameworks, the difficulties of so doing, and the potential benefits.

Source: IEG results framework analysis.

taining continued support motivated stakeholders to conduct necessary monitoring. And elsewhere, donor support helped build capacity for monitoring and evaluation of results (Benin).

Over time, in some countries with longer PRSC series, improvement has been observed (Benin, Ghana, Mozambique, Vietnam), although there has been less evolution elsewhere (Armenia, Nicaragua), which may also depend on the establishment of proposed new M&E capacity (Lao PDR).

These findings are broadly corroborated by task team leaders (box 3.7), who point to the challenges and difficulties in working with well-functioning results frameworks but who support their purpose and point to the resulting improvements in country-level monitoring and data collection.

Results Frameworks—PRSCs and Other IDA Countries

A comparison of results frameworks in PRSC countries and other IDA countries shows that, on average, PRSC countries score better than other IDA countries. Three aspects of results orientation have been examined in a database on 62 IDA countries (table 3.3).[19] The questions focused on (i) the degree to which monitoring data for the underlying PRS is collected and analyzed in a timely, regular, and systematic manner; (ii) the timely availability of quality information pertaining to the medium-term strategy and to public expenditures, including in local languages; and (iii) the degree of implementation of a country-led M&E system, which is organized with well-defined institutional responsibili-

Results shortcomings in PRSCs may also be due to upstream shortcomings in PRSs or difficulties in reaching donor agreements.

Table 3.3. PRSC and Other Countries: Comparison of Ratings on Results Orientation

	Composite rating		Quality of information		Access to information		Country-level M&E	
	2005	2007	2005	2007	2005	2007	2005	2007
PRSC countries (27 countries)	1.8	2.0	1.7	1.9	1.8	2.1	1.8	2.1
Non-PRSC IDA countries (CPIA 3+) (23 countries)	1.4	1.6	1.4	1.6	1.4	1.6	1.3	1.6
Difference from PRSC	–0.4	–0.5	–0.3	–0.3	–0.4	–0.5	–0.5	–0.5
Non-PRSC IDA countries CPIA <3 (10 countries)	1.2	1.2	1.3	1.1	1.2	1.5	1.0	1.0
Difference from PRSC	–0.6	–0.9	–0.4	–0.8	–0.6	–0.7	–0.8	–1.1

Source: World Bank 2007e.

ties, tracks indicators (input, output, and outcomes), and produces unified reports used by policymakers and external partners. Responses are scored on a five-point scale (0–4).

On average, PRSC countries score better than others on results frameworks, but this is not obviously linked to the PRSC.

PRSC countries perform better in all aspects, even when other well-performing IDA countries are considered. Information is of better quality, easier to access, and is monitored more regularly. Over time, PRSC countries have maintained their lead. A disaggregation by country, however, shows a high level of variability in performance on various aspects of results orientation. Overall performance does not appear to be linked to the length of time for which a country has had a PRSC.

PRSC Results Frameworks: An Africa Region Study

IEG findings are broadly corroborated by experience in the Bank's Africa Region, where designing and implementing results frameworks continues to be one of the most challenging dimensions of policy-based loans.[20] Among the challenges are insufficient attention to the definition and monitoring of baselines and targets and weak annual indicators due to lack of data at the country level. Indicators are generally better designed in social sectors, and least so in areas such as governance. This study also points to underlying issues such as weaknesses in the results frameworks of the associated PRS and its Annual Progress Review and the upstream CAS frameworks on which the PRSCs are supposed to build. It points out that donor harmonization can add to this due to both the wide range of indicators required by the donor group and differences in approaches to these indicators.

IEG findings are corroborated by information from other Bank studies.

Most PRSCs have only achieved modest quality in their M&E frameworks.

PRSC Countries' Monitoring and Evaluation—IEG ICR Reviews

IEG Implementation Completion Reports Reviews of projects rate the quality of design, implementation, and utilization of M&E systems of projects.[21] For operations such as PRSCs, the rating also assesses the extent to which these systems are used for PRSC monitoring. Ratings are assigned on a four-point scale (*negligible, modest, substantial,* and *high*).

Of the 51 PRSCs that have been rated, 30 have a rating for the quality of their M&E systems. The majority of these (20 operations in 10 countries) have been rated *modest* for their M&E quality. Two (Benin PRSC 1 and Nicaragua PRSC 2) have the lowest possible score, *negligible*, and 6 PRSC operations in 3 countries (Cape Verde, Rwanda, and Vietnam) have been evaluated to have *substantial* M&E quality. No PRSCs were scored in the highest category. The overall conclusion is that M&E in most PRSC countries could be substantially improved in quality and in consistency of the design and use of data collection. In many cases,

Box 3.8. Monitoring and Evaluation in PRSC Countries

Rwanda, one of the better performers among PRSCs (with a substantial rating for M&E), focused its monitoring on measurable outcome targets that could be associated with the Bank program. Surveys were undertaken at the household and firm levels to establish baseline data and enable monitoring of progress toward targets. A results framework was drawn up to track progress for 11 key indicators, and an impact evaluation of performance-based contracting in the health sector is also under way. Institutional reforms have led to improved coordination among statistics, planning, and budget. Sector cluster groups composed of representatives of donors and government counterparts have discussed M&E frameworks in a consultative framework.

Nicaragua, at the other extreme, had systemic problems with the M&E framework with important shortfalls in the design, implementation, and utilization of monitoring and evaluation. Concerning design, a key performance indicator of the proportion of the population living in extreme poverty was not constructed with a view toward ensuring that data would be available to track the outcome. Concerning implementation and utilization, data for 3 of the 12 performance indicators were not available. Moreover, the program document for PRSC I sets out a dozen expected results of the program, presumably to be achieved by the end of PRSC 2. Some are intermediate results, but others are presented as if they were independent objectives. These do not appear to have been tracked and are not discussed in the ICR. The ICR reports that the supervision mission for PRSC 2 used a number of incorrect performance indicators. It also reports that the government substantially changed its estimate of a number of performance indicators, which led Bank supervision missions to conclude that the project was *highly satisfactory*. This suggests that monitoring and evaluation was, at the very least, not given due attention and may even have been manipulated.

Source: IEG desk reviews and country case studies.

PRSCs have tried to build upon national systems that suffer from shortcomings that impede the development of results frameworks for PRSCs.

Finally, it must be remembered that PRSC alignment with recipient countries, and contributions to the reinforcement of domestic systems and processes, frequently occurred within the context of a multidonor budget support group, in which the PRSC played a variable part. The next chapter examines the role of the PRSC within the context of a wider donor support framework.

Chapter 4

Evaluation Highlights

- Despite stagnant shares in budget support, PRSCs made effective contributions to donor harmonization.
- Progress has been made in achieving harmonized matrixes, but conditionality may initially increase to accommodate all donors.
- Progress is limited in harmonizing reviews of the PRS and integrating it with the joint matrix, harmonized results indicators, or reporting arrangements.
- In a large Budget Support Group, the Bank may lose the ability to incorporate substantive issues in the agenda.
- The Bank's processing calendar may limit its voice in a joint process.
- Individual small donors can sometimes unduly influence the agenda.
- Recipients may prefer to leave major items off the agenda.
- Sector working groups have contributed little to harmonization.
- Reconciliation of Bank policy-based versus EU outcome-based aid is desirable.
- Harmonization has high transaction costs for Bank PRSC staff.

Display of flags at World Bank/IMF Annual Meetings.
Photo courtesy of the World Bank Photo Library.

PRSCs and Donor Harmonization

From their inception, PRSCs were intended to serve as vehicles for donor harmonization. The Interim Guidelines anticipated that donors could base their medium-term support on the PRSC program.[1] Bank commitment to aid harmonization deepened with the Paris Declaration on Aid Effectiveness (2005), which affirmed the principles of recipient country ownership, alignment with country systems, and aid harmonization around a results-based agenda.

New guidelines on policy-based lending (also applicable to PRSCs), prepared guidance on the establishment of budget support groups, joint Memoranda of Understanding and disbursing around a common PAF. Guidelines provided that the joint PAF would draw indicators from the PRSP, based on a joint Annual Performance Review of the PRS. Country-based systems would be used and country capacity building would be coordinated.[2] IDA-15 Harmonization Guidelines reinforced these principles.[3] This chapter reviews the extent to which the PRSC was an effective vehicle of donor harmonization as envisaged by the Bank.[4]

Overview of PRSC Contributions to Aid Flows

The contribution of the PRSC to aid harmonization must be viewed in the context of (i) an aggregate decline in the share of aid in national income in all PRSC countries; (ii) a stagnant or declining share of general budget support in total aid, which is still largely channeled through traditional investment projects; (iii) some decline in the share of the World Bank assistance to PRSC countries from 2005 to 2007; (iv) some decline in the share of the PRSC in total IDA assistance and in total aid flows; and (v) some trend decline in the PRSC share of national budgets, from around 7 percent to less than 3 percent of budget expenditures (table 4.1).

A disaggregated review reveals a heterodox pattern among countries (appendix table A1.4). Many countries, especially those in Africa with historically higher aid shares in national income and long PRSC series, remain significantly aid dependent. In Mozambique, aid shares hover around 25–26 percent; in Rwanda, 20–25 percent; in Tanzania, 13–17 percent; and in Uganda, around 15 percent. In contrast, there were declines in aid dependence in fast-growing East European PRSC countries, such as Albania, Armenia, and Georgia, to a third of 2001 levels, where the Bank was typically the sole source of budget support.

The PRSC typically accounted for a variable share of budget support in several African countries, many of which have well-established donor relations (two-fifths to two-thirds in Cape Verde, Ghana, Madagascar, and Uganda and between 20 and 40 percent in another nine countries). And the overall contribution of the Bank declined by at least a third in some major African countries with PRSC programs, such as Ghana (from 30.1

Table 4.1. All PRSC Countries: Aid Flows (%)

	CY01	CY02	CY03	CY04	CY05	CY06	CY07
Share of aid in national income	11.8	12.1	11.3	12.7	10.6	10.4	10.0
Budget support flow—share of total aid flow	18.4	14.2	16.9	17.1	17.5	19.1	17.3
World Bank share of total aid flows	19.7	20.8	20.2	20.4	19.1	17.7	17.8
PRSC share of total World Bank disbursements	50.2	40.8	49.2	38.0	38.2	34.2	36.1
PRSC share of total aid flows in PRSC countries	12.2	7.3	12.0	9.3	7.8	7.2	6.6
PRSC share of government expenditures	7.1	3.4	5.2	5.4	4.1	3.0	2.9
PRSC share of total budget support aid flows	57.0	67.1	74.9	58.7	47.3	64.5	34.1

Source: See appendix tables A4.1 to A4.7

Note: Data on budget support flows are not available for all countries, or for all points in time. CY = calendar year.

to 20.3 percent of total official development assistance flows) and Uganda (36.1 percent to 21.5 percent of official development assistance flows).

PRSCs are the sole source of budget support aid in some countries with short PRSC series and a limited donor process.

The relative share of budget support provided by the Bank declined in a number of countries: from two-thirds of the total to barely a sixth in Vietnam, from over half to about a third in Burkina Faso, and from 25 percent to 18 percent in Mozambique. Trend declines in the PRSC share of Bank aid are perceptible in other countries with long PRSC series: Burkina Faso, Madagascar, and Vietnam. This could be due to a deliberate exit policy where the declining share of World Bank engagement is then covered by other, typically smaller, donors.[5]

PRSC Programs: Modalities of Harmonization

Harmonization without a Jointly Negotiated PAF

Donor harmonization under the PRSC took different forms depending on the recipient aid architecture (appendix table A4.1). Many countries began to receive general budget support (GBS) aid, strongly resembling Bank/IDA policy-based lending, from many sources. Joint donor matrixes of policy actions, referred to as PAFs, were intended to "provide the basis for joint monitoring by all donors, for management according to a set of predefined common principles, however with disbursement still subject to individual donor decisions."[6]

Modalities of aid harmonization in PRSC countries range from simple coordination to clearly defined multi-donor processes.

Not all PRSC countries had joint budget support arrangements (table 4.2). Better-off countries in Eastern Europe and those elsewhere that were more politically fragile, such as Guyana, Honduras, Nepal, and Sri Lanka, have had little or no other budget support.[7] Yet there was coordination in the PRSC process and sometimes the hope of attracting future budget support

In another five countries, (Armenia, Ethiopia, Lao PDR, Moldova, and Pakistan), there were limited attempts at coordinated budget support offered by other donors.

Only one PRSC country fully meets the original expectations of donor harmonization around the focal point of the PRSC—Vietnam. The PRSC policy matrix constituted the single Performance Assessment Framework, derived from the PRSP (Comprehensive Poverty Reduction and Growth Strategy) for PRSCs 2–5. From PRSC 6, the underlying strategy document was merged with the government's formal planning process, and subsequent PRSC policy matrixes have been based upon annual reviews of the State Economic Development Plan. All PRSC cofinancers are cosignatories to the annual Vietnam Development Report, which maps PRSC progress.[8] The number of partners in the process had grown from 3 to 11 at the start of PRSC 6. Some concentrate attention on a select group of policy actions that

Table 4.2. PRSC and Donor Harmonization: The Nature of Budget Support Coordination

Type of support	Countries
No other budget support	Albania, Azerbaijan, Georgia, Guyana, Honduras,[a] Nepal,[b] Sri Lanka[a]
Other budget support, some of which is harmonized/ cofinanced	Armenia, Ethiopia, Lao PDR,[c] Moldova, Pakistan
Other budget support, based on Bank PRSC matrix, adopted by government and accepted by other donors	Vietnam[d]
Other budget support with a common PAF or PAF-like framework developing	Benin, Lesotho, Madagascar (government matrix), Senegal, Mali, Nicaragua (government matrix), Rwanda[e]
Other budget support, common PAF or PAF-like framework operational	Burkina Faso, Cape Verde, Ghana, Malawi, Mozambique, Tanzania, Uganda

Source: Appendix table A4.8, based on PRSC program documents, IDD and Associates 2006b, and IEG country case studies.

a. Joint budget support had been considered by two other donors but had not occurred by the beginning of FY08.

b. The Asian Development Bank had prepared budget support, but it was not delivered with the PRSC.

c. In Lao PDR, as in Vietnam, the government adopted the PRSC matrix as its own matrix.

d. The government adopted the PRSC matrix, which served as the basis of a joint matrix.

e. There was an initial partnership framework and a form of joint matrix, but it is used only by the African Development Bank and the World Bank.

Box 4.1. PRSC Donor Coordination—No Other Budget Support

In Honduras, PRSC 1 attracted donor interest in program-based assistance and representatives of Germany's *Kreditanstalt für Wiederaufbau* (KfW) and the Swedish International Development Cooperation Agency (SIDA) participated in its appraisal mission. Together with the Canadian International Development Agency (CIDA) and the U.K. Department for International Development, they also accompanied the preparation of a companion PRSC Technical Assistance Credit.

In Nepal, IDA and the U.K. Department for International Development jointly supported reforms in governance, health, and privatization, as well as in reforms to the Medium-Term Expenditure Framework. Coordination with other bilateral and multilateral agencies was evident in a number of sectors.

Coordination typically occurred first in the formulation of sector strategies and joint analytic work. In Albania, for example, a quarter of analytic work was undertaken with other donors, although only a tenth of missions were coordinated, and only 5 percent of aid was deemed to be program-based.

Source: IEG desk reviews and interviews.

Box 4.2. PRSC Donor Coordination—With Other Budget Support

In Lao PDR, Japan provided some cofinancing for PRSO 3. The PRSO 4–7 matrix was jointly appraised with Japan, the European Commission, and Asian Development Bank, which committed to cofinancing. The Bank undertook considerable sectoral coordination as well as joint analytic work. The government has expressed the view that it would like an annual Lao PDR Development Forum under its leadership, with a significant role for the Ministry of Finance, to replace the current triennial Donors' Roundtable process (jointly led by UNDP and the Ministry of Foreign Affairs). But so far it has not been willing to exercise leverage with donors to promote greater use of budget support.

In Armenia, where the Bank has been virtually the sole source of budget support, barring a small volume of EU funds, government representatives have not voiced any preference for joint support and are content to allow donors to follow their lead areas of expertise and inclination.

Source: IEG country case studies.

coincide with their priorities. Others fully adopt the PRSC matrix as a cross-sectoral component in their aid programs.

Harmonization with Other Budget Support Donors—The Joint Matrix

The more traditional model of harmonization, in 13 PRSC countries, is one where donors are already involved, each with their own visions of policy priorities. A common position must be negotiated. Twelve such PRSC countries are in Africa. In most, the process of adopting a common matrix has strengthened over time. By fiscal 2008, a joint PAF was fully operational in six countries. The process typically began with the adoption of Partnership Principles, followed by a more detailed Memorandum of Understanding where donors commit to a joint approach. Where donors have had their own matrixes, harmonization entails the merger of the Bank PRSC matrix with other donor matrixes.[9]

In Vietnam, the Bank's PRSC and the national development strategy merged in identity over time, and the Bank clearly led the donor process.

Budget support groups often have uneven membership with a few large core donors and a large number of smaller donors, as well as nonfinancing members, which find it desirable to have a seat at the table (table 4.3). Leading bilaterals sometimes enjoy a proportional contribution greater than the Bank. In all countries, donor groups have grown over time. By 2007, Mozambique had 19 donors, including 15 bilaterals and 4 supranational or international agencies; Tanzania had 13 and Ghana and Burkina Faso had about 10 each. Countries with long PRSC series have tended to have more donors.

Bank task team leaders attribute some of the growth to the PRSC contribution. While coun-

Table 4.3. Shares in Budget Support Recipient Country—Donor Contributions, 2007

	Total GBS received ($ millions)	w/o World Bank	World Bank (%)	European Commission (%)	Bilaterals (%)	Top 3 bilaterals and their shares (%)			Number of bilaterals	Donors/ MOU 2005	Donors/ MOU 2007
Tanzania	657.4	246	37.5	5.9	52.6	UK (24.3)	Sweden (6.9)	Dutch (5.6)	11	13	13
Mozambique	356.7	70	19.6	13.9	52.6	UK (18.1)	Sweden (7.6)	Dutch (6.3)	15	17	19
Ghana	321.9	110	34.2	5.5	0.0	UK (19.0)	Dutch (5.7)	Canada (4.4)	7	8	10
Uganda	248.8	126	50.7	15.5	35.7	UK (25.0)	Ireland (4.9)	Norway (4.0)	5	0	0
Burkina Faso	187.7	90	48.8	27.2	26.3	Dutch (12.0)	France (4.3)	Sweden (3.6)	5	9	9
Rwanda	171.9	52	30.0	12.9	39.3	UK (33.0)	Sweden (6.3)		3	3	6
Mali	146.0	46	31.5	21.2	25.5	France (9.5)	Dutch (8.6)	Sweden (7.4)	4	0	6
Madagascar	109.2	41	37.4	20.7	8.1	France (8.12)			1	4	4
Malawi	58.2	21	35.7	20.6	74.4	UK (61.1)	Norway (13.2)		2	0	4
Benin	34.6	30	87.4	30.5	68.4	Dutch (36.3)	France (16.3)	Denmark (13.8)	4	4	7

Source: Based on dataset from Strategic Partnership with Africa, U.K. Department for International Development, Overseas Development Institute, and the World Bank.
Note: MOU = Memorandum of Understanding.

tries that have successfully adhered to programmatic support have increased their budget support donors; attribution to the PRSC is difficult. The African Development Bank, for example, initially signed very few Memoranda of Understanding (3 in 2005), often waiting until the Bank/IDA was a cosignatory, but Memoranda of Understanding increased to 11 in 2007.

Achievements of PRSCs in a Multidonor Environment

Seven specific questions are addressed below, on the contribution of the PRSC to the harmonization agenda, based on evidence from IEG country case studies.

Did the PRSC Provide a Platform for a Donor-Harmonized Program?

While the Bank made important contributions to donor coordination, case studies suggest that only in Vietnam did the PRSC create a strategic platform around which other donors could coalesce in the aid process. In Vietnam, the Bank's PRSC matrix became synonymous with the national development policy matrix. The Bank clearly had a primary role in harmonizing and aligning donors around the PRSC matrix as the vehicle for budget support. Its success has been attributed also to the Bank's physical presence in Hanoi, its deep technical resources, analytical leadership, and financial resources. Continuity of the Bank's PRSC team leaders, and the sustained program, had cumulative impact. The Bank's role as senior partner was accepted by other donors. In Lao PDR, a similar approach was adopted but is less evolved.

Multidonor budget support groups are the more traditional modality for harmonization in the PRSCs, and they exist in most African countries.

Many governments have not voiced a preference for multidonor support groups.

The Bank played an important role in countries where donor coordination for budget support aid is less mature, though not through the focal

Box 4.3. Donor Harmonization—Negotiating a Common PAF

In Benin, Senegal, and Madagascar, a common performance framework appears to be emerging. Benin's PRSC matrix was harmonized with the African Development Bank from 2002. The European Commission and European bilaterals harmonized under a separate arrangement. In December 2007, a Memorandum of Understanding was agreed for a common matrix derived from PRSP among all donors. In Senegal, a joint Memorandum of Understanding to initiate harmonization was signed during PRSC 3.

In other countries, such as Madagascar and Nicaragua, the government has taken ownership of the process through its own matrix, around which donors are then expected to align. In Madagascar, for example, the government matrix is the Madagascar Action Plan, from which the PRSC and other donors derive conditions. The Bank and other donors still have their own performance frameworks and matrixes. From PRSC 4 onward, the government matrix is expected to function like a common PAF. In Nicaragua, similarly, the government had its own Performance Assessment Matrix (PAM), which is the joint matrix of policy actions to be agreed on with GBS donors. The PRSCs were not fully integrated with this.

A fully harmonized joint framework has been achieved already in Burkina Faso, Ghana, Mozambique, Tanzania and Uganda, which also have long PRSC histories. In Ghana, a multi-donor budget support (MDBS) group, established in 2003, committed itself to a set of common premises. The PRSC is now an integral part of the MDBS process, which in 2007 had 10 contributing donors and several observers, including the United States Agency for International Development (USAID), Japan, UN agencies, and nongovernmental organizations. Until 2006, the PRSC continued to derive its matrix separately from the PAF, albeit with limited differences. After 2006, the matrixes were merged and both use the same three-year rolling PAF. However, the Bank refrains from using outcome indicators as prior actions even though they are included in the joint policy matrix.

In Mozambique, the Bank signed a Memorandum of Understanding in 2004 committing itself to harmonizing PRSC support with budget support provided by the other GBS partners, and today is an integral party to its group of 19 development partners. While the PRSC-supported program, in itself, is limited to 8–10 measures or prior actions, the overall GBS program is substantially broader.

Source: IEG desk reviews, country case studies, and interviews.

The Bank played a pivotal role in donor harmonization in countries such as Lao PDR and Vietnam, where it led the process.

role of the PRSC. In Nicaragua, Bank participation gave credibility to the proposal of creating a budget support group. The Bank's technical expertise was a key factor because most donors did not have the capacity to analyze the government proposals.

The Bank's contribution is more difficult to identify separately in countries with a large number of donors. Government representatives in Ghana do not single out the Bank's financial contributions, although its leadership role has been recognized. In Mozambique, the government supports the alignment of the Bank's PRSC with the donor budget group and acknowledges the Bank's convening power. However, both donors and government counterparts suggest the Bank could show stronger leadership.

Has the Common Donor Matrix Been Aligned to the PRS Process?

While donor-harmonized policy matrixes typically reflect underlying poverty reduction strategies or national development strategies, they rarely appear to be linked to the annual review of the PRS and its implementation. Initially, it was envisaged that the Annual Progress Reviews of the PRS would yield information that would feed into disbursement decisions as well as formulation of the PAF.[10] In practice, annual reviews of the PRS often run in parallel to the PAF process, rather than as an integral element of it. Other authors have pointed out that PAF reviews bear little resemblance to PRSP Annual Progress Reports, because the former focus largely on policy measures, whereas the latter focus on descriptive reporting of achievements together with data on a limited number of PRSP priority indicators, which are based on measurable inputs, outputs, and outcomes, rather than policies or actions.[11] While harmonization through a common policy framework is accepted in principle, there is room for coordination of the annual review of countries' development strategies and PRSC or other budget support operations.[12]

Performance of multidonor sector groups has been highly variable, with limited support to the PRSC process.

Vietnam provides one example where joint annual evaluations of the PRS have been conducted in collaboration with other donors, translating national strategies into prioritized sets of policy actions.[13] Government officials indicate appreciation for the triangulation among the national plan, the annual development review, and the PRSC. This example suggests that achieving more complex consensus may be easier if there is a recognized lead player, whether it is the government or a donor partner.

Has the Donor Process Helped Achieve Unified Sectoral Strategies?

Coordinating sector policy within the multidonor framework has often been difficult. In most countries, sector coordination among some donors pre-

Box 4.4. Harmonization and Alignment with the PRS Process

Ghana is considered an example of good alignment between the underlying PRS and the donor-harmonized performance assessment framework. The Ghana Poverty Reduction Strategy (GPRS) is, in effect, the national development strategy, and the current version of the PAF is based on its objectives.[a]

Similarly, the Mozambique PAF is fully drawn from the strategic matrix of the government's PRS, which was determined in 2004. However, this has since become out-of-date. Basing the PRSC program on the PAF has therefore become a growing challenge because in many areas the matrix no longer adequately reflects the government's reform priorities.

In Benin, where the PRSC has occasionally contained measures outside the PRSP, these have sometimes been requested by the government, for example, a request to eliminate education fees in PRSC 4, although this was outside the scope of PRSP 2. In this case, the government ordered the measure, but not as part of the PRSC 4 matrix.

Source: IEG desk reviews, country case studies, and interviews.

a. Although, as pointed out in the Strategic Partnership with Africa (2006), the Performance Assessment Framework policy matrix in Ghana is derived from the PRSP, it also includes additional information from sectors and subnational governments. The PRSC matrix is also derived from the PRSP matrix but addresses politically sensitive cross-cutting issues, such as public financial management, transparency, corruption, and decentralization. The government prefers these to be excluded from the PRS policy matrix reported on in the annual performance review, making it difficult to reconcile the processes over time.

Box 4.5. Harmonization of Policy Matrixes and Sector Strategies

In Ghana, agendas of sector groups cannot reasonably be met through a single PAF, leading to donor-supported sector budget support funds (agriculture, natural resources) outside the multidonor budget support group. These funds employ very different ground rules and funding arrangements. The agriculture fund in Ghana is a mix of earmarked funding from the UK and Canada, and the Canadian money is not even on-budget. Another example is the Health Fund to which the Bank contributes through its funding for nutrition. Such funds have their own triggers, with differences in triggers among donors. The proliferation of sector funds raises questions about the future character of the core general budget support matrix and its role in sector inclusion. And core ministries are sometimes reluctant to take on measures where noncompliance would affect disbursement, if it is beyond their influence.

Source: IEG desk reviews, country case studies, and interviews.

Box 4.6. Harmonization of Policy Matrixes and Increases in Conditionality

In Benin, for example, even at the time of PRSC 4, the Government Policy Agenda matrix contained about 120 measures for a three-year period, or about 40 per year. According to some observers, the unwieldy nature limited its use, although the donor community consulted portions relevant to their programs. Country officials sense that multiple matrixes are sometimes superimposed, instead of harmonized. In Benin, there are still three matrixes in practice: the Bank's PRSC matrix, also supported by the African Development Bank, a second matrix supported by the EU and several of its members (*Approche Budgétaire Conjointe—Reduction de la Pauvreté*), and the government's own matrix.

Such parallel arrangements with the EU have also been present in other countries, such as Burkina Faso, where a single matrix has been achieved. In other cases, the PRSC matrix has been defined as a subset of the overall joint matrix. In Mozambique, the joint PAF includes a subset of 40–50 indicators. The PRSC draws a select number of measures, limited to 8–10 measures or prior actions.

Source: IEG desk reviews, country case studies, and interviews.

ceded the multidonor budget support process. With general budget support, some donor groups attempted arrangements for the alignment of sector policy as a part of the budget support/PRSC process, as in Benin, where donors have been grouped according to sector tables, which share information and contribute variably to developing joint strategies.[14]

The size of the Bank PRSC program can be an obstacle. Inadvertent limited treatment of individual sector policy areas has been pointed out in Vietnam, where multidonor alignment around general budget support unusually preceded sectorwide approaches. Another factor may be internal complexities at the sectoral level in Vietnam, where international departments in each ministry manage donor relationships through a series of international support groups (at the ministry level), partnership groups (in certain individual sectors), and technical advisory groups (on specific issues) of differing strengths and degrees of effectiveness. As in Ghana, sector and targeted budget support is starting to emerge with initial pilots in education and rural water, building on sectoral, medium-term expenditure frameworks. In some cases, this builds upon previous donor-supported sector arrangements.

Has Donor Coordination Helped to Simplify Conditionality?

A frequent finding has been that, at least in the early years of PRSC donor harmonization, the joint matrix tended to expand in size to accommodate all donors. A second limitation observed in joint matrixes is that donors may cluster around the lowest common denominator of policy content. This is reinforced by the actions of government counterparts who prefer to peg strategic conditionality on what is likely to be achievable, especially if there is a sense of donor unison, and delays in achievement could limit disbursements. Finally, the harmonization process can also imply loss of flexibility for the Bank in including new areas of importance in the joint agenda.

Sometimes the donor process limits the Bank's ability to bring substantive issues to the PRSC agenda and it has to use other means.

Has Harmonization Reduced Transaction Costs for Recipients?

Evidence suggests that donor mission coordination did reduce transaction costs, but not as much

Box 4.7. Harmonization of Policy Matrixes and Weakened Program Content

In Mozambique, the Bank provided valued technical advice on reforming the concession system for the natural resource extraction sector. However, actions in this area were outside the purview of the budget support group; the Bank had to rely on the IMF program to include implementation of key policy actions.

Ghana, with increasing energy dependence, grew vulnerable to price and subsidy increases, which had the potential of creating serious macro imbalances. PRSC conditionality focused first on deregulation of petroleum, and then on more efficient management of electrical power agencies, using cost recovery mechanisms. As a result, when oil prices increased, they were absorbed more easily. This was subsequently deemed a key area of Bank intervention in Ghana. The Bank was able to persuade other donors to include energy sector measures in the common matrix. While they were also triggers for the Bank, they were not triggers for the MDBS process.

Source: IEG desk reviews, country case studies, and interviews.

as hoped for by recipients, and not always to the satisfaction of other donors.[15] In Vietnam, where the Bank PRSC had a clear leadership role, the team was able to maintain a strict annual schedule, concentrated in the first semester of the year, geared to the target date of a June PRSC approval by the Board. Donors argue for a greater role before finalizing each year's PRSC, particularly in those areas in which Bank staff may not have a comparative advantage.[16] Government officials, however, appreciate the focus of the tight schedule, which maintains reform momentum. Notwithstanding, a number of measures have been taken in recent years to improve communications among participants in policy discussions.

Transaction costs for core ministries may have increased, compared with line ministries. In some countries, such as Ghana, donors have agreed to a mission-free period (September 15 to November 15), but this does not limit donor representatives to be present in Accra. Coordinated sector working groups, which are frequent offshoots of the general budget support process, are also time-consuming for governments.

Better harmonized disbursements are limited by differences in approach by the Bank and other donors.

Increased transaction costs for the Bank (and other donors) are another corollary. With large donor groups, the Bank may experience some loss in relevance if its own processing schedule is not well synchronized with the budget support group process. In Mozambique, the Bank's internal review comes too late for it to influence adequately the formulation of the joint policy matrix. This is a consequence of the inflexibilities of the budget support process.

Have Disbursements Been Harmonized? Are They More Predictable?

Budget support groups have helped provide governments with a more predictable source of funding. Between 2003 and 2006, annual disbursements in Ghana were within 5 percent of pledges, except for one year when it was still within 10 percent. However, internal transfers to individual ministries remain slow. Complaints remain about funds being released too late in the fiscal year to allow achievement of program outcomes.

In most PRSC countries, the European Union is also a general budget support provider. The Bank faces the challenge of harmonizing with the EU's dual-tranche system. Under this system, a fixed-amount tranche is tied to the fulfillment of basic conditions, typically in the areas of public financial management or macroeconomic stability and general adherence to the reform program.[17] A second, variable tranche is tied to policy targets achieved.[18] This reflects the EU philosophy of outcome-based conditionality in contrast to the Bank's policy-based conditionality. The Bank has expressed the belief that disbursements according to outcomes achieved are premature, as outcome indicators rarely change from year to year, the databases in countries to which the Bank disburses are typically unreliable, and attributions between policy measures and outcomes achieved are often difficult to establish.

EU tranche releases are often performed on a two-year cycle, making the task of predictable support harmonized with the PRSC especially difficult. In some countries (such as Benin and Burkina Faso), EU budget support was harmonized with other bilateral European budget support donors early on in the process. In Ghana, failure to meet the condition on share of primary education in the total education budget led to a 10 percent reduction in disbursements on the performance tranche.[19] Over time, however, the two approaches have shown some signs of converging, as seen in Benin.

Has Capacity Building Been Coordinated?

From the limited available evidence, capacity building for donor harmonization has received limited and erratic attention in PRSC programs, which have been substantially focused on public financial management. In Lao PDR, for example, efforts focused on the restructuring of the Financial Management Capacity Building Project and the creation of a multidonor trust fund to fund capacity development activities. There are now efforts in the ministries of education, health, and agriculture and forestry to develop sectoral capacity development frameworks. In Ghana, where there is substantial donor, as well as Bank, funding for capacity building, there is no systematic review process for assessing capacity needs arising from the PRSC/budget support process, although efforts are emerging in some areas.[20]

Joint Missions and Joint Analytic Work—PRSC and Non-PRSC Countries

Data from the 2008 Paris Declaration Monitoring Survey permit a comparison of groups of IDA countries in two dimensions of donor coordination—the share of coordinated analytical work and joint missions that donors undertake (appendix tables A4.2 and A4.3). Data on joint missions have been measured for two years by the Paris Declaration Monitoring Survey for 20 PRSC countries as well as non-PRSC IDA countries.

The average number of donor missions is not greatly different between PRSC and non-PRSC countries. About 18 percent of donor missions were coordinated, in 2005, to PRSC countries as well as to better-performing non-PRSC aid recipients. Both groups showed some improvements in 2007, compared with 2005, to 23 percent for PRSC countries, and to 21 percent for other well-performing IDA countries. For all non-PRSC IDA countries joint missions were initially higher, at 20 percent, and there was an increase to 22 percent in 2007.[21]

The Bank harmonized more missions than other donors in PRSC and non-PRSC countries, especially in weaker IDA countries.

The Bank/IDA performed better than all donors, on average, in terms of coordination in PRSC countries, and the Bank also shows a striking improvement in performance for PRSC countries of 11 percentage points between 2005 and 2007. Yet, Bank performance also improved in other IDA countries, and the Bank has also coordinated intensively in the more poorly performing IDA countries, possibly because of security issues.[22]

Another measure of the extent to which harmonization reduced burdens on aid recipient countries is the share of analytic work undertaken jointly by two or more donors. Joint analytic work often precedes joint missions, and both often occur in the absence of deeper agreement on harmonization.

A high proportion of analytic work was donor coordinated, especially by the Bank, but coordination was not higher in PRSC countries.

Data confirm that the proportion of joint analytic work, at 42 to 46 percent, over 2005 and 2007, is higher than the proportion of joint missions. There was some increase in joint analytic work between these years in PRSC countries.[23] And again, the Bank/IDA has performed better, on average, than the combined donor average, and has improved its own performance by seven percentage points. There does not appear to be a substantial difference in performance between PRSC countries and other comparison groups. Indeed, non-PRSC IDA countries seem to have done better initially on coordination than PRSC countries. Over time the groups have converged. For the Bank, coordination was initially the same between both groups of countries, however, coordination for other well-performing IDA countries improved somewhat less than for PRSC countries.

The Paris Declaration may have prompted some increase in coordination, especially on joint missions. Yet these must be interpreted with the caveat that data on numbers of coordinated missions and pieces of analytical work are incomplete in conveying the sense of a broader culture of collaboration, and it is not possible to infer a trend from two years and a limited number of countries.

Finally, data also suggest that PRSC countries may channel more aid through national public sectors (appendix table A4.4).[24] Data on donor use of national public financial management and national procurement systems show that in 2007, 43 percent of aid provided to governments was channeled through national public financial management systems for PRSC countries, compared with 29 percent for other well-performing IDA countries, and 24 percent for other IDA countries. Similarly, for procurement, 43 percent of aid to PRSC countries went through public procurement systems, compared with 35 percent for other well-performing countries, and 25 percent for other IDA countries. This suggests that PRSC countries do better in aligning their aid systems with domestic processes than non-PRSC countries.

Aid to PRSC countries was clearly channeled more through in-country systems.

This marked contrast may be associated with the special focus of PRSCs on public sector management. However, all countries with long PRSC series do not exhibit improvement. Drivers of success have particularly been those countries where the share of budget support in total aid increased—especially Vietnam and Mozambique.[25]

Views on Harmonization: Clients, Staff, and Donors

Country Client Perspectives

Bank Alignment with Country Strategy, and Harmonization with Other Donors. In response to a survey of country clients (annex 7), respondents generally believe that the PRSC was well aligned with other donors as well as with national strategy.[26] Almost all agreed that the PRSC policy matrix only included measures from the unified matrix (87 percent). An overwhelming proportion (97 percent) acknowledged that the Bank had made considerable effort to facilitate donor coordination and that the Bank's alignment with other donors had improved since the first PRSC-supported operation was introduced (92 percent). Yet harmonization with other budget support donors was only partial (43 percent). The donor matrix reflected an aggregation of submatrixes reflecting each donor's preferences. And each still wished to adopt its own reporting templates and internal procedures for disbursement.

Clients acknowledge Bank efforts in donor coordination.

Harmonization and Overall Conditionality. More than half of the respondents (58 percent) believed that the alignment of the PRSC with other donors had significantly increased the number of conditions that governments had to fulfill. However, others noted that the broader scope of the PRSC policy matrix warranted such an increase. Two-thirds (67 percent) agreed or strongly agreed that the joint donor budget support matrix contained too many actions. Yet one stakeholder, who appreciated the difference between program benchmarks and policy conditions, found it helpful to benchmark the activity of the executive branch.

Harmonization and Predictability. Three-quarters of stakeholders noted that donor alignment had brought about a reduction in transaction costs, reducing the effort spent preparing, negotiating, and reviewing budget support programs. Almost two-thirds of respondents believed that Bank assistance through the PRSC was "significantly more predictable" than other donors. More than three-quarters believed that donor coordination had reduced reporting requirements.

Client Country Perceptions—Data from the Strategic Partnership with Africa. Data from the Strategic Partnership with Africa (table 4.4) provides corroborating evidence on how recipients view the aid process. The strongest performing areas are the holding of joint reviews or missions and coordinating budget support conditions. There are also strong scores in supporting public financial management and minimizing reporting requirements. Support to statistical systems, while improving, is consistently weak. Reducing conditionality has shown improvement but also remains weak. Scores have improved

Table 4.4. Country Client Perceptions of Donor Coordination and Budget Support (average scores)

	2003	2004	2005	2006	2007	Scores improved (2006–07)	Scores constant (2006–07)	Scores worsened (2006–07)
Coordination of selection of GBS conditions?	2.71	3.36	3.79	3.57	4	1	9	1
Joint reviews or missions?	2.78	3.4	3.57	3.64	4.33	3	8	0
Minimize reporting requirements?	3.17	3.07	3.64	3.14	3.67	3	8	0
Support to public financial management?	2.94	3.27	3.57	3.43	3.75	1	10	0
Support to statistical systems?	2.35	3.13	3.29	3.21	3.25	4	5	2
Minimizing overall numbers of conditions?	n.a.	2.13	2.64	2.57	3.25	1	10	0
Usefulness of conditionality?	3.22	3.57	3.92	3.54	3.55	1	7	2

Source: Strategic Partnership with Africa 2009, based on a rating system where 1 = poor and 5 = excellent.

Note: Based on data from 13 PRSC countries in Africa (Benin, Burkina Faso, Cape Verde, Ethiopia, Ghana, Madagascar, Malawi, Mali, Mozambique, Rwanda, Senegal, Tanzania, and Uganda). Lesotho, another PRSC country in Africa, is not covered.

over time. These data, however, comment on the overall budget support process, not on the PRSC specifically.

Donor Harmonization—Implications for the Bank and Its Staff

Survey of Task Team Leaders. Almost 80 percent of Bank task team leaders believe the PRSC to be effective or very effective for donor harmonization around the national development strategy. Even in countries where there were no other GBS donors, half of the task team leaders surveyed believed that the PRSC had played this coordinative role. And most staff perceived that coordination had reduced, or substantially reduced, transaction costs for government counterparts (58 percent; see annex 5).

The converse is an increase in transaction costs to Bank staff, particularly additional time required for task processing. Bank task team leaders believe that, while the PRSCs made an important contribution to the harmonization of donor dialogue around a PRSP, transaction costs have increased as donor groups have grown. The PRSC was perceived to substantially increase transaction costs for team leaders (84 percent) as well as other PRSC team members (66 percent), sometimes to the detriment of substantive work and interaction with governments.

Costs are perceived to be high in countries with larger donor groups (such as Benin, Ghana, and Vietnam). By contrast, in countries with limited or no additional budget support (Albania, Armenia, Azerbaijan, and Nepal), the PRSC has been deemed marginally effective for donor harmonization around a common PRS, but task team leaders have reported lower, or no increases in transaction costs from the coordination process. Data from donor country case studies prepared by the Organisation for Economic Co-operation and Development's Development Assistance Committee (OECD-DAC) suggest that other donors also feel increased transaction costs in the coordination process.[27]

Clients believe that harmonization initially increased conditionality but improved predictability.

There is also a sense of limited acknowledgement within the Bank for increased staff transaction costs required for donor harmonization. Only 12 percent of task team leaders felt that their efforts were fully recognized and rewarded, in contrast to 44 percent who thought there was partial acknowledgment, and an equal number who thought these efforts were not acknowledged. Even if these perceptions are discounted somewhat, they remain large.

Bank staff feel that the transaction costs of donor harmonization for Bank staff are not adequately recognized.

Survey of Bank Sector Staff Team Members. A separate IEG survey of sector specialist team members who participated in PRSC teams suggests sharply divided views about donor harmonization and the PRSC. Over half of the respondents believe that PRSCs only partly help donor dialogue and coordination to reach agreement on sectoral priorities, if at all. Yet over a third believe the role of the PRSC is significant (annex 6).

Bank sector staff point to occasional undue influence of donors who may not be well informed in certain areas but who assume a strong role in roundtable discussions, to the detriment of sector policy. They also point out that country counterparts in a multidonor environment prefer to agree to easily achievable conditions rather than those that may be in the best interests of the sector. About a fifth feel that counterparts resist harmonization because it represents a coalition against country staff. Over half believe this to be at least partially true. While budget support/PRSC programs typically entail a number of important sector measures (education, health, water, and sometimes social protection), Bank sector staff are not convinced that the single common matrix framework can provide sufficient depth for sector policy reforms and believe that sector ministries are often poorly integrated into the general budget support/PRSC framework.

Other donors also feel burdened by the high transaction costs of harmonization.

Donor Harmonization—Other Donor Views

Based on limited evidence from IEG country case studies, other PRSC donors also feel burdened by high transaction costs involved in aid harmonization. Donors also point out that they face formal restrictions, such as political vetoes, to entering into common arrangements, and many believe that parallel rather than joint financing is less burdensome and has lower transaction costs.[28] Some donors hold the view that donor partnerships may undermine the position of governments that are weak already.[29]

Despite these frustrations, in most countries the budget support/PRSC group is seen as a desirable group to belong to because it brings advantages of information as well as a voice at the table. Many express appreciation for the leadership role of the Bank, its quality analytical work, and the dedication of its task team leaders. In some cases, as discussed above in the case of Vietnam, donors complain that the Bank sometimes appears too demanding for small donors and suggest a more effective division of labor toward donors who have expertise in a sector.

The following chapters of this evaluation focus on PRSC outcomes. Given that the PRSC was heavily focused on public sector and public financial management issues and the strengthening of the budget process, chapter 5 reviews outcomes in these areas and chapter 6 evaluates the contributions of the PRSC toward fostering poverty-reducing growth.

Chapter 5

Evaluation Highlights

- PRSCs acknowledged and addressed fiduciary risks and helped to advance PFMP reform.
- PFMP strategies in PRSCs were grounded in adequate diagnostics and harmonized among donors, but implementation was sometimes slow.
- PFMP results frameworks are an area of weakness.
- Objectives in budget formulation were achieved, especially in using standard classifiers, reducing expenditure variance, and reducing expenditure arrears.
- Efforts are needed to better integrate medium-term forecasting, reduce extra-budgetary funds, and include donor funds on budget.
- Improving the internal controls environment remains a challenge.
- Budget reporting has improved.
- Results on procurement seem to be harder to achieve.
- The one PRSC fragile state, Lao PDR, performed as well as others in PFMP reform.

Community loan and repayment schedule; India. Photo by Simone D. McCourtie, courtesy of the World Bank Photo Library.

PRSC Outcomes: Public Financial Management and Procurement

Recognition that budget support transfers can potentially enhance the allocative efficiency of aid flows has underpinned the design of PRSC operations.[1] However, channeling aid flows through recipient countries' domestic budget processes may require fiduciary risk mitigation to ensure that funds are directed efficiently toward their intended uses. Recognizing these needs, reforms of public financial management and procurement (PFMP) systems have been a core objective of PRSCs.[2]

PRSCs and Public Financial Management Reforms

The overall evaluation question addressed is: How effectively have PRSCs helped countries strengthen their public financial management systems? This overarching question is addressed through a review of three component questions (figure 5.1): (i) What was the extent of diagnostic work in PFMP undertaken as a part of the PRSC, and did this use Bank guidance? (ii) How well was PFMP reform designed, and to what extent was diagnostic work implemented? (iii) What were the results, and how can they be associated with the PRSC program? Answers have been constructed through a structured desk review of appraisal, completion, evaluative, diagnostic, and analytical work for 18 of the 27 countries in which PRSCs were approved during fiscal 2001–08.[3] The extent of progress is gauged on the basis of actual results achieved.[4]

New Diagnostic Tools for PFMP Quality

Bank diagnostic work for the design of public financial management reform has been based largely on principles and diagnostics developed in the years just before the introduction of the PRSC, adapted in 2001 from OECD principles, for a development setting.[5] Standardized assessment instruments, tracking, and scoring systems were introduced shortly after, most notably the Country Financial Accountability Assessments (CFAAs), for a comprehensive stocktaking of the financial accountability of budget and auditing systems. In parallel, Country Procurement Assessment Reports (CPARs) were redefined in 1998 to increase emphasis on national procurement systems. These two instruments represent the fundamental due diligence for fiduciary risk. Their assessment formed a part of the PRSC decision-making process.

Diagnostic tools used by PRSCs included a range of Bank instruments, such as Country Financial Accountability Assessments and Country Procurement Assessment Reports.

Such reports were generally deemed reliable and able to provide an adequate basis for an assessment of fiduciary risk. An IEG evaluation found that 64 percent of CPARs and 71 percent of CFAAs were of satisfactory quality.[6] A Bank review of 22 countries found that CFAAs/CPARs contribute to a greater focus on public financial management in subsequent Country Assistance Strategies and increased public financial management lending.[7]

Figure 5.1. Methodology of PFMP Evaluation of PRSCs

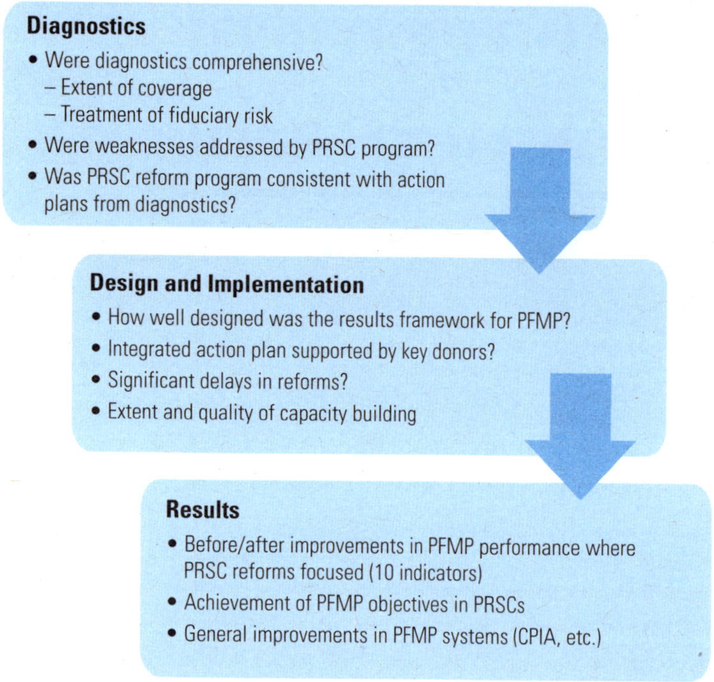

Diagnostics
- Were diagnostics comprehensive?
  - Extent of coverage
  - Treatment of fiduciary risk
- Were weaknesses addressed by PRSC program?
- Was PRSC reform program consistent with action plans from diagnostics?

Design and Implementation
- How well designed was the results framework for PFMP?
- Integrated action plan supported by key donors?
- Significant delays in reforms?
- Extent and quality of capacity building

Results
- Before/after improvements in PFMP performance where PRSC reforms focused (10 indicators)
- Achievement of PFMP objectives in PRSCs
- General improvements in PFMP systems (CPIA, etc.)

Other parallel instruments, which contributed to the design of PRSC PFMP reform components, include the IMF's Report on the Observance of Standards and Codes (ROSCs) on Fiscal Transparency (1998) for the quality of fiscal reporting and accountability mechanisms.[8] Additionally, the Heavily Indebted Poor Country (HIPC) tracking system, Assessment and Action Plan (AAP), evaluated PFMP systems according to 16 basic indicators with established benchmarks and proposed action plans. These were conducted in HIPC countries in two rounds (2001 and 2004).[9] The HIPC approach was updated in the joint IMF/World Bank Public Expenditure and Financial Assessment (PEFA) initiative, which has an evaluation framework with 28 indicators and identifies the roles of institutions in PFMP processes, for example, finance ministries, supreme audit institutions, etc., as well as donors. Eleven out of 16 HIPC Assessment and Action Plan (AAP) indicators can be reevaluated using corresponding PEFA ratings. This allows for a comparison of PFMP performance over time.[10]

Diagnostic Work

Minimum Levels of PFMP Quality as an Entry Condition for PRSCs

Operational guidance for PRSCs on minimum standards of fiduciary risk were not detailed initially and called for only an assessment of the "adequacy of public financial accountability arrangements."[11] In practice, and explicitly in the Africa Region, a broad criterion of institutional readiness has applied—a minimum overall CPIA score of about 3.5.[12] In the area of public financial management, more explicit questions are

Box 5.1. Linking Reforms in Public Financial Management to a Broader Policy Reform Agenda

Public financial management and procurement reforms achieved prominence in the 1990s with the OECD's Public Management program (OECD 1995). This initiative had eight components: (1) more robust central controls; (2) inclusion of expenditures for all government activities; (3) a multiyear budget linked to a clear fiscal policy and realistic revenue estimates; (4) use of performance information in monitoring against targets; (5) shift from cost accounting toward accrual accounting; (6) shift from compliance auditing toward performance auditing; (7) computerized information systems providing timely financial and related information to all parties in the budget process; and (8) greater use of devolved budget management and market mechanisms, such as user and capital charges, market testing, outsourcing, and performance agreements (Brumby 1999).

Development agencies increasingly realized that deficient in-country PFMP systems could undermine development assistance. Donors agreed that aid required not only physical investment but also good public sector management (Allen and others 2004). These principles were mainstreamed into country-based lending to help greater accountability of government provision of services (Batley and Larbi 2004).[a]

a. A recent OECD-DAC study of general budget supports reinforces this view, finding that countries with established track records that channel aid through country systems has strengthened budget processes, including comprehensiveness and transparency (IDD and Associates 2006a).

embedded in CPIA component question 13, which assesses: "the extent to which there is: (a) a comprehensive and credible budget, linked to policy priorities; (b) effective financial management systems to ensure that the budget is implemented as intended in a controlled and predictable way; and (c) timely and accurate accounting and fiscal reporting, including timely and audited public accounts and effective arrangements for follow-up." In practice, the Bank's approach to fiduciary risk in PRSCs has been a pragmatic balance of costs (fiduciary risk) and benefits (leverage to motivate reforms).[13]

Existence and Quality of PFMP Diagnostics

The existence and use of adequate diagnostic tools for PRSCs, in the form of a CFAA, a CPAR, and when available, a Public Expenditure Review, is evaluated for 21 PRSC series. Findings show that most PRSCs were based on diagnostics that systematically covered most relevant PFMP areas, less than three years before commencing the series. Only 3 out of 21 series were deemed to have inadequate or insufficient diagnostics (appendix table A5.1).

Links between the PRSC Reform Agenda and Diagnostic Work

To what extent did PRSC operations draw on the assessments and action plans derived from those diagnostics in a well-sequenced and prioritized manner?[14] The next three questions address the link between diagnostic work and the PRSC design, looking first at whether the relevant PRSC appraisal documents acknowledged fiduciary risks emerging from diagnostic work; second, at whether these risks were addressed; and third, at whether the overall PFMP strategy of the PRSC reflected these and acknowledged broader PFMP challenges raised in the diagnostics.[15]

Thirteen of the 21 PRSC series evaluated adequately acknowledged fiduciary risks. The remaining 8 series acknowledged some fiduciary risks. Those that did not include the program document for the first Rwanda PRSC series, which does not clearly acknowledge fiduciary risks raised in diagnostic work, although it focuses on a reform plan to deal with the risk. Vietnam also acknowledged risks partially in its early program. Its fifth PRSC was the first instance where appraisal documents discussed fiduciary risk.

HIPC indicators, PEFA assessments, and IMF Fiscal Transparency ROSCs have also been used.

Although only 13 out of 21 PRSC series adequately acknowledged fiduciary risks, in 12 of these the Bank took measures to address the diagnosed fiduciary risks. In Senegal, for example, the PRSC took measures to formalize the medium-term expenditure framework and implement it through subnational bodies, increase external audits, improve decentralization, and better match turnouts to budget amounts. Systems of internal controls, however, still need development. Only Georgia seems to have taken inadequate measures to address known fiduciary risks. PRSC conditions address only a quarter of the risks assessed in preceding analytic work and acknowledged in program documents. These include risks stemming from budget credibility issues, internal controls, and internal audit functions.

Evaluative findings suggest generally adequate recent diagnostic work.

Beyond attending to fiduciary risks, PRSC PFMP programs also incorporated measures for further developing PFMP capabilities. In eight of the series rated there was good correspondence. In another 10 series, or half of the projects rated, the PRSC matched a subset

PRSCs drew upon recent diagnostics and adequately acknowledged fiduciary risks.

Box 5.2. PFMP Diagnostic Work and Incorporation in PRSC Design

Lao PDR is a case where the CPAR and CFAA were dated. The CFAA coverage was incomplete. Particularly notable at the time was the lack of a discussion of differences between budgets approved and implemented and the role of extra-budgetary funds, relative to the total budget. It also had a low overall CPIA score and a particularly low score on the relevant component question (Q. 13) for public financial management. The Pakistan CFAA also did not adequately address the issue of extra-budgetary funds. The Vietnam Public Expenditure Review, prepared along with the first PRSC, is an example of good practice in this area; it specifies seven off-budget accounts and assesses their risks in detail.

Source: IEG analysis of PFMP components of PRSCs.

Most PRSCs also incorporated plans to further develop domestic financial management systems, beyond the minimal requirements for taking care of fiduciary risk.

of preceding analytic work.[16] Only 2 series of 21 were judged to have a PFMP strategy with limited overlap, with the focus of the AAA.[17]

A comparison was also undertaken of the prioritization and sequencing of PRSCs compared with diagnostic work. PRSC conditionality was largely consistent with action plans suggested by preceding analytic work regarding sequencing and timing (for example, Cape Verde, Lao PDR, Madagascar, Nicaragua, and Rwanda).[18]

Design and Implementation

Beyond diagnosis, to what extent did PRSCs adequately capture good practice in the design of their PFMP components? Specifically, did they have an appropriate results framework, linking the PFMP reform program to a country-based and donor-supported strategy? Did errors in design of the reform program, with respect to technical capacity or political feasibility, constrain implementation and lead to delays? Were capacity building needs met?

Quality of the Results Framework in PFMP Areas

Only about half of the countries reviewed had a complete or mostly complete results framework, which had been reported on at least once before the series was over. But in the other half, results frameworks were incomplete, inadequate, or not implemented.

Results frameworks were a weak link in the design of PFMP components of PRSCs.

The quality of results frameworks in the PFMP area generally improve over time, and countries where PRSC programs began after 2004 generally had better-designed frameworks.[19] Yet some late starters, such as Armenia and Cape Verde, were also found to have a results framework that was initially incomplete, although there were important improvements over time.

Existence of a Donor-Supported Integrated Action Plan

Key to a well-developed PFMP reform program is a single action plan that integrates guidance from diagnostic work, government policy goals, and donors. Such an integrated action plan, supported by all donors, was found in more than half the series evaluated (13 out of 21). In Ghana, for example, the government had a comprehensive Public Financial Management Reform Program, as well as a Short-Term Action Plan for Public Financial Management. These were incorporated into the reform agenda for the second PRSC series, as part of the Multi-Donor Budget Support framework, which was functional by PRSC 3 (table 5.1).

In the remaining eight series, three had something close to an integrated action plan with some donor backing. However, five had no integrated plan for public financial management reforms, limited donor support, or plan that were never implemented. Overall, most PFMP reform programs had integrated or nearly integrated action plans, with donor backing, usually coordinated among all key donors (appendix table A5.1).

Implementation Delays

Reasonably good implementation is also evidenced by the timeliness of execution, relative to

Box 5.3. PFMP Results Frameworks—Examples of Shortcomings

In Albania, results frameworks for PFMP components were incomplete, specifically regarding intermediate outcome indicators. The indicators available were not specific to PFMP functions or they were not tracked or drawn upon in the PRSC. By PRSC 3, some indicators referred to the period before the PRSCs, others referred to the post-PRSC period, but with no baseline. In some cases, it was not clear when outcomes occurred.

In Georgia, results were not presented until the last PRSC of the series. Not all indicators have been reported in PRSO 3, and there is no coherent presentation of whether desired outcomes were achieved. Many PFMP indicators are very broad. Although some are reported on fairly specifically in the last program document matrix, the series would have benefited from indicators that were better specified from the outset.

Source: IEG analysis of PFMP components of PRSCs.

Table 5.1. Government PFMP Strategy and Donor Support

Single integrated action plan Support by all key donors (14)	Nearly integrated action plan Some donor backing (3)	Government plan for public financial management reform; never implemented; OR Government plan, limited donor support; OR Donor support for PFMP reforms but no plan (4)
Benin	Georgia	Albania
Burkina Faso—Series 1	Pakistan	Armenia
Burkina Faso—Series 2	Senegal	Nicaragua
Cape Verde		Uganda—Series 1
Ethiopia		
Ghana—Series 1		
Ghana—Series 2		
Lao PDR		
Madagascar		
Mozambique		
Rwanda		
Tanzania		
Uganda—Series 2		
Vietnam		

the plan. Six PRSC series, out of 20 rated, showed no significant delay, and in another 12, progress was eventually achieved, although there was evidence of some delay. Only two series showed significant delays. Both political economy risks and capacity constraints appear to have been factors (box 5.4).

Capacity-Building Needs

The evaluation also looks at the extent to which PRSCs provide targeted and adequate capacity building. In most of the series rated (16 of 18), capacity-building needs for PFMP improvement were met, albeit by a variety of means and not exclusively through the PRSC.[20] There were four countries with separate, comprehensive capacity building operations. Capacity building in Pakistan, for example, enjoyed the support of two comprehensive public financial management capacity-building projects. One included a focus on auditing and reporting, areas of PRSC emphasis. An additional Public Sector Capacity Building project (2005) focused on skills in line ministries, including technical and statistical capacity for accounting. The ICR for the first project found progress in improved accounting and auditing skills, providing an enabling environment for PRSC-supported reforms.

In sum, countries performed reasonably well in developing a PFMP strategy harmonized among donors, in addressing capacity needs, and in avoiding excessive delays. Results frameworks, however, have been an area of weakness in design and implementation, although there was some evidence of improvement in later PRSC series, following Bank-wide initiatives on managing for results.

Most PRSCs had an integrated action plan for PFMP with adequate donor support.

Implementation delays occurred sometimes due to capacity or political economy factors.

PRSC Public Financial Management Programs—Results Achieved

To what extent did PRSCs achieve their objectives and obtain results on PFMP goals? We first compare progress in PRSC countries before and after the PRSCs were implemented, and then compare performance with areas emphasized in PRSC program conditionality.[21] Last, and more broadly, indicators such as CPIA scores and perceptions of PRSC performance are discussed. Findings are prefaced by the caveat that measuring PFMP improvements is difficult. Reform is a complex process where changes in one area can have unexpected impacts on others over an uncertain timeline. Precise causes and

PFMP results are measured in the four broad areas of budget formulation, execution, reporting, and procurement.

Box 5.4. Delays in Implementation of the PFMP Reform Plan—Examples

The first Burkina Faso series showed significant PFMP implementation delays. Three conditions were not fully implemented: (i) the strengthening of the Supreme Audit Institution, (ii) adoption of a procurement procedures manual, and (iii) verification that a large share of public procurement would be subject to competitive procurement practices, with public audit. By the second Burkina Faso series, delays in meeting PFMP triggers were reduced.

Lao PDR is an example of a country where there was relatively strong country ownership of public financial management reforms but the Bank was too optimistic about the speed at which key reforms could be implemented and may have attempted too much. These included a revised Chart of Accounts, a Medium-Term Expenditure Framework, and a harmonized procurement manual. There was some expectation in the Bank's program that implementation obstacles might occur. The response, in PRSOs 2 and 3, was to initiate many reforms and follow through on those with traction.

In Albania, frequent fiscal revisions, some in consultation with the IMF, made it very difficult for the government to properly execute its annual budget, an area of strong emphasis in the PRSC. This indication of challenges to reform is consistent with Albania's rating on reform ownership under Paris Declaration monitoring, which is lower than for many PRSC countries.

Source: IEG analysis of PFMP components of PRSCs.

effects are hard to identify, multiple stakeholders are interdependent, and there is no finish line.

Performance Ratings Relative to PFMP Benchmarks

Ten broad indicators of PFMP performance are first investigated for 21 PRSC series over 2001–08. The indicators used here follow closely from those applied in the 2001 and 2004 HIPC AAP assessments and subsequent Public Expenditure and Financial Accountability reports.[22] As discussed above, the combination of these sources permits an analysis of changes over time in a country's public financial management, which can be associated with the PRSC period. The review compares this performance with objectives emphasized in the PRSC for each country. Progress for each indicator was measured on a five-point scale, relative to key benchmarks established in the HIPC AAP methodology.

There are seven indicators for budget formulation that focus on themes such as standardized definitions, classifiers, inclusion of funds on-budget, and integration of medium-term expenditures in the budget cycle.

Results are assessed for indicators in the four areas of budget formulation and execution (appendix table A5.2), and reporting and procurement management (appendix table A5.3). Results below emphasize formulation, in part because HIPC AAP has more formulation indicators than indicators on execution, reporting, or procurement.[23] While this may be a limitation, formulation has also been the most emphasized area of PRSC PFMP reforms. Some aspects of formulation (such as expenditure predictability and classification) also significantly affect budget execution and reporting.

Questions in the areas of formulation focused on such issues as the use of standardized definitions of the government sectors; reductions in the use of extra-budgetary sources of funds; inclusion of donor and local government funds on-budget; reductions in the variance between budget formulation and execution; increased use of budget classifiers, based on administrative and economic areas as well as functional/programmatic divisions; and the integration of medium-term expenditure forecasts into the budget formulation cycle.

There are two indicators on budget execution, which focus on reductions in expenditure arrears and the use of internal control systems. The one indicator on reporting requires the presentation of a complete audited report of actual expenditures to the legislature on a semi-annual or annual basis. There is also a single broad-based indicator for procurement, which requires clear and enforceable rules for procurement that promote competition, transparency, and value, together with appropriate follow-up on such rules.

Overall performance was mixed across the three PFMP areas. Budget formulation enjoyed the highest average number of operations that had a benchmark before the PRSC and was maintained for the duration of the PRSC. The indicator on reporting seems to have had the greatest number of series that achieved a benchmark during the PRSC. No country achieved a benchmark in procurement, although there was some improvement.

Within the area of budget formulation, performance was relatively good across a large number of countries, in terms of using administrative and economic classifiers and reducing the aggregate variance of total budget expenditure. Fewer PRSC series were able to reduce the proportions of extra-budgetary funds brought on-budget, or include all donor funds on-budget. A limited number of series have also been able to achieve good progress with integrating medium-term expenditure forecasting with the budget cycle. In execution, greater progress was achieved in the reduction of expenditure arrears, although progress has been slower on improving the effectiveness of the internal controls environment. More than half the series have been able to achieve progress on budget reporting.

How does this compare with areas of PFMP reform emphasized by PRSC reform programs? Budget formulation and execution have been the areas of greatest emphasis, although many operations also emphasized procurement. Reporting was less emphasized, although reporting systems are weak in most PRSC countries, as discussed in the preceding section. Moreover, adequate reporting systems, especially on public expenditure, are important for country-level M&E, especially for countries receiving general budget support. A comparison of results in PFMP areas with emphasis in PRSC programs, based on 10 indicators (appendix table A5.2 and A5.3), shows that there was generally some improvement in many areas emphasized by the PRSCs.

A formal test of the correlation between improvement in PFMP indicators with the existence of core PRSC PFMP conditions suggested generally positive (but not often strong) correlation. However, in a few instances (classification, internal control) the correlation was negative, and only one correlation—on budget classification—was statistically significant. This suggests that there is no statistically justifiable relationship between particular indicator areas and PRSC conditionality, although a relationship may potentially exist.

There are two indicators on execution and one on budget reporting.

Budget formulation performed well except in the reduction of off-budget funds or inclusion of all donor funds on budget.

Previous results obtained by de Renzio and Dorotinsky (2007) permit a comparison of performance of 11 PRSC and 5 non-PRSC countries.[24] These data suggest that PRSC countries seemed to achieve a consistently higher share of benchmarks. Yet there was substantial progress only in the area of reporting, and this was also the case for non-PRSC countries. However, reporting was a weak area in our findings. Also, these data seem to indicate that execution over time deteriorated in both PRSC and non-PRSC countries, which is not consistent with our observed results. One explanation for these mixed results may be the variation in application of the evaluative criteria across the two periods in which the HIPC AAP assessment was undertaken. The IEG desk review does not face this disadvantage because it attempted to adjust for such implicit variations in rating criteria over time.

Yet improvement in reform indicators is not clearly linked to PRSC reform conditions.

Achievement of PFMP Objectives in PRSCs

Most of the 21 PRSC series achieved their PFMP objectives, stated at the beginning of each series, with only minor shortcomings (table 5.2). For example, Vietnam's PRSC series set out to achieve a PFMP objective of: "timely, consistent, comprehensive data from Treasury's public financial management system." An important step forward in meeting the overall objective was unification of the accounting systems of the state budget and the state treasury, enhanced by work on an integrated Treasury and Budget Management Information System. However, minor shortcomings exist in the deterioration in off-budget financing in recent years, which still needs attention. Both series in Burkina Faso were also judged to have minor

Table 5.2. PRSC Series: Achievement of PFMP Objectives

Evaluative rating	Countries/series
Fully achieved with no shortcomings	Burkina Faso–series 1, Burkina Faso–series 2, Cape Verde, Georgia, Ghana–series 1, Ethiopia, Mozambique, Nicaragua, Tanzania, Vietnam
Fully achieved with only minor shortcomings	
Achieved, but with significant shortcomings	Albania, Armenia, Benin, Lao PDR, Madagascar, Pakistan, Uganda–series 1
Not achieved	
Not enough evidence to rate	Ghana–series 2, Rwanda, Senegal, Uganda–series 2

Source: IEG ICR reviews, supplemented by World Bank ICRs, PPARs, PRSC program documents, and PEFAs.

ICRs show that most PRSCs achieved their PFMP objectives with only minor shortcomings.

shortcomings: its ICR rating of *moderately satisfactory* reflects some missing of targets and nonachievement of triggers, and it has also suffered from a paucity of indicators and nonachievement of particular benchmarks.

Armenia is an example of a series with some significant shortcomings in achieving objectives laid out at the beginning of the series. Emphasis was mostly on budget formulation, and there was apparent improvement in reducing extra-budgetary funding sources. There was some emphasis on internal audit as part of budget execution, and there has been some reduction of arrears, but no evidence of improvement in internal controls. Reporting was given little importance and showed no improvement. There was some emphasis on procurement, leading to the enactment of a new Law on Public Procurement.[25] Yet, a recent Bank PEFA review in Armenia found systemic weaknesses remaining in the procurement system.[26]

By comparison, there were significant shortcomings in Madagascar's PRSC series. There was limited progress in achieving budget management objectives, as indicated in the Implementation Completion Report of PRSCs 1–3. There was also limited progress in achieving the objective of improved formulation (budget classification), which seems to be a major part of the PFMP reform effort. All procurement triggers were modified (downward) or dropped. And while there was clear progress in meeting some objectives in Benin (such as rollout of computerized financial management systems, reporting), there were significant shortcomings in other areas (such as internal control, integration of accounts).

Improvement in Performance in Relevant Indicators from the Bank's CPIA

A final assessment of overall PFMP results in PRSCs is based on data from the CPIA indicators, where questions 13 and 14 are broad measures of PFMP performance. In half of the series rated (10 of 20) there was at least some improvement in this measure from the beginning to the end of the series. Others remained unchanged.[27]

A comparison was also undertaken by IEG of the performance of PRSC countries, over the period 1999–2006, with non-PRSC IDA and blend countries (CPIA question 13).[28] The results (table 5.3) indicate that PRSC countries have performed significantly better than non-PRSC IDA countries.[29]

We also examine ratings of the domestic accountability of PFMP processes over 2006–08 in PRSC

Table 5.3. PRSC and Non-PRSC Countries: Change in CPIA Indicators on Budget Management and Accounting (1999–2007)

Average change for PRSC countries	0.5577
Average change for non-PRSC IDA/blend countries	0.1531
Difference in means	0.4046
(P-value of result)	*(0.0089)*

Source: World Bank database.
Note: Allowing for unequal variances of samples and null hypothesis that difference is 0. *P*-value is calculated on the basis of a two-tailed, heteroskedastic *t*-test.

countries, with non-PRSC IDA and IBRD countries. These ratings are prepared by Global Integrity, a nonprofit group that examines transparency and accountability across countries. Results indicate that, overall, public financial management budget processes are more domestically accountable than in comparator IDA countries. Surprisingly, the opposite seems be the case for procurement systems. Supreme audit institutions, which ensure proper independent and external auditing of government expenditures and of the national accounts are more domestically accountable in PRSC countries than non-PRSC IDA countries, but less than in IBRD countries. This variation in scores illustrates difficulties in attributing outcomes to actions, except in broad terms.

Evaluation of the PFMP Approach of PRSCs: Bank Staff and Clients

Task team leaders in the Bank believed the PRSC led to a greater orientation toward public financial management in PRSC countries. This was deemed to be the second most successful element of PRSCs, according to survey results. Almost all task team leaders believed PRSCs to have been effective (43 percent) or very effective (51 percent) in accomplishing their public financial management goals. Procurement was also rated very highly, with 73 percent of response ratings of highly effective or effective. These responses were mirrored in the IEG survey of PRSC government counterparts, where 97 percent of respondents said that the PRSC was very effective or somewhat effective at strengthening public financial management systems.

The PRSC was also broadly perceived by task team leaders to have significantly improved the use of the budget as a policy tool (74 percent of respondents fully or partly agreed that it was mainly used to enhance the importance of the budget as a policy tool).[30] Government counterparts also felt that the process helped to make the budget a more important tool for policy formulation and implementation (87 percent of respondents agreed or strongly agreed). And 90 percent of counterparts agreed or strongly agreed that the PRSC helped to increase the role of the budget as a tool for accountability of line ministries and to improve interministerial dialogue.

Task team leaders corroborate the finding that PRSC achievements on public financial management were broadly effective.

On the efficiency and efficacy of public expenditures, government counterparts felt that the PRSC helped to facilitate alignment of public expenditures with priorities defined by the country's medium-term development strategy (92 percent agreed or strongly agreed). However, 71 percent of surveyed sector staff who worked on PRSCs believed that it was not true, or only partly true, that budget allocations were delivered to line ministries in a more timely and predictable manner. Although these are different questions, these findings signal a disconnect between the impression of sector staff and the views of task team leaders and government stakeholders regarding results achieved by PFMP reforms.

There was less success in some areas of efficiency of public expenditure processes, such as timely transfer to sectoral ministries.

Findings from Seven Country Case Studies

In-depth analysis of IEG country case studies awarded a moderately positive overall score to PFMP performance, with an average score of 3.7 out of 6 (table 5.4). The scores were highly variable: Lao PDR, for example, performed strongly on progress relative to initial conditions, while Nicaragua performed poorly because of the reversal of reform efforts after the 2006 election.

Table 5.4. PRSC Overall Scores on Improving the Public Financial Management System

Armenia	Benin	Ghana	Lao PDR	Mozambique	Nicaragua	Vietnam
4	4	3	6	4	1	4

Source: IEG country case studies.
Note: Scored on a scale of 0–6.

The case studies found that attempts to increase priority spending were largely successful in almost all countries, but in several (especially Benin and Ghana), budget execution, internal control, and internal audit mechanisms remained poor. In Benin, there was slow execution of the budget and continuing problems with procurement. The review of national accounts by the Court of Auditors was behind schedule. A large share of expenditures in Ghana occurred outside the formal budget process, through donor pools, which undermined much of the budget process. Mozambique failed to adopt an adequate budget classification system and to establish effective links between budget and PRSP priorities.

In many case studies (especially Benin, Mozambique, and Nicaragua), a significant part of the reform effort was directed toward developing and rolling out the Integrated Financial Management System. However, this is not evaluated as an aspect of PFMP performance since it is not a critical component of a well-functioning PFMP system. While a well-functioning Integrated Financial Management System can significantly improve the efficiency and quality of reporting of public expenditures (Mozambique's eSISTAFE in many ways has been successful in this regard), its existence does not guarantee that PFMP systems are functioning efficiently and effectively, or that fiduciary risks are being mitigated.

PRSCs made good progress in public financial management reforms, but it was harder to achieve procurement reform benchmarks.

In sum, PRSCs, with the parallel capacity building work that accompanied them, were reasonably effective in terms of design, helping to address recipients' needs in the areas of PFMP systems, harmonizing such programs among donors, and generally implementing them in a timely manner. The PFMP results framework remains an area of weakness. Efforts could also be made to improve some areas of budget formulation. PRSCs made good progress toward their objectives of addressing technical limitations in budget formulation, execution, reporting, and procurement, although progress has been uneven across countries and over time. Results in the area of procurement seem to be harder to achieve. Based on CPIA ratings for public financial management, countries appear to perform significantly better than comparator countries.[31]

Chapter 6

Evaluation Highlights

- PRSC countries have better growth and macro indicators, but this began before PRSCs; non-PRSC countries have also improved.
- Most PRSCs lacked comprehensive growth strategies.
- PRSC countries had a better record in poverty reduction, but PRSCs paralleled sector projects in pro-poor service areas.
- PRSC health and education components focused on better budget allocation, yet large proportions of resources remain off-budget.
- Objectives were fully met a third to half of the time; a high proportion of service delivery components had modest achievements.
- Overall, PRSCs performed more satisfactorily than prior adjustment lending, but differences are negligible when compared with all adjustment loans in the PRSC period.
- Tracking poverty outcomes is difficult due to limited indicators.

A local school in Ghana. Photo by Curt Carnemark, courtesy of the World Bank Photo Library.

Growth, Poverty, and PRSCs

Poverty Reduction Support Credits were introduced to support the implementation of IDA countries' Poverty Reduction Strategies, which embodied comprehensive national development plans for achieving poverty-reducing economic growth. To what extent did the PRSC, as the vehicle for the implementation of such strategies, help to achieve these objectives? Much debate remains regarding factors leading to growth (annex 8) or poverty reduction, and it is not clear that they can be generalized across countries. The PRSC is only one typically modest element in a range of factors contributing to country outcomes. With this caveat, this chapter describes observed growth and poverty outcomes of PRSC countries and the extent to which PRSCs reflected strategies to better enable poverty-reducing growth.

PRSC Countries—Creating a Growth-Enabling Environment

PRSC design typically reflected a pragmatic combination of growth and poverty reduction objectives. PRSCs recognized the role of growth in the long-term reduction of poverty and focused on building a growth-enabling environment through better public sector institutions and incentives for private sector development. Poverty relief was emphasized through pro-poor service delivery in areas such as health and education, basic service provision of water and sanitation, and the implementation of social safety nets.

Economic Performance and Growth in PRSC Countries—A Description

A comparison was undertaken of the growth performance of 22 PRSC countries with 74 IDA countries (appendix tables A 6.1–A6.3), as well as with a reduced set of better-performing non-PRSC countries having a CPIA score of 3.0 or better in 2007.[1] PRSC countries achieved growth rates superior to non-PRSC IDA countries in the PRSC period and rates somewhat better than other well-performing IDA countries.[2] These findings are true for per capita income growth as well as for the main economic sectors: agriculture, industry, and services. PRSC countries achieved higher rates of export growth and lower inflation rates than their comparators.

PRSCs had better macroeconomic results than others—both in the PRSC period and before.

However, looking at the pre-PRSC period, the same pattern is observed. In all cases, PRSC countries outperformed their comparators, including better-performing IDA countries. This suggests that some of the superior performance of the PRSC countries was not only due to PRSCs but also to better initial performance. This is not unexpected given that PRSCs were generally given to better performers.

Rates of growth in all sets of countries improved in the second period compared with the first

Other countries improved their performance too, sometimes more than PRSC countries.

(appendix table A6.1).[3] The proportional increase in growth rates for comparator countries was, in some cases, greater than for PRSC countries, especially for per capita GDP growth and agriculture. The clearest lead in performance improvement for PRSC countries is in industry, where PRSC countries outpace comparators. In the areas of export growth and service sector growth, the proportional improvement in non-PRSC IDA countries, taken together, was as good or better than in PRSC countries. Overall, the results suggest that although PRSC countries were superior performers, non-PRSC countries have also improved, and the degree of improvement in performance in non-PRSC countries is at least as good as in PRSC countries. It is therefore difficult to associate the better performance in PRSC countries with the PRSCs.

PRSC countries were superior performers, but non-PRSC countries also improved their performance.

It is also surprising that PRSC countries had the greatest lead in industrial growth, even though agriculture is usually considered more pro-poor by virtue of its high labor intensity.[4] Both PRSC and better-performing non-PRSC countries had slightly higher growth of agriculture in the PRSC period, and both increased agricultural growth by 0.4 percentage points. Many PRSCs have limited policy measures related to agriculture.[5] Industrial growth in the PRSC countries rose from 4.0 percent to 7.2 percent. Industrial growth also accelerated in non-PRSC countries, but by a smaller amount, from 3.2 to 5.6 percent. Thus, there was a widening of the gap in industrial growth that paralleled the widening of the gap in per capita GDP.

One area where PRSC countries exhibit a marked improvement in performance over time and relative to comparators is in their investment and savings rates (appendix table A6.4). PRSC countries clearly increased their rates of investment over the pre-PRSC period and over the level of non-PRSC countries. The average investment rate in PRSC countries was 24 percent during 2000–07, compared with 20 percent during 1985–2000. Investment in non-PRSC countries remained at about 22 percent during both periods (23 percent for the better performers). Savings rates in PRSC countries rose by five percentage points between the two periods; savings rates in non-PRSC increased only slightly (about 1.5 percentage points).

PRSC countries improved their institutional environment over time, but others increased about as much.

Curiously, however, increased investment seems to have been financed largely by an increase in domestic savings, and not by an increase in foreign capital transfers. The external deficit fell somewhat in the PRSC countries and in both groups of non-PRSCs. This is an interesting finding since this was the period of HIPC debt relief, when donors were supposed to increase their support for countries with poverty reduction strategies. True, the external balance also reflects other capital flows, including private borrowing and private direct investment. However, it is difficult to attribute higher rates of savings and investment to PRSC support.

An analysis of the extent to which PRSC countries were able to build a more growth-enabling environment was undertaken based on CPIA scores for institutional and fiduciary systems. Results suggest that being a PRSC country did not affect improvement of countries' enabling environment. Non-PRSC IDA countries also improved their performance over time and to a similar degree (appendix table A6.5).[6]

Comparing CPIA subcomponents for economic management and policies for social inclusion for 1999 and 2007 shows, again, that PRSC countries, as is known, had better initial conditions. Component scores are somewhat higher for PRSC countries in 1999.[7] All scores increase slightly over the period.[8] Better-performing non-PRSC countries improved their performance somewhat more than PRSC countries, in percentage terms, in all areas except public financial management. Among non-PRSC IDA countries, scores for social inclusion indicators improved as much as in PRSC countries, though improvements in economic management are somewhat lower.

These findings reinforce earlier ones. PRSC countries were generally better performers on macroeconomic management and social inclusion, but they began from better initial positions. And non-

PRSC IDA countries improved their performance almost as much as countries with the benefit of the PRSC program.

Measures to Support Growth—Evidence from Case Studies

Country case studies afford a complementary perspective on the role of the PRSCs in fostering poverty-reducing economic growth, tailored to local needs. They show that while measures to increase growth were included in most PRSCs, these usually did not add up to an overall growth strategy. It is difficult to trace a direct link from PRSC growth-related measures to country growth outcomes. In some successful countries, growth–oriented reform was already under way. In others, there were no attempts to make growth more pro-poor.

It is not possible to identify the PRSC with growth outcomes. Some countries achieved high rates of growth, but these were hard to ascribe to the PRSC. Armenia's projected growth rate of 6 percent, foreseen in PRSC 1, rose to 13 percent over 2004–06. But growth sources have been attributed to remittances, trade liberalization, infrastructure improvements, fiscal prudence, and low inflation. And economic growth in Lao PDR accelerated from the 5 to 6 percent level, which had characterized the 2000–04 period, to 7 to 8 percent during 2005–07. However, the acceleration appears to have been fueled by investments linked to the Nam Theun 2 project. In Ghana, growth rates accelerated during the PRSC period. The PRSC supported growth-protecting energy reforms but these remain incomplete.

PRSC growth measures were not usually based on a comprehensive growth diagnostic.

Other countries failed to achieve high growth but this, too, cannot be attributed to the PRSC. In Nicaragua, growth remained closely linked to commodity export prices and did not change materially with the PRSC, despite large amounts of external aid. Growth activities supported by the PRSCs were isolated measures, without a coherent strategy. And the PRSCs supported pension reform, which failed when its fiscal implications were ascertained. Benin, too, failed to achieve expected growth rates—but its lackluster performance in this regard is a continuation from the pre-PRSC period.[9] Expected reforms in key structural areas, such as the cotton sector and energy, failed to materialize over this period.

Box 6.1. PRSC Growth Orientation—Policies Supported

In Armenia, PRSCs focused on macroeconomic stability measures as a precondition for growth, also strengthening governance, sharpening competition, and modernizing the rural economy. Ghana, through the joint donor matrix, emphasized issues related to the investment climate and the commercial court system. The most significant PRSC growth-related measure was in the energy sector, where the Bank boosted measures to end subsidies for electricity and fuel. But negligible attention was given to agriculture, where other donors provided special budget support.

In Mozambique, growth-related issues formed the core of PRSCs 1 and 2, and focused on macroeconomic stability, public financial management, financial sector issues, and the investment climate for business. Mozambique also sought in PRSCs 3 and 4 to improve the potential for agricultural sector growth through enhancing productivity and improving connectivity of the rural sector and the rest of the economy. In Lao PDR, both PRSO series emphasized the role of growth in reducing poverty over time. The series also spanned investment climate issues, private sector development, regional and global integration, and improved resource management.

In other cases, the PRSC supported a pattern of development that had more pro-poor growth elements. For instance, in Benin, the PRSCs focused on the cotton sector and rural transport. In Nicaragua, the PRSCs focused largely on reforms more directly targeted to the poor, including indigenous property rights, health, education, water, and social protection. And in Vietnam, PRSCs evolved from a focused-growth orientation toward a more broad-based strategy, due to the view that Vietnam's exceptional record in reducing poverty in the 1990s (from 57 percent in 1992 to 37 percent in 1998) was closely linked to its rapid economic growth. Poverty declined further, to 16 percent by 2006, although the pillars of the Vietnam strategy remained unchanged.

Table 6.1. Overall Scores on Policy Dialogue and Influence on Growth

Country	Influence of PRSC process on government policy dialogue	Relevance and effectiveness in supporting a pro-poor growth strategy
Armenia	5	4
Benin	4	3
Ghana	3	5
Lao PDR	5	4
Mozambique	4	4
Nicaragua	4	1
Vietnam	5	5
Average	**4.3**	**3.7**

Source: IEG country case studies.
Note: Rankings are done by authors of case studies using the following scoring system for achievement of stated objectives: 6 = fully achieved without any shortcomings; 5 = substantially achieved with only minor shortcomings; 4 = achieved with moderate shortcomings; 3 = significant shortcomings; 2 = major shortcomings; and 1 = severe shortcomings in achieving stated objectives.

Vietnam is one example where high growth was achieved (more than 7.5 percent during 2001–06), exceeding previous periods, attributed to achievements in the five policy areas related to the PRSC's growth objectives (trade, private sector development, infrastructure, state enterprise reform, and banking reform). The PRSC therefore supported the achievement of growth, even though it is difficult to establish any causality. And scores attributed by case study authors to the effectiveness of supporting a pro-poor growth strategy average 3.7 on a scale of 1 to 6, in seven countries (table 6.1).

PRSC countries show a marked reduction in income poverty, even when compared with control groups.

PRSC Countries—Helping Poverty Alleviation

Poverty Rates in PRSC and Non-PRSC Countries—Poverty Lines

A review of the evolution of poverty rates in PRSC and non-PRSC countries shows that poverty rates fell in both sets of countries between 1999 and 2005 (table 6.2 and appendix table A6.6),[10] by 19 percent in PRSC countries and by 11 percent in non-PRSC countries.[11] However, as with growth, PRSC countries' performance in reducing poverty had also been superior in the period before the PRSC.

PRSC countries also do better on nonincome measures of poverty as defined by the Millennium Development Goals.

During 1985–99, poverty fell 16 percent in the PRSC countries versus only 12 percent in the control group.[12] The superior outcome for PRSC countries is more pronounced than the relative outcomes in terms of growth. However, the extent to which this was related to a greater pro-poor focus or due to measures incorporated in their PRSCs requires further exploration.

Other Measures of Poverty—Millennium Development Goal Indicators

Poverty has other aspects beyond income, such as access to health, education, and employment. The Millennium Development Goals not only call for a reduction in the numbers of persons living on less than $1 per day but also for reductions in infant and child mortality, hunger and malnutrition, maternal mortality, and malaria and HIV/AIDS infection. The Millenium Development Goals also emphasize increased access to primary school education and to clean water and sanitation.

Results (table 6.3) show that in all indicators covered, with the exception of secondary school enrollment, PRSC countries, on average, performed better than other groups with which they are compared. Primary school enrollment increased, infant and child mortality declined, and access to safe drinking water and sanitation improved more in PRSC countries than in all IDA countries, or even in better-performing IDA countries (appendix table A6.7). Moreover, improvement in the PRSC period was faster than in the previous period, in all areas except access to clean water and sanitation, where remarkable progress had already been achieved in the period before the PRSC. PRSC countries were able to better their performance more than non-PRSC countries in all areas except secondary school enrollment.

Together, these data suggest that PRSC countries had a better record in many dimensions of poverty reduction than other IDA countries, including better-performing IDA countries. And improvement was more marked in the PRSC period. In many dimensions PRSC countries did not have a marked advantage relative to comparators at the start of the periods examined (1990/91).

Table 6.2. Poverty Rates for PRSC and Non-PRSC Countries (percentage of population living on less than $38 per month)

Year	PRSC countries (20)[a]	Better performing non-PRSC (24)[a]	Non-PRSC countries (36)[a]	All IDA countries (56)[a]
1984	51.6	49.1	45.0	47.5
1990	48.8	45.2	51.1	46.9
1999	43.2	42.9	44.1	43.7
% change *(1984–99)*	–16.2	–12.6	–2.1	–7.8
2005	34.9	37.3	39.3	37.6
% change *(1999–2005)*	–19.3	–13.0	–10.8	–14.1

Source: IEG estimates based on World Bank POVCAL database (see appendix table A6.3).
Note: Figures are averages of data per country and are not population weighted data.
a. Figures in parenthesis are the number of countries in the sample for which data are available. The poverty line is in 2005 purchasing power parity at $38 per month or $1.25 per day.

Table 6.3. PRSC and IDA Countries on Millennium Development Goals (percentage of population)

	1990	1991	1995	2000	2006	Difference (%) (1990/91–2000/01)	Difference (%) (2001–06)
Primary enrollment, net							
PRSC	n.a.	62.8	n.a.	68.9	79.1	9.7	14.8
All IDA countries	n.a.	62.8	n.a.	70.1	76.5	11.6	9.1
Secondary enrollment, gross							
PRSC	n.a.	31.2	n.a.	40.1	49.3	28.5	22.9
All IDA countries	n.a.	34.6	n.a.	42.8	53.2	23.7	24.3
Infant mortality (per 1,000)							
PRSC	82.8	n.a.	76.2	67.1	58.2	–19.0	–13.3
All IDA countries	86.2	n.a.	80.7	73.7	66.6	–14.5	–9.6
Child mortality (per 1,000)							
PRSC	125.6	n.a.	115.3	101.3	87.5	–19.3	–13.6
All IDA countries	130.7	n.a.	122.0	110.9	99.9	–15.1	–9.9
Access to safe water							
PRSC	57.3	n.a.	64.6	68.9	73.9	20.2	7.3
All IDA countries	61.2	n.a.	65.4	68.9	72.2	12.6	4.8
Access to sanitation							
PRSC	25.5	n.a.	38.4	41.5	46.2	62.7	11.3
All IDA countries	33.1	n.a.	42.0	44.3	46.1	33.8	4.1

Source: World Bank, World Development Indicators data, and appendix table A6.7, which has comparisons of PRSC countries with better-performing non-PRSC IDA countries, and with all non-PRSC IDA countries.
Note: Years were chosen on the basis of most complete observations.

Basic Service Provision

A major thrust of the PRSC was to improve the access of the poor to basic services, particularly health, education, and water and sanitation. An analysis of HIPC data on pro-poor expenditures for 15 PRSC countries suggests some trend increase in such expenditures, especially in countries with long PRSC series, and in contrast to non-PRSC HIPC countries (appendix table A6.10). Over the PRSC period, the Bank also increased its use of diagnostic tools for poverty reduction, but these were, at best, moderately used to influence operational design.[13]

Using the health and education sector as examples, a portfolio review of PRSC components in these sectors looked at the following broad areas: (i) Did PRSC objectives address the provision of basic social services? (ii) To what extent did any expansion of service focus on the poor, or on those presently excluded? (iii) What was the focus of service delivery improvements in PRSC operations, and how were quality aspects addressed? (iv) Was there an adequate framework for the monitoring of outcomes? (v) Was expansion in service associated with improved pro-poor outcomes.[14]

Inclusion of Social Services as an Overall Objective. Most operations included objectives in health and education, and about half also included water supply and sanitation (table 6.4).[15] But some lacked PRSC-specific measures to address them. In most cases, PRSCs were primarily a complementary vehicle of Bank sector-specific lending in the country and not the only vehicle of sector support. There was an active sector-specific country lending program in 85 percent of PRSC projects with health sector components, 81 percent with education components, and 65 percent with water supply and sanitation components. This may explain why the frequency of PRSCs with explicit social sector objectives among their core objectives was low: only 30 percent in health, 31 percent in education, and 44 percent in water supply and sanitation.[16]

Most PRSCs included health and education but usually as a complement to other Bank lending.

Table 6.4. Number of PRSCs with Social Sector Objectives, FY01–08

Social sector	PRSC series	PRSC operations	Operations not included
Health	36	83	4
Education	35	81	6
Water supply and sanitation	24	48	39
Total	**38**	**87**	

Source: IEG social sector portfolio review.

Improving Service Delivery to the Poor as an Objective

Improving access for the poor was mentioned as an explicit objective in 55 percent of PRSCs that included health sector conditions, 43 percent for the education sector, and around a quarter (27 percent) in water supply and sanitation. However, a smaller proportion of operations focused on improvement of the quality of access by the poor or translated stated objectives into specific measures to achieve these objectives. For health, only 38 percent of operations had explicit actions to improve access by the poor. In water supply and sanitation, 83 percent of operations were not explicitly designed to improve access of the poor. Indeed, only one operation could be identified (Nicaragua PRSC 1) that was designed to improve the access of the poor to sanitation. Fewer measures were framed in terms of improving overall outcomes for the poor—13 percent of PRSCs in health and 20 percent in education attempted to frame such measures.

Social Sector Focus in PRSCs. A high proportion of measures incorporated in individual PRSCs, to support the achievement of sectoral objectives in health, education, and water supply and sanitation, focused on budget and public finance. The highest proportion of conditions in the health sector focused on the formulation, execution, and allocation of the sectoral budget (20 percent of legally binding conditions and 17 percent of program benchmarks). In the education sector, 15 to 18 percent of conditions focus on the sectoral budget. High proportions of conditions also lie in areas related to public subsidies. However, in the education sector, the highest attention is given to teacher recruitment and remuneration. In both sectors, human resource management is also an important area, which can stem from the budgetary need to focus on recurrent costs (appendix table A6.9).

This distribution of measures may reflect the fact that PRSCs take place largely in tandem with parallel projects in the social sectors. As such the PRSCs provide support largely to those elements of sectoral dialogue, such as budget planning and execution, that need to be taken up with core ministries and where the PRSC is best positioned to provide support through strengthened public sector management. And budget rationalization was often a first step toward the realization of deeper structural changes in the sector, for example, shifting resources toward priority areas, providing for recurrent costs, and rationalizing expenditures.

Monitoring and Evaluation. Questions concerning monitoring and evaluation were answered for each PRSC series rather than for individual operations, since a monitoring framework is typically devised for the series as a whole (table 6.5). In the majority of the PRSCs, the monitoring and evaluation framework included indicators relevant to the sector (69 percent for health, 83 percent for education, and 71 percent for water supply and sanitation). However, in most cases, sector-specific indicators were not consistently monitored over the series. Only 22 percent of indicators in health, 36 percent in education, and 35 percent of the water supply and sanitation indicators were consistently monitored.

Baseline data were only available in about half the series for each sector, making it difficult to gauge progress. Baseline data were more likely to be available in water supply and sanitation than in health or education. As for access by the poor, in health only 11 percent of the series' monitoring systems included information on access by the poor. For education, 17 percent of the series included this information, and for water supply and sanitation, only 8 percent.

A high proportion of PRSC sectoral objectives pertained to budget and public finance issues.

These data suggest gaps among objectives, measures, and monitoring for service delivery to the poor. Although a good percentage of operations set out to improve access by the poor to such services, a smaller percentage contain specific measures to do so. Monitoring systems to ensure that the poor have access have been incomplete, with baseline data that changed, indicators that were not consistent, and shifting standards of what needed to be monitored.

Measuring outcomes in pro-poor service delivery is hampered by a poor monitoring and evaluation framework.

Outcomes. On the key question of whether sector indicators improved over the course of the PRSCs, results from the portfolio review are not conclusive due to the shortage of relevant indicators. Ratings could not be applied, or were not relevant, to almost 40 percent of PRSC series' health components and to over 50 percent of PRSC series' education components. Excluding these cases, around a third of monitorable indicators were met in the health sector, and another half were somewhat realized.[17] For education, about half of the indicators were met, and another third were partially realized (table 6.6). In water supply and sanitation, a large proportion of indicators (over 40 percent) were not met. On average, even after the exclusion of PRSCs that ended after a single operation, and

Table 6.5. Monitoring and Evaluation in PRSC Series (% positive)

Sector	M&E framework includes indicators relevant to sector	Specific indicators were consistently monitored over the series	Baseline data were available	Indicators are linked to policy actions to measure progress achieved	Monitoring system includes information on access of the poor to services	Monitoring system includes information outcomes among the poor
Health	69	22	53	41	11	6
Education	83	36	54	48	17	6
Water supply/sanitation	71	35	69	67	8	n.a.

Source: IEG portfolio review.

Table 6.6. PRSC Social Sectors—Success in Meeting Specific Objectives, as Measured by Their M&E Systems (%)

Were specific targets met?	Health	Adjusted % health	Education	Adjusted % education	Water supply/ sanitation	Adjusted % WSS
Yes	19	0.31	20	0.44	17	0.29
No	0	0.00	0	0.00	25	0.43
Somewhat	28	0.46	14	0.31	8	0.14
Unclear	14	0.23	11	0.24	8	0.14
	61		**45**	**1.00**	**58**	**1.00**
Not applicable	39		54		42	

Source: IEG portfolio review of PRSC operations, based on IEG questionnaire.
Note: Not applicable refers to series with only one operation completed or those in which monitoring was not consistently undertaken.
Percentages are calculated excluding "not applicable" operations.

Table 6.7. PRSC Social Sectors—Project Ratings

Sector	Total series for sector	How many series had ICR ratings		ICR sector-relevant rating substantial		ICR sector-relevant rating modest	
		Number of series	%	Number of series	%	Number of series	%
Health	36	19	52.8	8	42.1	11	57.9
Education	35	19	54.3	9	47.4	10	52.6
Water supply and sanitation	24	11	45.8	4	36.4	7	63.6

Source: IEG PRSC ICR review.

While not conclusive, about a third to a half of monitorable indicators for health and education were fully met, and targets were somewhat met in another 30–40 percent of projects.

those where monitoring was not adequate to permit measurement, only some 30–45 percent of targets were met in the three sectors and somewhat met in another 30–40 percent of projects for health and education.

PRSC social sector objectives were usually ancillary to their core objectives; translation of objectives into specific measures was mixed.

These findings are largely corroborated by IEG ratings of PRSC outcomes (table 6.7). Somewhat less than half of all PRSC project components in health and education, and about a third of all projects in water supply and sanitation, received substantial outcome ratings, and the rest were deemed to be modest.[18]

To summarize core findings from the portfolio review, PRSC social sector development objectives were usually ancillary to core objectives. Components ran in parallel to sector projects and included a substantial focus on budgetary aspects of social service delivery. Only two-fifths of PRSCs in education, and over half of PRSCs in health, had an explicit pro-poor focus. Proportions for water supply and sanitation were lower, at less than a fifth.

Translation of objectives into specific measures to achieve program results was largely incorporated in education components, but less so in health components, at about 70 percent. Tracking achievement of objectives is hampered by shortfalls in the monitoring framework, despite sector-relevant indicators, due to missing baseline data or, especially, a lack of indicators specific to the poor. And indicators were not tracked consistently over series. Overall, there were gaps among objectives, measures, and monitoring.

Regarding outcomes, and subject to caveats of coverage, indicators have been fully met one-third to half of the time across the three sectors. However, adding those projects where outcomes are somewhat met raises the total to three-quarters. A large proportion of service delivery components had modest achievements.[19]

These findings do not, by themselves, permit judgment of the extent to which observed outcomes in the service delivery sectors can be attributed to the PRSC. Such an association would require a comparison of these outcomes with those achieved through non-PRSC projects. A rough comparison is available for investment projects in the health sector, over the period 1997–2007; a recent IEG evaluation found that about two-thirds were deemed to have had satisfactory outcomes.[20] These results appear to be better than those found for PRSC outcomes in the health sector. To the extent that comparisons are possible, these results suggest that health outcomes in PRSCs may be less successful than in other projects.

These findings of limited achievement in PRSC pro-poor components may appear at odds with the preceding section, which finds that PRSC countries fare better than comparators on poverty and social indicators. But one explanation for their better outcomes may be a greater pro-poor policy orientation outside of PRSC areas. Another may be that these relatively better outcomes reflect support through other sector projects or other donors. Finally, the limited coverage of the above measures must be remembered.

Case Studies—Service Delivery to the Poor

Health. Case studies in seven countries provide a more detailed account of outcomes of social service delivery components in PRSCs and indicate mixed results (annex 9). In the health service area, all case study countries included health objectives as a major focus of poverty reduction. Almost all countries tried to increase resources for health services for the poor either by increasing the overall budget envelope (Benin, Ghana, Lao PDR, Mozambique) or by achieving efficiencies that permitted reallocations of resources (Armenia).

Efforts were made to incorporate a pro-poor focus into health components in case study countries.

In addition to increased budget resources, health programs often included a more timely and regular release of sector funding down to the provincial level (Benin, Ghana, Mozambique). More efficient resource use was also emphasized by improving sector budgeting, establishing management contracts, and shifting toward the private provisions of services. Reimbursement schemes for hospitals were improved in several countries, thus lowering costs (Armenia, Benin). And many programs included improvements in health information and monitoring (Benin, Lao PDR, for example).

Efforts were made to explicitly recognize pro-poor objectives in most PRSC health components, in some cases through improvements in service delivery to excluded groups, such as the rural poor. In many countries this was incorporated though the delivery of a minimum package targeted at the poor (Benin, Lao PDR), including health insurance schemes for the poor and free healthcare for the most vulnerable groups (Vietnam). Fees for health services were eliminated for the poor (Armenia, Ghana) or resources were reallocated toward pro-poor services (Armenia).

Attributions of larger outcomes to the PRSC are more difficult because, in virtually all case study countries, Bank support via the PRSCs was ancillary to support via sector-specific projects (Armenia, Benin, Ghana, Lao PDR, Mozambique, Vietnam). However, findings indicate that the goal of increasing resources for health was achieved in many countries. Access by the poor improved in many (Benin, Mozambique, Vietnam) but not all (Armenia, Nicaragua). Many countries showed improved health indicators but often below what was expected (Ghana).[21] Even in successful countries, the problem of reaching down to the very poor remained a challenge despite PRSC-supported reforms (Mozambique, Vietnam). In a few countries there has been no material progress in improving health indicators

Attribution of results is difficult due to parallel sector projects—large shares of expenditures are off-budget.

(Armenia, Nicaragua), and in some, inadequate definition of sector goals and monitoring makes the tracking of results difficult or impossible (Lao PDR, Mozambique).

Education was not a substantial area of focus in any PRSC.

One complication for achieving results has been the fact that large shares of expenditures for health have been off-budget, including in countries that receive generous donor support (Ghana, Mozambique). This has made it difficult to achieve resource efficiencies across health spending and has also made it difficult to track resource use. Another difficulty has been the continuing limitations of public budgetary systems, which make it difficult to use these as vehicles of sectoral support (Benin, Lao PDR). Finally, as pointed out by officials in some countries (Ghana), achieving health outcomes is complex, long-term, and in some cases, depends on actions outside the sector. Clean water, for example, can be a significant ingredient in achieving health outcomes.

Education. In education, as in health, many countries focused on increasing resources as well as the improvement of resource management (Armenia, Benin, Ghana; annex 10). However, education was not an area of substantial focus in the PRSCs of some countries (Lao PDR, Mozambique), apart from budget management issues, and in some cases, dialogue was focused on too limited a number of objectives to form the basis of a sector strategy (Vietnam). Many countries increasingly rely on parallel sector projects as their primary vehicles of intervention (Lao PDR, Mozambique, Vietnam). Objectives also included measures to expand access: raising enrollment rates (Ghana, Vietnam), raising school completion rates, increasing the number and quality of teachers, improving their regional distribution, and increasing the timely availability of classroom materials.

While budget processes improved and funding increased, there is less evidence of better outcomes.

Access for the poor in some countries was improved by eliminating school fees (Ghana, Mozambique), reducing regional and gender inequalities, and decentralizing management (Benin, Nicaragua). However, in some countries, an early poverty focus shifted toward growth-oriented educational strategies, emphasizing technical and vocational training in an effort to address growing skilled-labor shortages (Ghana). Mozambique's growth-focused PRSC did not include education. In Armenia, total enrollments went up, but primary and preschool enrollments were static.

Overall results scored in case studies are modest.

Many countries were able to achieve increases in enrollments and/or completion rates (Benin, Ghana, Vietnam) and the number of trained teachers (Benin, Mozambique) during the PRSC period. In some, progress was made in reducing gender gaps in enrollments and completion rates (Benin). Education quality lagged in some countries (Benin) and may have actually gone down in some cases during the process of rapid enrollment expansion (Ghana, Mozambique).

While emphasis has been given to improving budgetary processes for the education sector, countries lag in their ability to link budgetary inputs with results and outputs. Donor coordination however has been less of an issue in education compared with health. Donor groups in education were relatively successful in some countries (Ghana, Vietnam).

There is little evidence of monitoring of results through achievement scores. Where monitored, a decline in quality has been observed (Ghana). The issue of continued disparities between richer urban and poorer rural regions continues to be an issue in many countries (Benin, Vietnam).

Table 6.8 gives an overall assessment, from country case studies, of effectiveness in each of three sectors for the seven countries, in response to the question: "How effectively has the PRSC helped advance the dialogue and achieve results in sectors that deliver services to the poor?" ranked on a scale of 1 (severe shortcomings) to 6 (achieved without any shortcomings).

Results reflect modest overall achievements. The overall ranking of 3.5 falls midway between significant and moderate shortcomings. Country scores vary from a high of 4.7 in Armenia to a low

Table 6.8. PRSC Country Scores: Achieving Results in Sectors That Deliver Services to the Poor

	Armenia	Benin	Ghana	Lao PDR	Mozambique	Nicaragua	Vietnam	Average
Education	4	4	4	3	3	3	5	3.7
Health	4	4	2	3	3	1	4	3
Water supply[a]	6	4	4	2	2	5	3	3.7
Average	4.7	4	3.3	2.7	2.7	3	4	3.5

Source: IEG country case studies.

Note: Rankings are done by authors of case studies using the following scoring system for achievement of stated objectives: 6 = fully achieved without any shortcomings; 5 = substantially achieved with only minor shortcomings; 4 = achieved with moderate shortcomings; 3 = significant shortcomings; 2 = major shortcomings; and 1 = severe shortcomings in achieving stated objectives.

a. For Armenia, this ranking refers to social protection, not water supply. Eliminating Armenia reduces the average score for Armenia to 4, and somewhat reduces the overall average to 3.4.

of 2.7 in Lao PDR and Mozambique. With sectors, there seems to have been somewhat more success in education and water supply and less in health. In short, the case studies broadly support the portfolio review findings of mixed results in realizing sector objectives via PRSCs.

PRSC Outcomes—IEG Ratings and IEG Surveys

PRSC Outcomes Compared with Other Policy-Based Lending

How have PRSC overall outcomes compared with those of other forms of adjustment lending? Table 6.9 analyzes overall outcome ratings in a database of 813 policy-based loans, to compare outcome ratings for PRSCs with (i) ratings for adjustment lending before the PRSC period (fiscal 1980–2000) and (ii) ratings of other policy-based loans during the PRSC period; (iii) two subperiods of the PRSC are also compared to see if ratings changed over time.

On average, PRSCs performed 13 percentage points better than previous adjustment lending in all countries and almost 16 percentage points better than loans to other IDA (and blend) countries. These differences are significant. Comparing PRSCs to policy-based loans in PRSC countries alone, the difference declines to around 8 percentage points. This suggests that, although PRSCs have done better than other forms of adjustment lending, at least some of the differential may have been due to the better performance of PRSC countries, even before the advent of the PRSC.

Overall outcomes of PRSCs are better than previous adjustment lending but not noticeably different from other adjustment lending.

Compared with parallel adjustment lending during the PRSC period, results show, again, that PRSCs performed roughly 12 percentage points better than all policy-based loans in IDA and blend countries. But the differential is negligible if compared with other policy-based loans made in PRSC countries. It is not possible to attribute direction of causality. Other policy-based loans at a sectoral level in PRSC countries may have performed better due to the presence of the PRSC, or both forms of adjustment lending may have benefitted from a more conducive institutional environment. If PRSCs are compared against the universe of all adjustment loans in the period fiscal 2001–08, including IBRD loans, overall performance differences are negligible.

Finally, separating earlier and later PRSCs, there is a marked change in relative ratings obtained by PRSCs, compared with other policy-based loans in the earlier and later periods. PRSCs performed better than other IDA and blend policy-based loans over fiscal 2001–04 by 19 percentage points, but not much better than that same group over fiscal 2005–08. The difference, compared with all adjustment lending including IBRD lending, declined to even lower levels in the second subperiod. These findings suggest that while PRSCs were more successful than adjustment lending and

Table 6.9. Outcome Ratings: PRSCs and Other Adjustment/Development Policy Lending (FY1980–2008)

	Number of projects	Projects with satisfactory outcome ratings[a]	Difference in mean relative to PRSC (% points)
PRSCs 2001–08 (all rated PRSC projects)	51	84.3	
PBLs in PRSC countries FY1980–2000	142	76.1	–8.3
PBLs in all IDA and blend countries FY1980–2000	324	68.5	**–15.8*** **
PBLs in all IBRD, IDA, and blend countries FY1980–2000	571	71.3	**–13.0** **
PBLs in PRSC countries (other than PRSCs) FY2001–08	33	84.8	0.5
All IDA and blend PBLs (other than PRSCs) FY2001–08	60	71.7	**–12.6***
All PBLs (other than PRSCs) (IBRD, IDA, and blend) FY2001–08	191	83.2	–1.1
PRSCs 2001–04	21	90.5	
All IDA and blend PBLs (other than PRSCs) FY2001–04[b]	60	71.7	**–18.8** **
All PBLs (other than PRSCs) FY2001–04[b]	136	85.3	–5.2
PRSCs 2005–08	30	80.0	
All IDA and blend PBLs (other than PRSCs) FY2005–08[c]	27	77.8	–2.24
All PBLs (other than PRSCs) FY2005–08[c]	55	78.2	–1.80

Source: IEG data.

Note: * 10% significance level, **5% significance level, and *** 1% significance level.

a. Satisfactory includes projects rated highly satisfactory, satisfactory, and moderately satisfactory by IEG.

b. Percentage point difference calculated relative to PRSCs for 2001–04.

c. Percentage point difference calculated relative to PRSC for 2005–08.

early development policy lending, as time passed the differential disappeared. And policy-based lending has generally done better in PRSC countries, regardless of whether such loans are PRSCs. Performance differences, as far as it is possible to tell, may be ascribed as much to country selection as to the PRSC. And these differentials are eroding over time.

PRSC Overall Outcomes—IEG and Staff Assessments

Staff ratings of PRSC performance tend to be more rosy than those of IEG. Table 6.10 compares outcome ratings given by staff in PRSC completion reports (ICRs) and IEG reviews (ICR reviews). Of the 51 operations that have been assigned outcome ratings so far, three-quarters have

Table 6.10. Poverty Reduction Support Credits—Outcomes (FY01–08)

	Number of rated PRSCs	Percent of rated PRSCs
Total number of rated operations	51	
Of which staff rated satisfactory	39	76%
IEG rated satisfactory	25	49%
Of which staff rated moderately satisfactory	12	24%
IEG rated moderately satisfactory	18	35%
Of which staff rated moderately unsatisfactory	0	0
IEG rated moderately unsatisfactory	8	16%

Source: World Bank database.

Note: Poverty Reduction Support Grants and Operations are also included here. For part of the FY01–08 period, Bank ICRs gave a single rating to the entirety of a PRSC series while IEG applied individual ratings to each operation in a series.

been rated *satisfactory* by Bank staff (76 percent) compared with half by IEG (49 percent). Over half have been rated *moderately satisfactory* (35 percent) or *moderately unsatisfactory* (16 percent) by IEG. These differences suggest a need for more careful staff scrutiny of lessons that can be learned from PRSC outcome reviews.

Task Team Leader Views on PRSC Achievements in Social Sectors. An IEG survey of PRSC outcomes in the social sectors has results similar to those in overall outcome ratings. Two-thirds of team leaders in health, and three-quarters in education, believe PRSCs have been effective or very effective in achieving results. Social protection and water supply/sanitation receive lower scores (half or less than half). Team leaders also give high marks (75 percent or more) to the PRSC as a vehicle for "improving the poverty focus of public expenditures" and "improving access to basic services." The overall average ranking of responses is close to the mean of 3.5 of the case studies.[22]

Sector staff hold divergent views on whether accomplishments of the PRSC could have been realized through a free-standing sector operation. A majority reject general budget support as a sole vehicle for delivering results in their sector. Sector achievements of the PRSC were therefore perceived more positively by team leaders, who typically did not represent specific sectors, compared with sector staff.

PRSC countries had reasonably good CAS outcomes, which generally coincided with PRSC outcomes, though there were some instances of disconnect.

PRSCs and the Achievement of Country Program Objectives

Finally, to what extent have PRSCs helped overall achievement of Bank country programs, as envisaged in Country Assistance Strategies? A review of CAS completion reports suggests a good correspondence between successful country programs and successful PRSCs (88 percent); compared with non-PRSC IDA countries (62 percent). Whether the PRSC was instrumental, however,

Box 6.2. PRSCs and Bank Country Program Successes

Country Outcomes and PRSC Outcomes: A comparison of ratings ascribed to PRSC countries' CAS completion reports and ratings given to 40 PRSC operations in these countries shows that 88 percent (15 out of 17) had satisfactory or moderately satisfactory ratings compared with 62 percent of 26 non-PRSC IDA countries. And 33 of the 40 PRSC operations in these countries (82 percent) received satisfactory *(satisfactory or moderately satisfactory)* ratings for their overall outcome. In most cases, there was a broad corroboration between country ratings and PRSC ratings, although in a few cases there were differences in ratings (Ethiopia, Madagascar, and Uganda).

Sectoral Pillars—PRSCs and CASs: There is also broad correspondence in outcomes for specific sectors. The few cases of marked differences in ratings for specific pillars in PRSC outcomes (ICRs) and country outcomes (CASCR reviews) are detailed below.

ICR satisfactory/CASCR unsatisfactory:

- Ethiopia (public financial management, governance, and other public sector)
- Ghana (human and social development)
- Azerbaijan (industry and trade, finance)

ICR unsatisfactory/CASCR satisfactory:

- Ghana (public financial management, governance, and other public sector)
- Tanzania (human and social development)
- Ethiopia (industry and trade, finance)

Sectoral Pillars—PRSCs and CAEs: An alternative comparison of country evaluations, based on IEG Country Assistance Evaluations and PRSCs, also indicated relative consistency, but with dissonance in two countries—Ethiopia and Uganda. In Ethiopia, while PRSC's contribution to public financial management, governance, and other public sector was rated substantial, the CAE, like the CASCR review, rated the same pillar moderately unsatisfactory. In Uganda, the CAE, like the CASCR review, rated the human and social development pillar moderately satisfactory, while PRSC's achievements in the same pillar were negligible.

cannot be inferred because PRSCs were typically given to willing reformers.[23]

Overall findings suggest mixed achievements on outcomes—not better than parallel sector projects and not distinguishable from other adjustment lending.

In sum, findings suggest mixed results of PRSCs on achievement of outcomes (box 6.2). While PRSC countries have performed better in some regards than comparators, especially in poverty-related areas, it is not easy to trace these outcomes back to PRSC-associated actions. Limitations in the monitoring framework compound the difficulty of tracing outcomes. Based on limited available evidence, PRSCs do not appear to have done better than parallel sector projects. While PRSCs appear to have done better than preceding adjustment loans, their performance is hard to distinguish from other policy-based loans today.[24]

Impact becomes even more muted if one considers the problem of selection bias. PRSC operations were undertaken in countries chosen for good performance and high reform commitment.[25] Thus, one would expect the PRSC countries to do better than the average non-PRSC country. Caveats are the countries' public budgetary systems or donor coordination issues, which may have limited the PRSC's role. Finally, achieving outcomes in many areas of social service delivery is complex, long-term, and may depend on actions outside of the sector.

Chapter 7

Student writes in lesson book. Photo by Curt Carnemark, courtesy of the World Bank Photo Library.

Conclusions and Recommendations

When it was introduced in early 2001, the PRSC signaled a new modality for adjustment lending to low-income IDA countries. It was intended to help implement countries' comprehensive, partnership-oriented, and poverty-focused development strategies as embodied in their Poverty Reduction Strategies. Interim Guidelines for PRSCs reflected a new approach toward conditionality that was less onerous and more flexible than previous adjustment lending. The programmatic nature of the PRSC resource flow was intended to enable predictable medium-term commitments, disbursed in alignment with countries' budget cycles. PRSCs emphasized the use of domestic institutional and budget processes and provided for reinforcement of budgetary and procurement systems. PRSCs were also intended to be a platform for aid harmonization and to focus on achieving results.

Today, PRSCs are a part of Development Policy Loans and Credits, and there are no guidelines for PRSCs as a distinct lending instrument. The PRSC Interim Guidelines were never formalized. New Bank guidelines for adjustment lending, introduced in 2005, subsumed the PRSC Interim Guidelines and bore many of its characteristics. Nevertheless, the PRSC label remains as a brand name reserved for broad-based programmatic Bank support to well-performing IDA countries, specifically those with a sustained reform commitment, to support their strategies to achieve poverty-reducing growth.

Development Policy Loans bearing the PRSC label remain the Bank's most important policy lending vehicle in many IDA countries, especially in Africa, where new PRSC operations continue to be added each year. In view of its continued prominence, a central objective of this evaluation has been to examine the PRSC's present relevance and effectiveness as an instrument of Bank group lending for poverty reduction.

Findings on Design and Process

Country Selection

While PRSCs were intended to support the implementation of PRSPs and provide programmatic, broad-based support for the achievement of poverty-reducing growth to countries with strong reform commitment, they came to be directed toward countries that already had stronger policy and institutional quality. Early PRSCs sometimes failed to identify political reform commitment, leading to the early termination of a number of PRSCs, for example, in Nepal, Nicaragua, and Sri Lanka. Later, PRSCs were more careful about country commitment. PRSC country selection could benefit from greater attention to outcomes of past adjustment lending.

Country Ownership and Alignment with National Strategies

PRSCs enjoyed a higher level of country ownership compared with preceding structural adjustment lending, particularly at the level of core ministries. PRSCs helped to improve dialogue between core and line ministries, but engagement with parliament and civil society has been much less.[1]

PRSCs reflect good, though not perfect, alignment with national development strategies, improving over the PRSC series. Stronger alignment is possible where the PRSP/national development strategy has a prioritized and costed framework and a strong annual review process. PRSCs occasionally include measures outside the national development plan, reflecting evolving issues, sometimes solicited by clients.

Sector Focus, Conditionality, and Predictability

The sectoral focus of the PRSC showed a marked shift away from macroeconomic adjustment, trade, and private sector development, toward public sector management and social service delivery. Over time, the PRSC continued to emphasize the new areas. Yet, differences relative to parallel non-PRSC adjustment lending have diminished as all Bank adjustment lending has reoriented toward the areas of PRSC emphasis.

Conditionality

PRSCs from the outset had significantly fewer legally binding conditions than other adjustment loans. Initially, nonbinding program benchmarks rose rapidly in PRSC programs, often reflecting attempts to adopt a common donor matrix. These declined over time. Following new guidelines for development policy lending in fiscal 2005, conditionality of all policy-based lending declined. By fiscal 2008, there was little difference in the number or distribution of PRSC conditions relative to other policy-based lending.

PRSCs were markedly more flexible in the interpretation of conditions compared with past adjustment lending and a high proportion of triggers, or indicative conditions for subsequent operations, were modified. Over time, flexibility was more selectively used.

Clients' beliefs that there are still too many conditions are partly due to blurred perceptions of the difference between legally binding conditions—in the form of prior actions already achieved, triggers or indicative prior actions—and program benchmarks, which are not legally binding. Donor coordination through a common Performance Assessment Framework is a contributing factor, especially in the early stages. Some clients also believe that the Bank does not adequately appreciate implementation constraints.

Predictability and Reliability in Financing

Overall, program support through PRSCs was somewhat more stable than under previous adjustment lending. The regularity of PRSC disbursement also improved, though there is scope for further improvement in alignment with the budget cycle. The Bank was able to balance inherent tensions between program regularity and predictability, and adherence to program content, with recourse to delays and downward adjustments in cases of program slippage. The Bank was prepared to exit PRSC series that faced severe difficulties, though following termination, the Bank often remained engaged through other instruments, sometimes with disbursements almost as large as under the PRSCs.

Results Frameworks, Monitoring and Evaluation

PRSC results frameworks, and particularly the monitoring and evaluation systems on which they depend, were initially weak in many operations, with varying improvement over time. Although outcome indicators and targets are increasingly specified, not all are quantifiable or consistent. Shortcomings remain in intermediate milestones, baseline data, and links between actions and outcomes. There is a paucity of indicators for pro-poor outcomes, in part because this cannot be extracted from underlying budget classifications. Yet there is clear evidence of improvement over time.

Difficulties in tracking results in some countries are also due to upstream shortcomings in associated results frameworks for the parallel PRSPs and limited alignment between PRSCs and CAS monitoring. Lack of statistical capacity or experience in data collection are also factors, as well as low incentives in those countries where governments do not use such indicators to guide policy.

Multidonor groups sometimes lead to large numbers of indicators in results frameworks with annual renegotiations of targets and milestones. Sometimes difficulties in agreement on indicators are based on differences in approaches. Yet, in some cases, common donor positions have emerged.

Findings on PRSC Outcomes

Creating an Enabling Environment for Growth and Poverty Reduction

Although PRSC countries performed well on growth and other elements of macroeconomic performance over the PRSC period, comparator countries also performed well. PRSC countries had better initial conditions. Differences in creating a growth-enabling environment, as reflected in CPIA scores on institutional quality, are small. While accelerating economic growth was a prominent part of the PRSC agenda in most countries, most PRSCs did not have a comprehensive set of actions constituting a growth strategy. It is difficult to trace a direct link from PRSC growth-related measures to country growth outcomes.

PRSC countries have a better record in many dimensions of poverty reduction than other IDA countries, including better IDA performers, despite broadly similar initial conditions. This includes better performance on income poverty as well as on the achievement of the Millennium Development Goals. A portfolio review of PRSC operations shows that most PRSCs had program objectives for pro-poor service delivery, though often in parallel with sector projects. Social sector development objectives were usually ancillary to core objectives.

PRSC program components in health and education included a substantial focus on budgetary aspects of social service delivery, raising resources and allocating them more efficiently. But only about two-fifths of PRSC objectives in education and over half of PRSCs in health had an explicit pro-poor focus. Proportions for water supply and sanitation were less than a fifth. Some program objectives were not matched by specific measures to achieve program results. And countries lag in their ability to link budgetary inputs with results and outputs. In most countries, the PRSC was not able to make the budget the vehicle for sector policy dialogue and intervention, and large proportions of resources allegedly remain off-budget.

Tracking pro-poor outcomes is especially difficult due to limitations in the monitoring framework. Where measurable, targets have been fully met only a third to half of the time in health, education, and water supply and sanitation. A large proportion of service delivery components had modest achievements. And a comparison with non-PRSC projects suggests that health outcomes in PRSCs may be less successful than in other Bank projects. Better poverty outcomes achieved by PRSC countries may result also from other Bank and donor support as well as government efforts. Achieving outcomes in many areas of social service delivery is complex, long–term, and in some cases depends on actions outside the sector. These exacerbate issues of attribution.

Outcomes: Public Financial Management and Procurement

PRSC countries performed moderately well in developing an appropriately sequenced and usually donor-supported PFMP strategy and addressing capacity needs. Overall, PRSC countries have performed better on public financial management reform than comparator groups of non-PRSC IDA countries. Implementation has sometimes been slower than expected. One area of weakness is the design and implementation of a public financial management results framework, which only half of the countries had mostly completed.

Most PRSC PFMP programs were able to address some technical weaknesses in budget formulation, execution, reporting, and procurement. Performance on budget formulation has been good in the use of administrative and economic classifiers and in reducing aggregate variance of total budget expenditure. Some countries achieved good progress in integrating medium-term expenditure forecasting with the budget cycle. Areas of remaining weakness are reductions in the proportions of extra-budgetary funds brought on budget and inclusion of all donor funds on budget. More than half the series have been able to achieve some progress on budget reporting, although reporting systems remain weak.[2]

Progress has been achieved in the reduction of expenditure arrears, but is slow in the more complex reform area of improving the effectiveness of internal controls.

Findings on PRSC Contributions to Donor Harmonization

PRSCs effectively contributed to donor harmonization in countries where there was limited general budget support as well as those where budget support assumed a large role. Where the Bank was a senior partner (as in Vietnam) it provided leadership, aided by its technical depth and physical presence. In large budget support groups, where the Bank is one of several donors, the Bank has less influence in shaping the overall agenda and may not be able to respond flexibly to emerging policy issues. The Bank has sometimes reverted to arrangements outside of joint budget support, underscoring trade-offs between budget support and policy goals. The PRSC did usually serve as a catalyst for attracting donor funding to general budget support.

Within budget support groups, progress has been the greatest in reaching agreement on a common policy matrix or joint PAF. Less has been achieved on harmonizing annual reviews of the PRS/national development strategy and integrating it with the joint policy matrix. More also remains to be achieved on harmonization of results indicators, reporting arrangements, and especially capacity building.

Harmonization helped recipients to reduce transaction costs, but there are high transaction costs for Bank PRSC staff. Where the Bank has been a senior partner, other donors have complained about less voice in the process of reaching decisions. These reflect a trade-off with Bank efforts to keep the program on track. Efforts have been made to address this issue.

The Bank's effectiveness is also curbed by limited synchronization of its internal processing calendar with the donor cycle. Where Bank commitment to financing is required substantially in advance, internal reviews come too late to influence the joint working group.

Findings on PRSC as an Instrument of Sectoral Support

The PRSC is an imperfect single vehicle for sector support with loss in depth of sectoral engagement. PRSC engagement focuses on core ministries, and while dialogue with line ministries has been strengthened, the depth of engagement of Bank staff is diluted, with some loss in their sense of ownership. Bank sector staff acknowledge the PRSCs' value in addressing cross-cutting constraints but express reservations about its role in details of sectoral programs, capacity issues, or even ensuring timely resource transfer. Although envisioned by some staff and management at the time of its introduction, few support it today as a sole vehicle for sectoral engagement. The PRSC was rarely able to subsume sector lending. When attempted, the Bank usually reverted to parallel sector financing.

Joint budget support arrangements have revealed further tensions in sector support. The establishment of parallel sector working groups has become commonplace, with limited effectiveness. Many reflect varied financing arrangements counter to the philosophies of joint budget support. Some donors, driven by their constituents' agendas, feel the need to maintain sector support programs that are directly disbursed to line agencies or even off-budget. And counterparts in recipient countries sometimes resist the sectoral harmonization of donor positions.

The Bank's incentive framework also limits recognition for sectoral team participation, compared with free-standing sectoral projects. Resource availability may be more constrained and is less predictable. Sector managers, too, are alleged to have some preference for a focus on deliverables within their own units' work programs. Finally, outcomes of sectoral components of PRSCs, especially in the social service areas, to the extent that comparisons are possible, are somewhat weaker than in direct sectoral lending.

Recommendations

1. Phase out the PRSC as a separate brand name for development policy lending or clarify when its use is appropriate

Convergence in the design and content of PRSCs and other development policy lending, in terms of conditionality and sector focus, suggests that there is limited rationale for the separate existence of the PRSC today. However, there are also implicit criteria backing the PRSC label. If the PRSC brand name is still important, clear guidelines (which are currently lacking) and criteria for eligibility should be spelled out and applied.

2. Simplify the language of conditionality for PRSCs/DPLs by eliminating the term "triggers" and by transferring program benchmarks to the monitoring framework

In line with its use of the term "prior actions," the Bank could further simplify its lending framework by dispensing with the term "triggers" and substituting the term "indicative prior actions for future lending." Lending would then be based simply on prior actions already achieved and indicative prior actions for future lending. This would exhibit greater flexibility and improve understanding.

To clearly delineate legally binding conditions from program benchmarks, which are still referred to as binding and nonbinding conditions by clients and others in the aid community, program benchmarks should be removed from the policy matrix/Performance Assessment Framework and, instead, combined with program monitoring framework.

3. Enable more effective participation of the Bank in a multidonor budget support lending framework by better synchronizing Bank internal process with donor processes

At present, Bank commitments in a multidonor framework must sometimes be made before the Bank's internal review of the PRSC. This can limit the Bank's substantive contributions and comments on program content. Synchronizing the Bank's internal processing schedule with country and donor group processes would ensure Bank input in PRSC/DPL formulation.

4. Underpin operations with comprehensive diagnostics

PRSCs (and DPLs) should reflect country-specific growth diagnostics, which are undertaken based on analytic underpinnings that identify an overall growth strategy reflecting the linkages among growth, poverty reduction, and broader social development.

5. Strengthen PRSC/ DPL results frameworks, link them with the underlying PRS/national development strategy, and increase their poverty focus

Results frameworks of PRSCs should be consistently linked to those in the PRS or national development strategy and its annual reviews, and should be simplified to a small set of core outcomes. Adequate baseline and intermediate indicators and pro-poor results indicators should be required and built on country monitoring systems to the extent feasible.

6. Focus sector content in policy loans to high-level or cross-cutting issues

PRSC/DPL sector content should focus on areas where it has been consistently effective—cross-sectoral or central ministry issues critical to facilitating key sectoral reforms and strengthening sector budget processes. Complementary parallel sector lending, linked to PRSCs/DPLs, remains important to address detailed technical issues and facilitate program ownership by line ministries.

Girl drinking water from a community water pipe. Photo by Dominic Sansoni, courtesy of the World Bank Photo Library.

Appendixes

Table A1.1. PRSCs: Shares in Bank Lending, by Volume of Disbursement

	Fiscal years									Memo items	
	FY01	FY02	FY03	FY04	FY05	FY06	FY07	FY08	Total FY01–08	FY09	Total FY01–09
PRSC amounts disbursed ($m)	0.0	294.7	643.8	709.3	1,450.8	1,236.3	1,285.2	973.3	6,593.3	852.2	7,445.5
PRSC approvals by region ($m)											
AFR		194	335	459	951	893	737	743	4,312.8	636	4,948.8
EAP		101	160	107	104	104	110	190	876.1	147	1,023.1
ECA			21	19	32	59	59	40	229.8	70	299.8
LAC				49	61	30	25		166.1		166.1
MNA											
SAR			128	75	303	150	353		1,008.6		1,008.6
PRSCs and policy-based lending[a]											
All IDA policy-based loans (PBLs)(US$m)	1,276	1,919	3,018	1,554	2,515	2,425	2,227	2,713	17,645.6	1,872	19,517.6
All policy-based loans (IBRD+IDA) (US$m)	5,673	6,845	8,502	6,033	6,272	7,824	6,496	6,298	53,941.5	11,004	64,945.5
PRSCs/All IDA policy-based loans (%)	0%	15%	21%	46%	58%	51%	58%	36%	37%	46%	38%
PRSCs/All PBLs (IBRD+IDA) (%)	0%	4%	8%	12%	23%	16%	20%	15%	12%	8%	11%
PRSCs and all lending[a]											
All loans to IDA countries (US$m)	5,056	5,965	6,996	6,548	8,582	8,493	8,091	8,583	58,314.7	8,482	125,111
All loans to IDA/IBRD countries (US$m)	17,276	17,857	19,275	17,170	18,672	20,743	19,635	19,650	150,277.5	27,784	328,339
PRSCs/(All IDA loans) (%)	0%	5%	9%	11%	17%	15%	16%	11%	11%	10%	6%
PRSCs/All Bank loans (IDA+IBRD) (%)	0%	2%	3%	4%	8%	6%	7%	5%	4%	3%	2%
IDA policy-based loans/ All IDA loans (%)	25%	32%	43%	24%	29%	29%	28%	32%	30%	22%	16%

Source: World Bank database.

Note: The evaluation covers the period FY01–FY08. Data for FY09 are added as a memo item.

a. Two-tranche PRSCs counted as a single operation. IDA countries includes blend countries.

Table A1.2. PRSCs: Shares in Bank Lending, by Number

	Fiscal years										Memo items		
	FY01	FY02	FY03	FY04	FY05	FY06	FY07	FY08	Total FY01–08	FY08%	FY09	Total FY01–09	FY09%
PRSCs approved	2	2	7	10	17	15	19	15	87		12	99	
Regional distribution of PRSC approvals													
AFR	1	1	4	5	11	11	11	10	54	62%	10	64	65%
EAP	1		1	1	2	2	2	2	11	13%	2	13	13%
ECA		1		1	3	2	4	3	14	16%		14	14%
LAC			1	2			1		4	5%		4	4%
MNA										0%			
SAR			1	1	1		1		4	5%		4	4%
Supplemental PRSC credits						1		1	2			2	
PRSCs and policy-based lending[a]													
IDA policy-based loans (PBLs) (Nos)[b]	15	23	24	23	31	30	35	29	210		33	243	
PBLs to all countries (IBRD+IDA)	30	44	45	41	53	51	57	45	366		67	433	
PRSCs/All IDA policy-based loans (%)	13%	9%	29%	43%	55%	50%	54%	52%	41%		36%	41%	
PRSCs/All policy-based loans (IBRD+IDA) (%)	7%	5%	16%	24%	32%	29%	33%	33%	24%		18%	23%	
Memo item: Number of all supplemental PBLs	16	7	5	2	3	2	0	2	37			37	
PRSCs and All Lending[a]													
PBLs+Other Loans All IDA Countries (Nos)	127	133	141	158	162	173	187	199	1,280		176	1,456	
All PBLs+Other Loans (IDA+IBRD)	218	229	240	245	277	286	298	298	2,091		301	2,392	
PRSCs/(All IDA Loans) (%)	2%	2%	5%	6%	10%	9%	10%	8%	7%		7%		
PRSCs/All Bank Loans (IDA+IBRD) (%)	1%	1%	3%	4%	6%	5%	6%	5%	4%		4%		

Source: World Bank database.
Note: The evaluation covers the period FY01–FY08. Data for FY09 are added as a memo item.
a. Two-tranche PRSCs counted as a single operation. IDA countries includes blend countries.
b. Not including supplemental operations.

Table A1.3. PRSCs, by Country and Date (FY01–08)

	PRSC Name	Approval FY	Series	Country FY	Dates of disbursement	Volumes of PRSC IDA disbursements (US$ mil.)	Volume of total IDA disbursements in country (US$ mil.)	PRSC disbursements as share of total IDA disb. in PRSC FY
1	Albania PRSC 1	2002	1	Jan–Dec	08/31/2002	21.2	75.6	28.0%
2	Albania PRSC 2	2004	1	Jan–Dec	12/31/2003	19.0	63.5	29.9%
3	Albania PRSC 3	2005	1	Jan–Dec	12/31/2004	10.6	66.4	16.0%
4	Armenia PRSC 1	2005	1	Jan–Dec	12/31/2004	21.2	75.1	28.2%
5	Armenia PRSC 2	2006	1	Jan–Dec	04/30/2006	20.3	55.0	36.9%
6	Armenia PRSC 3	2007	1	Jan–Dec	04/30/2007	28.6	85.1	33.6%
7	Armenia PRSC 4	2008	1	Jan–Dec	03/31/2008	19.7	82.0	24.0%
8	Azerbaijan PRSC 1	2005	1	Jan–Dec	03/31/2006	18.8	57.1	32.9%
9	Benin PRSC 1	2004	1	Jan–Dec	08/31/2004	19.7	43.8	45.0%
10	Benin PRSC 2	2005	1	Jan–Dec	12/31/2005	28.3	51.3	55.2%
11	Benin PRSC 3	2007	1	Jan–Dec	01/31/2007	30.2	59.9	50.4%
12	Benin PRSC 4	2007	2	Jan–Dec	04/30/2008	43.1	88.1	49.0%
(1)[4]	Benin PRSC 5	2009	2	Jan–Dec				
13	Burkina Faso PRSC 1	2002	1	Jan–Dec	10/31/2001	46.4	76.1	60.9%
14	Burkina Faso PRSC 2	2003	1	Jan–Dec	11/30/2002	37.3	74.5	50.0%
15	Burkina Faso PRSC 3	2004	1	Jan–Dec	10/31/2003	50.6	127.5	39.7%
16	Burkina Faso PRSC 4	2004	2	Jan–Dec	07/31/2004	60.2	119.2	50.5%
17	Burkina Faso PRSC 5	2005	2	Jan–Dec	09/30/2005	58.2	143.7	40.5%
18	Burkina Faso PRSC 6	2006	2	Jan–Dec	09/30/2006	62.1	150.8	41.2%
19	Burkina Faso PRSC 7	2008	3	Jan–Dec	09/30/2007	91.6	173.0	52.9%
(2)	Burkina Faso PRSC 8	2009	3	Jan–Dec				
20	Cape Verde PRSC 1	2005	1	Jan–Dec	05/31/2005	14.5	29.8	48.6%
21	Cape Verde PRSC 2	2006	1	Jan–Dec	07/31/2006	10.3	24.5	42.1%
22	Cape Verde PRSC 3	2007	1	Jan–Dec	07/31/2007	10.4	19.5	53.2%
(3)	Cape Verde PRSC 4	2009	Transitory	Jan–Dec	10/30/2008	(9.5)	(14.4)	(66.0%)
23	Ethiopia PRSC 1	2004	1	8 July–7 July	03/31/2004	123.3	422.0	29.2%
24	Ethiopia PRSC 2	2005	1	8 July–7 July	12/31/2004	137.0	373.3	36.7%
25	Georgia PRSO 1	2006	1	Jan–Dec	11/30/2005	19.7	75.4	26.1%
26	Georgia PRSO 2	2007	1	Jan–Dec	12/31/2006	20.4	70.5	28.9%
27	Georgia PRSO 3	2007	1	Jan–Dec	07/31/2007	20.2	96.0	21.1%
28	Georgia PRSO 4	2008	1	Jan–Dec	08/31/2008	21.8	40.8	53.5%
	Georgia PRSO 4–Suppl. Fin.		1		12/2/08	37.9	40.8	93.0%
29	Ghana PRSC 1	2003	1	Jan–Dec	06/30/2003	128.2	228.9	56.0%
30	Ghana PRSC 2	2005	1	Jan–Dec	07/31/2004	127.5	321.5	39.7%
31	Ghana PRSC 3	2006	1	Jan–Dec	08/31/2005	123.4	435.6	28.3%
32	Ghana PRSC 4	2006	2	Jan–Dec	06/30/2006	143.1	435.6	32.9%
33	Ghana PRSC 5	2007	2	Jan–Dec	06/30/2007	110.1	225.9	48.7%
34	Ghana PRSC 6	2008	2	Jan–Dec	06/30/2008	98.1	222.4	44.1%

(continued on next page)

Table A1.3. PRSCs, by Country and Date (FY01–08) *(continued)*

	PRSC Name	Approval FY	Series	Country FY	Dates of disbursement	Volumes of PRSC IDA disbursements (US$ mil.)	Volume of total IDA disbursements in country (US$ mil.)	PRSC disbursements as share of total IDA disb. in PRSC FY
(4)	Ghana PRSC 7	2009	2	Jan–Dec				
35	Guyana PRSC 1	2003	1	Jan–Dec	12/31/2003	13.4	20.9	63.8%
36	Honduras PRSC 1	2004	1	Jan–Dec	11/30/2004	61.2	209.2	29.3%
37	Lao PDR PRSC 1	2005	1	Oct–Sept	09/30/2005	9.7	36.3	26.7%
38	Lao PDR PRSO 2	2006	1	Oct–Sept	09/30/2006	8.3	53.4	15.5%
39	Lao PDR PRSO 3	2007	1	Oct–Sept	1/30/08	10.6	50.7	20.9%
40	Lao PDR PRSO 4	2008	2	Jan–Dec	08/31/2008	9.6	18.1	53.4%
(5)	Lao PDR PRSO 5	2009	2	Jan–Dec				
41	Lesotho PRSC 1	2008	1	1 April–31 March	8/22/08	8.1	12.6	11.2%
42	Madagascar PRSC 1	2005	1	Jan–Dec	08/31/2004	125.1	324.3	38.6%
43	Madagascar PRSC 2	2006	1	Jan–Dec	08/31/2005	79.2	212.9	37.2%
44	Madagascar PRSC 3	2007	1	Jan–Dec	08/31/2006	40.1	183.3	21.9%
45	Madagascar PRSC 4	2008	2	Jan–Dec	09/30/2007	40.9	224.0	18.2%
46	Madagascar PRSC 5	2008	2	Jan–Dec	08/31/2008	48.5	103.9	46.7%
(6)	Madagascar PRSC 6	2009	2	Jan–Dec				
47	Malawi PRSC 1	2008	1	July–June	12/31/2007	20.8	79.5	26.1%
(7)	Malawi PRSC 2	2009	1	July–June				
48	Mali PRSC 1	2007	1	Jan–Dec	08/31/2007	45.9	178.6	25.7%
49	Mali PRSC 2	2008	1	Jan–Dec	06/30/2008	42.6	178.6	23.8%
(8)	Mali PRSC 3	2009	1	Jan–Dec				
50	Moldova PRSC 1	2007	1	Jan–Dec	04/30/2007	10.3	42.8	24.0%
51	Moldova PRSC 2	2008	1	Jan–Dec	08/31/2008	9.8	18.9	52.1%
(9)	Moldova PRSC 3	2009	1	Jan–Dec				
52	Mozambique PRSC 1	2005	1	Jan–Dec	09/30/2004	60.0	223.0	26.9%
53	Mozambique PRSC 2–1st Tranche	2006	1	Jan–Dec	10/31/2005	60.0	307.5	19.5%
	Mozambique PRSC 2–2nd Tranche				03/31/2006	60.0	307.5	19.5%
54	Mozambique PRSC 3	2007	2	Jan–Dec	02/28/2007	69.7	263.7	26.5%
55	Mozambique PRSC 4	2008	2	Jan–Dec	03/31/2008	61.8	206.0	30.0%
(10)	Mozambique PRSC 5	2009	2	Jan–Dec				
56	Nepal PRSC 1	2004	1	16 July–15 July	12/31/2003	74.9	100.9	74.3%
57	Nicaragua PRSC 1–1st Tranche	2004	1	Jan–Dec	03/31/2004	36.0	141.6	25.4%
	Nicaragua PRSC 1–2nd Tranche				03/31/2006	30.3	77.5	39.1%
58	Nicaragua PRSC 2	2007	1	Jan–Dec	01/31/2007	25.2	54.7	46.0%
59	Pakistan PRSC 1	2005	1	Jan–Dec	09/30/2004	303.4	984.4	30.8%
	Pakistan PRSC 1–Suppl. Fin.				10/31/2005	149.9	1,211.8	12.4%

(continued on next page)

Table A1.3. PRSCs, by Country and Date (FY01–08) *(continued)*

	PRSC Name	Approval FY	Series	Country FY	Dates of disbursement	Volumes of PRSC IDA disbursements (US$ mil.)	Volume of total IDA disbursements in country (US$ mil.)	PRSC disbursements as share of total IDA disb. in PRSC FY
60	Pakistan PRSC 2	2007	1	Jan–Dec	05/31/2007	352.9	1,189.3	29.7%
61	Rwanda PRSC 1	2005	1	Jan–Dec	12/31/2004	69.2	138.1	50.1%
62	Rwanda PRSC 2	2006	1	Jan–Dec	12/31/2005	53.8	101.3	53.1%
63	Rwanda PRSG 3	2007	1	Jan–Dec	05/31/2007	51.5	107.1	48.1%
64	Rwanda PRSG 4	2008	2	Jan–Dec	03/31/2008	72.4	139.9	51.8%
(11)	Rwanda PRSG 5	2009	2	Jan–Dec				
65	Senegal PRSC 1	2005	1	Jan–Dec	01/31/2005	31.3	217.7	14.4%
66	Senegal PRSC 2	2006	1	Jan–Dec	09/30/2006	30.8	151.8	20.3%
67	Senegal PRSC 3	2007	1	Jan–Dec	08/31/2007	20.7	96.6	21.4%
68	Sri Lanka PRSC 1	2003	1	Jan–Dec	06/30/2003	127.5	202.3	63.1%
69	Tanzania PRSC 1	2003	1	Jul–Jun	08/31/2003	132.6	336.9	39.3%
70	Tanzania PRSC 2	2005	1	Jul–Jun	09/30/2004	150.5	459.8	32.7%
71	Tanzania PRSC 3	2006	1	Jul–Jun	11/30/2005	149.6	339.3	44.1%
72	Tanzania PRSC 4	2006	2	Jul–Jun	07/31/2006	206.4	415.6	49.7%
73	Tanzania PRSC 5	2007	2	Jul–Jun	09/30/2007	195.2	505.3	38.6%
(12)	Tanzania PRSC 6	2009	2	Jul–Jun	11/30/08	(150.3)	(267.7)	(56.2%)
(13)	Tanzania PRSC 7	2009	2	Jul–Jun				
74	Uganda PRSC 1	2001	1	Jul–Jun	12/31/2001	147.7	167.1	88.4%
75	Uganda PRSC 2	2003	1	Jul–Jun	05/31/2003	168.7	256.2	65.8%
76	Uganda PRSC 3	2004	1	Jul–Jun	05/31/2004	152.9	353.6	43.2%
77	Uganda PRSC 4	2005	1	Jul–Jun	04/30/2005	155.3	291.0	53.4%
78	Uganda PRSC 5	2006	2	Jul–Jun	06/30/2006	137.0	315.5	43.4%
79	Uganda PRSC 6	2007	2	Jul–Jun	06/30/2007	126.1	296.4	42.6%
80	Uganda PRSC 7	2008	2	Jul–Jun				
(14)	Uganda PRSC 8	2010	3	Jul–Jun				
81	Vietnam PRSC 1–1st Tranche	2001	1	Jan–Dec	10/31/2001	100.6	331.5	30.4%
	Vietnam PRSC 1–2nd Tranche				01/31/2003	160.2	457.9	35.0%
82	Vietnam PRSC 2	2003	1	Jan–Dec	12/31/2003	106.7	426.8	25.0%
83	Vietnam PRSC 3	2004	1	Jan–Dec	10/31/2004	103.6	407.9	25.4%
84	Vietnam PRSC 4	2005	1	Jan–Dec	12/31/2005	94.8	418.9	22.6%
85	Vietnam PRSC 5	2006	1	Jan–Dec	01/31/2007	102.2	489.9	20.9%
86	Vietnam PRSC 6	2007	2	Jan–Dec	12/31/07	179.4	649.2	27.6%
87	Vietnam PRSC 7	2008	2	Jan–Dec	10/24/08	141.4	330.0	42.8%
(15)	Vietnam PRSC 8	2009	2	Jan–Dec				
(16)	Zambia PRSC 1	2009	1	Jan–Dec				
	Total Disbursements (FY01–08)					6,592	19,585	33.7%

Source: World Bank database.
Note: Shaded lines are operations in the pipeline for FY09 or FY10 and dates and figures should be considered indicative.

APPENDIX B: ADDITIONAL DATA AND ANNEXES AVAILABLE

Appendix tables A1.4–A6.10, in their entirety, are available on this report's website at www.worldbank.org/ieg/prsc.

A1.4	PRSCs in Proportion to Country Income, Budget and Aid Flows (CY1999–2008)
A2.1	CPIA Scores: PRSC Countries and other IDA Countries (FY01–07)
A2.2	PRSC Legal Conditions and Corresponding Sector Projects—No. of Countries
A2.3	PRSC Program Benchmarks and Corresponding Sector Projects
A2.4	PRSC Operations: Intended and Actual Replacement of Sectoral Lending (FY01–08)
A2.5	PRSC Countries: Non-PRSC Sectoral Lending—Examples from Health and Education
A2.6	PRSC Legal Conditions, Benchmarks and Corresponding Sector Projects
A2.7	Conditions and Benchmarks in Adjustment Operations (1980–2008)
A2.8	Country Series—Trends Over Time in Triggers and Prior Actions (FY01–08)
A2.9	PRSC Prior Actions / Triggers—Trends over Time by Country
A2.10	Modifications to Triggers by Nature and by Country (2001–08)
A2.11	PRSC Countries' Policy-Based Lending Gross Disbursements (FY1995–2008)
A2.12	Years with Adjustment Lending—Pre and Post PRSC (FY1996–2008)
A2.13	PRSCs Compared with Past Adjustment Lending—Variability of the Volume of Lending
A2.14	PRSCs Compared with Past Adjustment Lending—Variability of the Share
A2.15	Budget Support Commitments and Disbursements: 11 PRSC Countries
A2.16	PRSCs—Regularity of Disbursements by Quarter
A3.1	PRSC Results Frameworks: End-of-Series Outcomes and their Indicators
A3.2	PRSC Results Frameworks: Baseline and Intermediate Indicators
A3.3	PRSC Operationalizing National Strategies through Budgets—Select PRSC Countries
A4.1	The PRSC and Donor Harmonization: Frameworks for Joint Support
A4.2	PRSC Aid Harmonization: Coordinated Missions (2005–07)
A4.3	PRSC Aid Harmonization: Coordinated Analytic Work (2005–07)
A4.4	PRSC and Other Countries: Program-Based Aid, Budget Support (2005–07)
A5.1	PRSC Public Financial Management and Procurement Desk Review
A5.2	PRSC PFMP Performance Indicators for Results—Budget Formulation
A5.3	Results-Execution, Reporting, and Procurement
A6.1	Growth Rates Disaggregated—PRSC and other IDA Countries (% per year)
A6.2	Growth Rates of Per Capita Income in 22 PRSC countries (% per year)
A6.3	PRSC and Non-PRSC Countries' Growth Rates: Sample Selection Effects

The following annexes are also available at www.worldbank.org/ieg/prsc.

Annexes

Chapter 1

1. *Guidance to Bank Staff on Adjustment Lending,* detailed in Operational Directive (OD) 8.60, December 1992. The *Interim Guidelines for Poverty Reduction Support Credits* were issued as official guidance to staff in March 2001. This evaluation includes Poverty Reduction Support Grants, which use IDA grants instead of credits.

2. Ex-post conditionality means that the loan is approved by the World Bank/IDA Board of Directors after the agreed upon policy measures have been implemented. Ex-ante conditionalities are conditionalities that the government agrees to undertake at a future time, prior to approval of an operation or its subsequent tranches.

3. *Operational Policy OP 8.60—Development Policy Lending*, August 2004, World Bank.

4. Management points out that OP/BP 8.60 eliminated the need for any separate guidelines on PRSCs and disagrees with the statement that PRSCs remain a subset of programmatic development policy operations reserved for well-performing IDA countries. There is no subset of operations defined by their title. As per operational policy and since 2004, there is no difference, either in processing, design, or implementation between an operation that carries the title "Poverty Reduction Support Credit" (or Grant) and any other Development Policy Operation with a different title.

5. "PRSC countries," in this evaluation, refer to countries that have received a PRSC—although some may also have received other forms of policy-based lending.

6. This evaluation uses the term "policy-based lending" to refer to all forms of adjustment lending under OD 8.60 of 1992, and development policy lending under OP 8.60 of August 2004.

7. Appendix tables and annexes, in their entirety, are available on the IEG website and are also available upon request.

8. Despite debate in the case of Lao PDR, given poor institutional conditions.

9. Based on evidence from CASs in Africa, the PRSC was actively considered in the CAS programs for the Gambia, Guinea, Kenya, Mauritania, and Niger; and as a possibility in Cameroon, Chad, Nigeria, and Zambia. In Europe and Central Asia, Kyrgyzstan and Tajikistan also considered the PRSC as a possibility. Bangladesh, Bolivia, Cambodia, and Mongolia also considered the PRSC. However, it was usually associated with a case where there was strong government commitment to, and capacity for, reform. Reasons for not adopting the PRSC were low country commitment and less than adequate reform effort vis-à-vis key triggers, or fiduciary readiness. Some of these countries (such as Bangladesh, Bolivia, Niger, and Tajikistan) instead had adjustment lending operations that covered essentially the same terrain as the PRSC.

10. IEG identified distinguishing features implicitly used to distinguish PRSCs from other IDA DPLs: policy-based lending as part of a programmatic series, providing broad-based support to country-owned national development strategies, policy reform packages oriented toward poverty-reducing growth, a well-performing macro environment and adequate financial management capacity, and finally, a demonstrated record of sustained reform commitment. Other than PRSCs, a detailed review of the all IDA policy-based lending over this period shows that type-2 errors are rare; that is, IDA DPLs that are not called PRSCs, which meet all these criteria.

Chapter 2

1. This evaluation uses the term "adjustment lending" to refer to all structural adjustment loans and credits made under directive OD 8.60 of December 1992, excluding PRSCs. "Development policy lending" refers to operations guided by the new OP 8.60 of August 2004 on development policy lending, but excluding PRSCs for purposes of analysis of the PRSC instrument. The term "policy-based lending" is used to refer to all forms of loans that disburse directly to a government's budget, whether they belong to the structural adjustment period before the revised operational guidelines or to the development policy loan period after the introduction of OP 8.60. Policy-based loans include PRSCs.

2. See chapter 1, endnote 4.

3. Details of the analysis are in annex 3 to this report. Subject to measurement error in the CPIA (Gelb, Ngo, Ye 2004) and subsequent impacts on misallocation (Eifert and Gelb 2005). These are underlying unresolved issues about the use of the CPIA for selection.

4. Overall Public Sector Average (questions 12–16 of the CPIA) and Quality of Budget and Financial Management (question 13). This finding reflects their large weight in the CPIA (IEG 2009b).

5. Consistent with findings in the Bank's retrospective on development policy lending (2006) that better-performing countries were selected for policy-based lending. Better performers that did not have a PRSC often had similar loans (for example, Development Support Credits in Bangladesh).

6. The Government Stability Index, within the PRS Group's ICRG Political Risk database, measures both (i) the current regime's ability to stay in office, and (ii) its ability to carry out its declared program(s).

7. Replaced in mid-2009 by the Development Policy Actions database and now available on the World Bank website. The updated database revises the terminology used to refer to previous adjustment lending, reflecting new policy toward development policy lending since 2004. It also 'unbundles' the numbers counted for program benchmarks to increase transparency.

8. The 10 broad categories used are based on an aggregation of ALCID sectors, based on topics of interest to the PRSC evaluation, and is similar to the Operations Policy and Country Services PRSC Stocktaking (World Bank 2005c). Other classifications have been used: the OPCS review of conditionality (World Bank 2005j) uses five broad categories; *Conditionality Revisited* (World Bank 2005i) uses eight. Wood (2005) looks more broadly at 17 sectoral categories to single out specific areas of emphasis or neglect.

9. Studies by the Agriculture and Rural Development sector board (World Bank 2004i, 2005b) point to the limited relative emphasis of agricultural and rural development reforms in PRSCs.

10. This confirms early impressions in a study by the Norwegian Agency for Development Cooperation (NORAD 2007), which also found less privatization emphasis in conditionality. It also puts into perspective findings in Wood (2005), which point to the overly privatization-focused nature of PRSCs. While privatization policies have been incorporated in some PRSCs, this represents a small share of conditions, especially legally binding conditions.

11. As shown in the PRSC Stocktaking (World Bank 2005c).

12. Reviewers such as ActionAid (2006) argue that 20 percent of all PRSC conditions, in its review, were focused on economic policy and therefore PRSCs maintained the status quo of policy emphasis from the adjustment lending period. But the actual content of these reforms has shifted dramatically away from the private and financial sector, or industry and trade, into public sector governance and management.

13. This may reflect the successful Education for All (EFA) programs in many IDA countries, which were sometimes used as dedicated parallel reform programs outside the PRSC. The EFA initiative is an international commitment launched in 1990 to bring the benefits of education to "every citizen in every society." The Bank engages in EFA lending and nonlending services via its EFA Fast Track Initiative in 37 partners' low-income countries.

14. Consistent with the vision of World Bank (2004g) "Adjustment Lending to Development Policy Lending: an Update of World Bank Policy," which lays out a strategic vision for all policy-based lending that is similar to PRSCs. The OPCS's Review of Conditionality in Development Policy Lending (World Bank 2007b) also shows a growing share of public sector governance and generally declining shares of trade, financial, and private sector development.

15. World Bank (2005c).

16. These conclusions echo World Bank (2007b) "Conditionality in Development Policy Lending."

17. Devarajan, Rajkumar, and Swaroop (1999) and Devarajan, Swaroop, and Zou (1996) discuss the allocative efficiencies of general budget support, which ideally would be able to incorporate all sector lending once country fiduciary systems are adequate. These reasons were also discussed in the World Bank Strategy for the Africa Region (World Bank 2003b). These reasons for budget support aid were also held by other donors, notably the DfID (2006, 2008), and are reflected in increasing budget support assistance over the early PRSC period (appendix table 1.4). Management points out that this vision has not been stated in Bank guidelines or in the operational policy governing development policy lending.

18. PRSC Stocktaking (World Bank 2005c). Replacement of preexisting sector engagement by the PRSC was not intended to be appropriate for all sectors, as described in the Africa Region's stocktaking of the Uganda PRSC. Government reform commitment and implementation capacity are preconditions for success (Miovic 2004). These objectives were also reflected in guidelines prepared by the Water Supply and Sanitation Sector Board, which developed a list of preconditions in their guidelines for task teams for budget support in rural water supply and sanitation (Iyer and others 2005).

19. Even after August 2004, when OP 8.60 was passed, there were 8 operations correponding to 3 CASs in 3 countries (Cape Verde, Rwanda, Uganda) where replacement of sector lending was mentioned. The Lesotho CAS 2006–09 also states that some sector programs will be subsumed in its PRSC series, starting with PRSC 2. However, this operation is outside the scope of this evaluation.

20. In Uganda, the Education Structural Adjustment Credit closed in 2000, and its Primary Education and Training operation was approved in 2009. However, a general caveat to this discussion is that the elements of sectoral operations that closed or reopened, or that were within the sphere of the PRSC, may have different areas of focus with varying degrees of substitutability.

21. One study comments that the inclusion of education in the PRSC was possible largely because of the preceding education SWAp (Sectorwide Approach), which set the stage for successful incorporation (Miovic 2004). External commentators have also pointed out that the budget support approach was undermined in cases of parallel external funding for SWAps (IDD and Associates 2006a).

22. In Uganda, PRSCs 1–6 subsumed investment projects in health, however, starting with PRSC 7 in 2008, there is a new health investment project.

23. See annex 5 for details of the task team leader survey.

24. Consistent with other findings by the World Bank (2005c) and outside (IDD and Associates 2006a), and with sectoral guidelines regarding budget support, prepared by, for example, the water supply and sanitation group.

25. Details of the survey are provided in annex 6 of this report.

26. Sector specialists could include, for example, PREM staff from public sector or public financial management units, or from economic policy units, if they assumed the role of a sector specialist for a PRSC operation, for example, because of expertise in that sector.

27. In mid-2009 the Bank's ALCID database was brought into line with the terminology of development policy lending and is now available as the Development Policy Actions database. This database has also remapped the terminology of the ALCID database so that legally binding conditions of Board presentation or effectiveness are called "prior actions" and legally binding conditions of tranche release are called "prior actions for future tranche." Desired actions during implementation that are not legally binding are referred to as "program benchmarks."

28. There was an apparent strong decline in the number of legal conditions after the introduction of PRSCs in 2001, from 36.0 in fiscal 2001 to 9.5 in fiscal 2008. However, this result is driven by a single outlier, Vietnam, which had 56 legal conditions in the first year, in a two-tranche operation, originally designed to be a structural adjustment credit. Because this operation began preparation as an adjustment credit, it is not considered a PRSC.

29. For example, as in Killick (2005) and Koeberle and Stavreski (2005).

30. ActionAid (2006) and Wood (2005). Discussions with task team leaders and government stakeholders suggest that the shift from legally binding conditions to program benchmarks reflected a combination of the pressures to decrease conditionality from Bank management and the pressure to include additional policy measures from other donors involved in policy matrix negotiations.

31. Three pre-PRSC adjustment operations in 26 countries, and two in 20 countries, between 1987 and 2005. These combine single-tranche and multi-tranche operations. However, since the operation was defined and negotiated at the same time, the analysis below looks at conditionality for each operation as a whole.

32. Omitting one observation (Vietnam PRSC 1), which had an unusually high number of 43 prior actions, the average decline is –0.39 conditions per year and is significant only at 10 percent. Adding back Vietnam, the annual decline increases to –0.88, significant at 1 percent. This early operation was essentially a late con-

version of a structural adjustment operation and had an unusually high number of conditions.

33. As is consistent with the need for overall vision, articulated, for example, in Killick (1999).

34. In 26 PRSC countries, for a total of 72 non-PRSC DPLs and 1,967 conditions.

35. Another interpretation could be that, initially, the Bank took risks selecting countries that were not the best performers, in the hopes of a turnaround, though later a more conservative approach was adopted.

36. Findings elsewhere on the predictability of budget support are mixed. A joint evaluation of multidonor budget support to Ghana (Lawson and others 2007) also found evidence of higher predictability with multidonor budget support, compared with other aid modalities. By contrast, the 2005 joint evaluation of budget support to Tanzania (Lawson and others 2005a) initially found predictability to be very poor (budget support was deemed the least predictable source of government revenue from 2000–02), but it improved significantly by 2004/05. The IDD and Associates (2006a) evaluation of budget support in seven countries found the short-term predictability of partnership general budget support to be a "frequent problem," but that "mitigating measures are having an effect."

37. Other measures of predictability have been used in prior analyses of aid flows. Celasun and Walliser (2008) compare actual budget support disbursements with predicted disbursements, based on information available to the country in the preceding six months. Their study of eight African countries (all PRSC recipients) showed low prediction errors on the whole, with a small decline in prediction errors in the period 2000–04, compared with 1993–99. Analyses of the Budget Support Working Group of the Strategic Partnership with Africa (2004) measure predictability by comparing commitments with disbursements, which suggests some decline in the lost percentage (from 20 percent to 9 percent) over 2003 to 2004.

38. These results are broadly consistent with Celasun and Walliser (2008), although they suggest a somewhat lower reduction in predictability. However, their data cover only the first four years of our eight-year PRSC period and are based on different measures.

39. The remaining 24 operations were not included in the Country Assistance Strategy/Country Partnership Strategy because they came toward the end of the CAS period and were not predicted.

40. Using data from the Strategic Partnership with Africa (SPA) for 11 PRSC countries. Reduction in gaps between commitments and disbursements is erratic.

41. As set forth in the Interim Guidelines (World Bank 2003a. The importance of granting countries more policy space was discussed in the conditionality review of OPCS (World Bank 2005j). The subsequent update to this study (World Bank 2007b) finds that the Bank has been successful in the incorporation of such policy space, especially in the PRSC.

42. Also found by IDD and Associates (2006a) in the summary report of the evaluation of general budget support undertaken by OECD/DAC and ODI, which states that "alignment with government budget cycles is generally improving, with more efforts to align the cycle of partnership general budget support discussions with government budget calendars and to give reliable advance notice of disbursements."

43. Celasun and Walliser (2008) also comment on the pattern of backloading in SPA quarterly data. The high proportions of disbursements in the first quarter suggest an improvement over previous SPA findings, which indicated bunching in the second and third quarters (SPA 2004).

Chapter 3

1. IEG (2004).

2. Extremely strong affirmations from country clients may partly reflect a diplomatically polite response, a desire to protect ongoing programs, or hesitation about the independence of IEG. However, while these considerations may dilute the results reached, the broad direction would remain robust. Conclusions are based on such broad directions rather than on the precise percentages of responses. Note also that the OECD/DAC evaluation of general budget support (IDD and Associates 2006a) concurred in all of its seven case study countries, that budget support "contributed to greater policy alignment of aid," although the degree of this alignment depended ultimately on "the quality and ownership of government strategies."

3. Also pointed out in the ODI review of budget support in Ghana (Lawson and others 2007).

4. A finding echoed in previous studies of budget support aid (IDD and Associates 2006a; UK Audit Office 2007 and NORAD 2007).

5. A key potential benefit of budget support is enhanced interministerial dialogue in elevating sectoral is-

sues to the level of national policy dialogue (Koeberle and Stavreski 2005; IDD and Associates 2006a).

6. Donor harmonization issues including the joint Performance Assessment Framework are dealt with in greater depth in chapter 4.

7. An early IMF/World Bank joint review of the PRSP process that was largely comfortable with implementation was queried by external reviewers who pointed to the need for the articulation of the budget within the PRSC (Nilsson 2004, for SIDA).

8. Discussions of the extent to which annual reports for PRSPs (APRs) have been integrated into annual budget reporting are described in the Driscoll, Christiansen, and Booth (2005) report for Japan International Cooperation Agency (JICA), which concludes that integrated reporting on APRs within a common PAF framework and linkage to operationalization has only been partially achieved.

9. These data were collected at the request of the OECD-DAC joint venture on the monitoring of the Paris Declaration. They cover all countries that have had Poverty Reduction Strategies or interim or transitional versions of such strategies since March 2006. Forty-eight of the countries in the database are signatories to the Paris Declaration. The analysis scores countries in the database on a five-point scale to permit aggregation and comparison of results across groups of countries. More information on the database and its five-point LEADS scale is available in "Results-Based National Development Strategies" (World Bank 2007e).

10. Based on World Bank, BMZ, and GTZ 2007. The study provides descriptive information on the questions discussed. Numeric scores have been attributed by IEG, based on the information provided.

11. A more in-depth assessment of the role of the PRSC in reinforcing budget processes and strengthening public financial management is undertaken in chapter 5 of this study.

12. IDA participated actively in global roundtables on Managing for Development Results (2002, 2004, 2007). IDA's results measurement system was launched in 2002 and enhanced in 2004 to strengthen IDA's focus on results (World Bank 2009b).

13. World Bank 2005c, 2005f, 2005k. See also, World Bank 2008k.

14. Because the third series is incomplete, results by series are presented only for Series 1 and Series 2.

15. The first PRSC in Mozambique sought to use the PAF as a results framework.

16. One reason could be that these early operations sought to use the results frameworks of the jointly supported PAF.

17. Objectives are achieved with shortcomings to the following degrees—6: none; 5: minor; 4: moderate; 3: significant; 2: major; 1: severe.

18. Driscoll, Christiansen, and Booth (2005) attribute problems with indicators in part to the limited reporting built into the Annual Performance Review process, which ideally should feed into the PAF.

19. World Bank database.

20. Klugman 2008 examines results frameworks in Burkina Faso, Ghana, Madagascar, Mozambique, Rwanda, Tanzania, and Uganda, with reference to the three key requirements of the 2005 OPCS guidelines: (i) a results framework; (ii) a system of performance indicators; and (iii) arrangements for the collection of information.

21. M&E quality rating is a relatively new phenomenon for ICR Reviews, it has only been used as a standardized method since July 2006. As such, PRSCs evaluated in ICR Reviews before then do not carry this rating, although some include evaluative comments on the quality of M&E.

Chapter 4

1. World Bank (2001d).

2. World Bank 2005l.

3. World Bank (2006d, 2006f).

4. This chapter focuses largely on harmonization issues although the usual context in the Paris Declaration agenda is the wider concept of harmonization and alignment. The preceding chapter examines issues of PRSC alignment.

5. The PRSC has achieved prominence in budget expenditures in a limited number of countries; Rwanda and Uganda (about 10 percent of expenditures) and in Burkina Faso, Madagascar, and Tanzania (about 5 percent of expenditures).

6. Lawson, Gerster, and Hoole 2005b.

7. The relatively small donor budget support groups may be partly due to lack of interest, as the share of official development assistance in national income has declined. Also, the United States, which does not provide general budget support, has been a significant donor in some Eastern European countries. Moreover,

as these countries strive toward alignment with the European Union, government policymakers are reluctant to place poverty reduction at the center of their agendas. While they do not object to the budget support received under PRSCs, they are reluctant to commit to the PRSP/ PRSC instrument, which they perceive as typical for poorer countries.

8. Several additional signatories are not cofinanciers of the PRSC and enjoy observer status.

9. On this basis, early evaluations of budget support at a country level have distinguished between PAF general budget support and full general budget support with World Bank funds belonging in the latter category (IDD and Associates 2006b, Uganda country report). This underlines the stages necessary in the harmonization process to reach full agreement on a common basis for decisions.

10. Booth, Christiansen, and de Renzio (2005) point out that donors have focused their attention on working jointly and with governments on an agreed PAF that is broadly identified with the goals of the PRSP but quite different in character from the APR. These negotiations parallel the production and discussion of the APR.

11. Booth, Christiansen, and de Renzio (2005).

12. The divergence of reporting requirements was pointed out in Ethiopia, where the PAF matrix contained more than 100 indicators, in an attempt to meet the reporting requirements of all donors. In Tanzania, government reports to donors now use the Poverty Reduction Budget Support performance assessment framework, based on a single annual progress report.

13. The annual review of 2007 had 16 cosigners and also included contributions from the United Nations and nongovernmental organizations.

14. Ghana's sector budget support funds are also mentioned by Lawson and others 2007.

15. Lawson and others (2007) note in the ODI evaluation of multidonor budget support to Ghana that such support entailed lower transaction costs, although they were still perceived as "higher than necessary and amenable to further reductions." On the other hand, the 2005 ODI evaluation of general budget support to Tanzania (Lawson and others 2005a) was unable to reach a conclusion on whether GBS there had reduced transaction costs (particularly in line ministries) and noted that, if anything, the distribution of transaction costs had changed—that is, costs were lower in some areas but higher in others. The OECD/ DAC joint evaluation of general budget support (IDD and Associates 2006a) found that transaction costs often increased for client governments up front but then decreased later as aid was scaled up, provided other aid modalities such as project aid and sector baskets did not continue in parallel.

16. These drawbacks have not been perceived externally as a major issue. Recent evaluations of aid effectiveness in Vietnam by OECD-DAC and an International Monitoring Team (IMT) for the Vietnam Partnership Group on Aid Effectiveness (PGAE) both note that increasing budget support in general, and the PRSC in particular, represent the most effective mechanism in Vietnam to achieve the harmonization and alignment goals, which have been the two lagging areas of the Paris Declaration.

17. The amount released is calculated using the aggregate performance score in percentage terms. If less than 100 percent of the tranche is released, the remainder can be, and is in practice, carried forward to the next year.

18. The fixed tranche was intended originally to be pegged to the achievement of PRS benchmarks, as laid out in its indicators matrix.

19. Until that point most of the donors had split their commitments in half between the two tranches, but when faced with the implications of this for their disbursements, the UK, Canada, and the Netherlands decided to reduce their allocation to the performance tranche to 20 percent.

20. Country teams point to efforts emerging in the areas of agriculture, public financial management, education, natural resource management, health, and transport, where there are annual review meetings to discuss, among other things, capacity-building needs.

21. Disaggregated data (appendix table A4.10) show that while several PRSC countries had high proportions of coordinated missions (Benin, Cape Verde, Ghana, Madagascar), there were also high proportions of coordinated missions to other IDA countries with better CPIA scores (such as Bangladesh, Bolivia, Kenya, Papua New Guinea, Sierra Leone, and Yemen); and to countries such as Afghanistan and Côte d'Ivoire (37 percent and 65 percent of all missions, respectively), where security may have been an issue.

22. However, the data and results presented here are subject to caveats. Data represent two relatively prox-

imate years and thus cannot identify or reject sustained change. In many cases, the PRSC was concluded or ended before or after one or both of the dates in the series. There is an increase in the sample countries for the 2007 observations. The sample includes 20 of 27 PRSC countries for 2007, and 17 for both dates. IDA countries below CPIA 3.0 have only five countries with data points for both years. Finally, it is hard to measure the degree of actual participatory undertaking in joint missions or joint analytic work.

23. The surprisingly high proportion of joint Bank work for IDA countries in 2005 with CPIA <3.0 may reflect the inclusion of Afghanistan.

24. Benin, Burkina Faso, Ghana, Mozambique, Rwanda, Tanzania, Uganda, and Vietnam. Lao PDR and Madagascar also meet this criterion but are omitted due to lack of data for 2005.

25. See appendix table A4.2. In Vietnam, budget support in total aid increased from about 10 percent to 27 percent of aid between 2001 and 2007, and in Mozambique it increased from about 9 percent to 22 percent over the period.

26. About two-thirds of the respondents reported that there was a joint performance assessment framework shared by development partners providing budget support. This is greater than the proportion of countries that have already achieved a unified matrix and could be attributed partially to low response from some countries where there was a limited common approach, and also to perceptions of a common approach, even when full alignment has not been achieved, in some other countries.

27. As an example, "Transaction costs on the donor side are generally perceived to have risen substantially" (Germany 2008, p. 42).

28. Dabelstein and others 2008.

29. Netherlands evaluation, as cited in Dabelstein and others 2008.

Chapter 5

1. Devarajan, Swaroop, and Zou (1996); Reinikka and Svensson (2003). These follow Campos and Pradhan (1996), which shows how institutional arrangements surrounding budget processes affect the efficient use of public resources.

2. PRSC Interim Guidelines (World Bank 2001d).

3. Only countries with two or more PRSC operations are included in the review. As a result, PRSCs for Azerbaijan, Guyana, Honduras, Lesotho, Malawi, Mali, Moldova, Nepal, and Sri Lanka are not reviewed.

4. These findings limit attribution of results to PRSCs because the funds, conditionality, and dialogue provided by PRSCs are often combined with other interventions by the Bank and other donors. The relative importance of the PRSCs in this mix is hard to estimate.

5. World Bank (1998). The principles were: comprehensiveness and discipline, legitimacy, flexibility, predictability, contestability, honesty, information, and transparency and accountability. One tangible sign of the Bank's heightened realization of the importance of PFMP was a sharp increase in lending, from about 17 PFMP loans (including tax administration reform) per year during 1987–92, to about 41 per year during 2000–06.

6. IEG 2008a.

7. In 13 of the 22 countries, the country CAS proposed Development Policy Loans (DPLs) with PFM prior actions and conditions. Only four CASs proposed such lending prior to the completion of the CFAA/CPARs. Likewise, there were twice as many CASs with proposed PFM investment lending than was the case previously (Allen and others 2004).

8. Reports on the Observance of Standards and Codes (ROSCs), which are often undertaken jointly with Bank staff.

9. World Bank and IMF (2003b, 2004).

10. As applied in de Renzio and Dorotinsky (2007).

11. PRSC Interim Guidelines (World Bank 2001d). However, Bank policy under OP 8.60 spelled out requirements for the assessment of the country's overall fiduciary risks and can identify additional steps needed to secure acceptable fiduciary arrangements for the operation.

12. Cambodia's low CPIA scores were an obstacle to its receiving a PRSC (Minutes from the Regional Operations Committee meeting; January 31, 2007). Yet PRSCs have been approved for countries with low CPIAs if government commitment to reform is considered strong. For example, Lao PDR was approved for a PRSC with an overall CPIA score of 2.98 and a score of 2.5 on the public financial management component question of the CPIA.

13. Realism is needed to assess how quickly fiduciary risk levels can be improved (Shand 2006). Case studies from Uganda and Tanzania show how, in the

right environment, budget support aid can help to motivate PFMP improvements (Williamson 2005).

14. PRSC Interim Guidelines (World Bank 2001d).

15. Based on requirements of OP 8.60 and examples cited in the associated Good Practice Note 3.

16. In this and subsequent cases, we could not obtain enough evidence to rate all 21 series; thus one or more series were not rated.

17. In one, the first Uganda series, the PRSC emphasized budget formulation, an area little reflected in preceding analytical work. However, the second Uganda series showed improvement.

18. Armenia is an exception, where there was only one legally binding condition for PFMP in three PRSC operations, despite many shortcomings and recommendations flagged in previous analytic work.

19. Also found in chapter 3 of this report. This was assisted by new Bank guidance on results as well as increased experience. Guidance included, among others, World Bank 2002b; the Roundtables on Results in 2002 and 2004, the 2004 Bank-wide event, "Results: Everybody's Business"; the Managing for Results initiative, and the 2005 Paris Declaration.

20. Three series could not be rated for this question because of insufficient information.

21. Using a scaled-down version of the HIPC Assessment and Action Plan indicators. The first evaluative approach discussed in this paragraph is a before-and-after comparison, the later approach more closely approximates an objectives-based evaluative approach.

22. Based on de Renzio and Dorotinsky (2007). A scaled-down version is used here, applied to a larger set of countries, however, with added evidence from additional sources, where there is no PEFA or HIPC AAP to provide ex-ante or ex-post performance data.

23. Also in part due to the need to drop some indicators because of lack of comparability between HIPC AAP and PEFA.

24. There is no procurement score because this HIPC AAP indicator was not tracked by de Renzio and Dorotinsky (2007).

25. Which decentralized procurement to the line ministries and permits the use of e-Government procurement. With the passage of an accompanying decree, a detailed functional and technical design of a modern system of electronic government procurement appropriate to Armenia's needs is being prepared.

26. Such as use of noncompetitive practices. More work has also been identified, for example, to develop an electronic database of goods, works, and services; standardization of bidding documents; a pilot e-Tendering system; and developing a detailed design for the introduction of an e-Procurement system.

27. Question 13 is explained above. Question 14 measures the overall pattern of revenue mobilization—not only the tax structure as it exists on paper but revenue from all sources as they are actually collected. (World Bank 2006b).

28. The 1999–2006 time span is used because comparable CPIA data are available for these years and all the series evaluated took place during at least part of the period. The analysis is limited to question 13 because the areas measured by this question were the main focus areas of the PRSCs being evaluated.

29. Although the first PRSC was not approved until 2001, it is relevant to look at the period since 1999 because PFMP improvements between 1999 and the approval of the first PRSC may have helped to achieve entry conditions for PRSC support. Yet even looking at the shorter timespan of 2001–06, the difference between improvement on CPIA question 13 for PRSC countries (0.43) and for non-PRSC IDA and blend countries (0.05) remains statistically significant ($p = 0.0121$).

30. A similar question was asked of TTLs regarding how effective they found the raising of importance of the budget to be. Eighty-two percent of TTL responses stated they felt this to be very effective or just effective.

31. The joint OECD/DAC evaluation of general budget support (IDD and Associates 2006a) finds that budget systems were greatly strengthened in all countries that were able to bring general budget support funds on-budget and that line ministries have, as a result, engaged directly in the national budget process. Nonetheless, the report finds the need for greater "systematic collaboration" in supporting countries' national PFM capacity and a need to strengthen "links between public expenditure and policies."

Chapter 6

1. Albania, which is not an IDA country, received two PRSCs and is therefore added to the PRSC and IDA groups. Five PRSC countries are excluded because they received their first PRSC after 2005. They are: Georgia (FY06), Malawi (FY08), Mali (FY07), Moldova (FY07), and Lesotho (FY08). These countries were

omitted partly because the impact of their PRSCs would need time to show up and because some data only extend to 2006. Of the remaining 22 countries, 5 received only one PRSC (Azerbaijan, Guyana, Honduras, Nepal, and Sri Lanka). It would be tempting to exclude these countries as non-PRSC since they did not continue with a longer-term program of reforms supported by a series of PRSCs. In the interest of not biasing the sample, these five are considered PRSC countries. Eliminating them does not, however, materially change the results (appendix table A6.1). And five IDA countries are excluded from the comparator group due to data gaps: Afghanistan, Myanmar, São Tomé, Somalia, and Timor-Leste.

2. Although PRSCs were received at different times by the 22 countries, their performance is examined together for the period, 2000–07, and for the prior period, 1985–99. Even countries that received their first PRSC late spent a considerable period drafting and refining their poverty strategies, including the development of an I-PRSP (Interim Poverty Reduction Strategy Paper). PRSCs are generally single-tranche operations disbursed once the policy actions have been taken. It can be argued that the impact of the entire package of PRS and PRSC began before the actual approval of the credit. Appendix table A6.1 shows data for the full 27-country sample, the 22-country sample, and a smaller sample of 17 countries that have had two or more PRSCs. The differences are minor.

3. The source of this growth seems to derive particularly from accelerated growth in three countries, Armenia, Azerbaijan, and Ethiopia. Eliminating these countries during 2000–07 would reduce the overall PRSC growth rate to 3.4 percent, and raise the growth rate for 1985–99 to 1.6 percent.

4. Perry and others (2006). Surprisingly, little was said about agriculture in the recent Report of the Commission on Growth and Development (World Bank 2008j).

5. However, in the case studies developed for this review, five of the seven countries did have some actions related to agriculture, including a focus on increasing farm productivity and improving agro-processing in Armenia, and liberalization of the cotton sector in Benin.

6. Chapter 2 of this evaluation.

7. Before 2004, the CPIA consisted of 20 indicators.

8. Since CPIA scores are relatively stable over time, the intervening years are not shown.

9. Benin also suffered external shocks due to the closure of its border with Nigeria and a sharp drop in cotton prices.

10. This discussion is in terms of the headcount poverty measure. Appendix table A6.3 shows the results for the poverty gap and the squared poverty gap. The conclusions relative to the headcount measure do not change if these alternative measures of poverty are used.

11. Purchasing power parity adjusted, at 2005 prices.

12. The control group is smaller due to missing data. There are only about 56 IDA countries with poverty data, 21 PRSC, and 35 non-PRSC.

13. IEG (2009c).

14. The portfolio review covered the 36 PRSC series and 87 PRSC individual operations between fiscal 2001 and fiscal 2008, and included program documents (PDs) as well as Implementation Completion Reports (ICRs) and ICR reviews. The review focused on three sectors with the high potential impact on poverty reduction—health, education, and water supply and sanitation—and four topics of interest—objectives, design, monitoring and evaluation, and outcomes. Data were compiled using a standard questionnaire for each operation or series of operations.

15. Only the PRSCs for Malawi and Sri Lanka did not contain any objectives or conditions for health, education, or water supply and sanitation.

16. All sector-specific objectives mentioned, by frequency, are detailed in appendix table A6.4.

17. Not applicable: only one operation was completed or monitoring was not undertaken consistently, or results were unclear from the data provided.

18. Of the 23 PRSC series completed through fiscal 2008, ICRs and corresponding IEG ICR reviews are available for 19 with health and education components and 11 with water supply and sanitation components. Since overall PRSC objectives are generally not sector-specific, ICRs and ICR reviews do not provide a sector-specific outcome rating. However, there are sector-relevant ratings under headings such as "service delivery."

19. The 2006 IDD and Associates evaluation of general budget support also finds clear evidence of inputs but mixed evidence on outcomes. Despite greater spending on, and expansion of, basic services (especially

education and health), there was often a "deterioration in quality." On overall poverty outcomes, the authors note "clear links from [partnership general budget support] to improved basic services, through funding and through a collective commitment of donors and government to service delivery targets."

20. IEG (2009a).

21. Although outside the time of reference of this study, new information from a household survey of 2008 suggests that Ghana made further significant progress on most health-related Millennium Development Goals, compared with the survey of 2003.

22. The midpoint of the scale of 1–4 is 2.5; the midpoint of the scale of 1–6 is 3.5. Note that the four-point scale uses 1 as the best, so 2.0 is above the mean in a positive direction. However, the six-point scale uses 6 as the best; an above-average score would be higher than 3.5.

23. However, there are also some cases where the overall country program was rated *moderately satisfactory* even though the PRSC was *moderately unsatisfactory* (Ethiopia, Madagascar), while in one case the PRSC was *moderately satisfactory* but the country program was rated *moderately unsatisfactory* (Uganda).

24. Management notes that because PRSCs are, in fact, Development Policy Operations there is no surprise in noticing that the performance of DPOs with the PRSC title is similar to that of other policy-based operations. However, IEG notes that the analysis here refers to comparisons of PRSC countries with all IDA countries and not only those receiving other DPOs.

25. IEG analysis also shows that alternative definitions of PRSC operations do not materially affect these findings. IEG analyzed results on growth and poverty outcomes separately considering the omission from the PRSC sample of type-1 error PRSCs (that is, those operations that bear the PRSC name but that did not exhibit some implicit PRSC characteristics, such as sustained reform commitment or poverty-focused growth) as well as type-2 error PRSCs (that is, other IDA DPLs that could possibly have been considered PRSCs, although some implicit PRSC characteristics may have been absent). The underlying conclusion that PRSC countries do not significantly outperform others remains robust.

Chapter 7

1. Management points out that according to Bank policy (OP 8.60, paragraph 6), the Bank advises borrowers to consult with key stakeholders and engage their participation in formulating development strategies. It is not the Bank's responsibility, therefore, to engage in such consultations.

2. The OECD/DAC evaluation of general budget support in seven countries (IDD and Associates 2006a) also found that parallel off-budget aid persists, undermining progress on the use of budget mechanisms. The ODI joint evaluation of multi-donor budget support to Ghana (Lawson and others 2007) had similar findings.

ActionAid International. 2006. *What Progress? A Shadow Review of World Bank Conditionality*. Johannesburg: ActionAid.

Alesina, Alberto, and David Dollar. 2000. "Who Gives Foreign Aid to Whom and Why?" *Journal of Economic Growth* 5 (1): 33–63.

Alexander, Nancy. 2008. "Budget Support and the New Approach to Conditionality: How the World Bank Contravenes Its 'Good Practice Principles' for Conditionality." Report to the U.S. House of Representatives, Financial Services Committee. World Bank, Washington, D.C.

Allen, Richard, S. Schiavo-Campo, and T.C. Garrity. 2004. *Assessing and Reforming Public Financial Management: A New Approach*. Washington, D.C.: World Bank.

Barro, Robert. 1998. *Determinants of Economic Growth: A Cross-Country Empirical Study*. Cambridge, Mass: MIT Press.

Barro, Robert, and Xavier Sala-i-Martin. 1997. "Technological Diffusion, Convergence, and Growth." *Journal of Economic Growth* 2 (1): 1–26.

Batley, Richard, and George A. Larbi. 2004. *Changing Role of Government: The Reform of Public Services in Developing Countries*. Basingstoke Hampshire (UK): Palgrave Macmillan.

Bojö, Jan, Kenneth Green, Sunanda Kishore, Sumith Pilapitiya, and Rama Chandra Reddy. 2004. "Environment in Poverty Reduction Strategies and Poverty Reduction Credits." Paper No. 102. Environment Department, World Bank, Washington, D.C.

Booth, David, Karin Christiansen, and Paolo de Renzio. 2005. "Reconciling Alignment and Performance in Budget-Support Programmes: What's Next?" World Bank conference, Practitioners Forum on Budget Support, Cape Town, South Aftrica, May 5–6.

Bourguignon, Francois, and S.R. Chakravarty. 1999. "A Family of Multidimensional Poverty Measures." In D.J. Slottje, ed., *Advances in Econometrics, Income Distribution and Methodology of Science: Essays in Honor of C. Dagum*. London: Springer-Verlag.

Bourguignon, Francois, and Danny Leipziger. 2006. *Aid, Growth, and Poverty Reduction: Toward a New Partnership Model*. Washington, D.C.: World Bank.

Brautigam, Deborah, and Stephen Knack. 2004. "Foreign Aid, Institutions, and Governance in Sub-Saharan Africa." *Economic Development and Cultural Change* 52(2): 255–85.

Brumby, Jim. 1999. "Budgeting Reforms in OECD Member Countries." In Salvatore Schiavo-Campo and Daniel Tommasi, eds., *Managing Government Expenditure*. Manila: Asian Development Bank.

Bulir, A., and A.J. Hamann. 2003. "Aid Volatility: An Empirical Assessment." *IMF Staff Papers* 50(1): 64–89.

———. 2008. "Volatility of Development Aid: From the Frying Pan into the Fire?" *World Development* 36 (10): 2045–102.

Burnside, Craig, and David Dollar. 2000. "Aid, Policies, and Growth." *American Economic Review* 90 (4): 847–68.

Calderisi, Robert. 2006. *The Trouble with Africa: Why Foreign Aid Isn't Working*. New York: Palgrave MacMillan.

Campos, Ed, and Sanjay Pradhan. 1996. "Budgetary Institutions and Expenditure Outcomes: Binding Governments to Fiscal Performance." Policy Research Department, World Bank, Washington, D.C.

Celasun, Oya, and Jan Walliser. 2008. "Predictability of Aid: Do Fickle Donors Undermine Economic Development?" *Economic Policy* 23 (7): 545–94.

Chauvet, L., and P. Guillaumont. 2007. "Aid, Volatility and Growth Again: When Aid Volatility Matters and When It Does Not." CERDI, Etudes et Documents, Clermont-Ferrand: Université d'Auvergne.

Ciccone, Antonio, and Marek Jarocinski. 2008. "Determinants of Economic Growth: Will Data Tell?" ECB Working Paper No. 852. European Central Bank, Frankfurt.

Collier, Paul. 1997. "The Failure of Conditionality" In *Perspectives on Aid and Development Policy,* eds., C. Gwin and J. Nelson. Washington, D.C.: Overseas Development Council.

———. 1999. "Aid Dependency: A Critique." *Journal of African Economies* 8 (4): 528–45.

———. 2007. *The Bottom Billion: Why the Poorest Countries Are Failing and What Can Be Done About It.* Oxford, UK: Oxford University Press.

———. 2009. *Wars, Guns, and Votes: Democracy in Dangerous Places*. New York. HarperCollins.

Collier, Paul, Patrick Guillamont, S. Guillaumont, and Jan Willem Gunning. 1997. "Redesigning Conditionality," *World Development* 25 (9): 1399–407.

Corbo, Vittorio, and Patricio Rojas. 1991. "World Bank–Supported Adjustment Programs: Country Performance and Effectiveness." Country Economics Department Working Paper 623. World Bank, Washington, DC.

Corbo, Vittorio, Stanley Fischer, Steven Webb. 1992. "Adjustment Lending Revisited: Policies to Restore Growth." A World Bank Symposium.

Dabelstein and others. 2008. *Evaluation of the Implementations of the Paris Declaration: Synthesis Report.*

Dasgupta, Partha. 1995. *An Inquiry into Well-being and Destitution*. Oxford, UK: Oxford Univ. Press.

———. 2004. *Well-being and the Natural Environment*. Oxford, UK: Oxford University Press

Datt, Gaurav, and Martin Ravallion. 1992. "Growth and Redistribution Components of Changes in Poverty Measures: A Decomposition with Applications to Brazil and India in the 1980s." *Journal of Development Economics* 38 (2): 275–95.

de Renzio, Paolo, and James Dorotinsky. 2007. "Tracking Progress in the Quality of PFM Systems in HIPCs—An Update on Past Assessments Using PEFA Data." PEFA Secretariat, World Bank, Washington, D.C.

de Renzio, Paolo, and Warren Krafchik. 2007. "Budget Monitoring and Policy Influence—Lessons from Civil Society Budget Analysis and Advocacy Initiatives." Briefing Paper 16. Overseas Development Institute, London.

de Soto, Hernando. 1989. *The Other Path: The Invisible Revolution in the Third World*. New York: Harper and Row.

Department for International Development (DfID). 2006. "Assessing the Volatility of International Aid Flows." DfID, London.

———. 2007. "Donor Consultation on Parliamentary Development and Financial Accountability Report." Hosted by the Government of Belgium, May 21–22, Brussels, Belgium.

———. 2008. "Poverty Reduction Budget Support." A DfID policy paper. DfID, London.

Devarajan, Shantayanan, Andrew Sunil Rajkumar, and Vinaya Swaroop. 1999. "What Does Aid to Africa Finance?" Development Research Group, World Bank, Washington, D.C.

Devarajan, Shantayanan, Vinaya Swaroop, and Heng-fu Zou. 1996. "The Composition of Public Expenditure and Economic Growth." *Journal of Monetary Economics* 37 (2): 313–44.

Dollar, David, and Craig Burnside. 1997. "Aid Policies and Growth." *The American Economic Review* 90 (4):847–68.

Dollar, David, and Paul Collier. 2002. "Aid Allocation and Poverty Reduction." *European Economic Review* 46 (8):1475–1500.

Dollar, David, and Aart Kraay. 2002. "Growth is Good for the Poor." *Journal of Economic Growth* 7 (3): 195–225.

———. 2004. "Trade, Growth, and Poverty." *The Economic Journal* 114 (493):F22–F49.

Dollar, David, and Lant Pritchard. 1998. "Assessing Aid." World Bank, Washington, D.C.

Dollar, David, and Jakob Svensson. 2000. *What Explains the Success or Failure of Structural Adjustment Programmes*. Oxford, UK: Blackwell Publishers.

Donovan, Donal. 1981. "Real Responses Associated with Exchange Rate Action in Selected Upper Credit Tranche Stabilization Programs." *IMF Staff Papers* 28 (4): 698–727. International Monetary Fund, Washington, D.C.

———. 1982. "Macroeconomic Performance and Adjustment under Fund-Supported Programs: The Experience of the Seventies." *IMF Staff Papers* 29 (2): 171–203. International Monetary Fund, Washington, D.C.

Dorotinsky, W., and S. Pradhan. 2007. "Exploring Corruption in Public Financial Management." In J. E. Campos and S. Pradhan, eds., *The Many Faces of Corruption*. Washington, D.C.: World Bank.

Doucouliagos, Hristos, and Martin Paldam. 2005. "The Aid Effectiveness Literature. The Sad Result of 40 Years of Research." Department of Economics, Working Paper 2005–15, University of Aarhus, Department of Economics, Aarhus, Denmark.

Driscoll, Ruth, Karin Christiansen, David Booth. 2005. "Progress Reviews and Performance Assessment in Poverty-Reduction Strategies and Budget Support: A Survey of Current Thinking and Practice." ODI and JICA, London and Tokyo.

Durlauf, Steven, Andros Kourtellos, and Ching Ming Tan. 2008. "Are Any Growth Theories Robust?" *The Economic Journal* 118 (March): 329–46.

Easterly, William. 1999. "The Ghost of Financing Gap: Testing the Growth Model of the International Financial Institutions." *Journal of Development Economics* 60 (2): 423–38.

———. 2003. "Can Foreign Aid Buy Growth?" *Journal of Economic Perspectives* 17 (3): 23–48.

———. 2005. "What Did Structural Adjustment Adjust?" *Journal of Development Economics* 76 (1): 1–22.

Easterly, William, M. Kremer, L. Pritchett, and L. Summers. 1993. "Good Policy or Good Luck? Country Growth Performance and Temporary Shocks." *Journal of Monetary Economics* 32 (3): 459–83.

Easterly, William, Ross Levine, and David Roodman. 2003. "New Data, New Doubts: Revisiting Aid, Policies, and Growth." Working Paper Number 26. Center for Global Development, Washington, D.C.

Eifert, B., and A. Gelb. 2005. "Improving the Dynamics of Aid: Toward More Predictable Budget Support." In S. Koeberle, Z. Stravreski, and J. Walliser, eds., *Budget Support as More Effective Aid?: Recent Experiences and Emerging Lessons*. Washington, DC: World Bank.

Elbadawi, Ibrahim. 1992a. "Have World Bank-Supported Adjustment Programs Improved Economic Performance in Sub-Saharan Africa?" Working Paper No. WPS 1000, World Bank, Washington, D.C.

———. 1992b. "World Bank Adjustment Lending and Economic Performance in Sub-Saharan Africa in the 1980s: A Comparison of Early Adjusters, Late Adjusters, and Nonadjusters." Policy Working Paper No. 1001, World Bank, Washington, D.C.

Elbadawi, Ibrahim, and John Randa. 2003. "Assessing the Development Impact of CDF-Like Experiences." IEG Working Paper. World Bank, Washington, D.C.

Elbers, Chris, Jan Willem Gunning, and Kobus de Hoop. 2009. "Assessing Sector-Wide Programs with Statistical Impact Evaluation." *World Development* 37 (2): 513–20.

European Commission. 2001. "Report on the Management, Monitoring and Control Arrangements Governing the Use of Counterpart Funds and Budgetary Support in Development Aid." Internal Audit Service, Brussels.

Gelb, Alan, Brian Ngo, and Xiao Ye. 2004. "Implementing Performance-Based Aid in Africa: The Country Policy and Institutional Assessment." Africa Region Working Paper Series No. 77. World Bank, Washington, D.C.

Germany, Federal Ministry for Economic Cooperation and Development. 2008. *Evaluation of the Implementation of the Paris Declaration: Case Study of Germany.* Bonn: BMZ.

Gerster, Richard. 2005. "Risks of General Budget Support: A Tale of Experience." Summary document on GBS for Swiss Seco.

Gilbert, Christopher, Andrew Powell, and David Vines. 1999. "Positioning the World Bank." *Economic Journal* 109.

Global Integrity. 2008. "Global Integrity Report: Global Integrity Indicators" http://www.globalintegrity.org Last accessed 06/12/2009.

Goldsmith, Arthur. 2007. "Is Governance Reform a Catalyst for Development?" *Governance: An International Journal of Policy, Administration, and Institutions* 20 (2): 165–86.

Goldstein, Morris, and Peter Montiel. 1986. "Evaluating Fund Stabilization Programs with Multicountry Data: Some Methodological Pitfalls." *IMF Staff Papers* 33 (2): 304. International Monetary Fund, Washington, D.C.

Grindle S., Merilee. 2004. "Good Enough Governance: Poverty Reduction and Reform in Developing Countries." *Governance: An International Journal of Policy, Administration, and Institutions* 17(4).

Haque, Nadeem, and Mohsin Kahn. 1998. "Do IMF-Supported Programs Work?: A Survey of the Cross-Country Empirical Evidence." IMF Working Paper No. 96/169. International Monetary Fund, Washington, D.C.

IDA and IMF (2008) "Heavily Indebted Poor Countries Initiative and MDRI Initiative. Status of Implementation." September.

IDD and Associates. 2006a. "Evaluation of General Budget Support: Synthesis Report." *Joint Evaluation of General Budget Support, 1994–2004: Burkina Faso, Malawi, Mozambique, Nicaragua, Rwanda, Uganda, Vietnam.* Commissioned on behalf of the OECD-DAC Evaluation Network. International Development Department, School of Public Policy, University of Birmingam, Birmingham, U.K.

———. 2006b. "Uganda Country Report." *Joint Evaluation of General Budget Support, 1994–2004: Burkina Faso, Malawi, Mozambique, Nicaragua, Rwanda, Uganda, Vietnam.* Commissioned on behalf of the OECD-DAC Evaluation Network. International Development Department, School of Public Policy, University of Birmingam, Birmingham, U.K.

———. 2007. "Evaluation of General Budget Support—Note on Approach and Methods A Joint Evaluation of General Budget Support." 1994–2004

IEG (Independent Evaluation Group). 1986. *Adjustment Lending: A First Review of Experience,* Operations Evaluation. Report No. 6409. World Bank, Washington, D.C.

———. 1997. *Annual Review of Development Effectiveness: The State in a Changing World.* World Bank, Washington, D.C.

———. 1998. *The Impact of Public Expenditure Reviews: An Evaluation*. World Bank, Washington, D.C.

———. 1999. *Annual Review of Development Effectiveness: Toward a Comprehensive Development Strategy*. World Bank, Washington, D.C.

———. 2000. *Evaluation and Poverty Reduction: Proceedings from a World Bank Conference.* World Bank, Washington, D.C.

———. 2003. *Toward Country-Led Development: A Multi-Partner Evaluation of the Comprehensive Development Framework: Synthesis Report*. World Bank, Washington, D.C.

———. 2004. *The Poverty Reduction Strategy Initiative. An Independent Evaluation of the World Bank's Support Through 2003*. World Bank, Washington, D.C.

———. 2006. "Debt Relief for the Poorest: An Evaluation Update of the HIPC Initiative." IEG Special Study. World Bank, Washington, D.C.

———. 2008a. "Project Performance Assessment Report: Ethiopia Poverty Reduction Support Credits 1–2." World Bank, Washington, D.C.

———. 2008b. "Country Financial Accountability Assessments and Country Procurement Assessment Reports: How Effective Are World Bank Fiduciary Diagnostics?" World Bank, Washington, D.C.

———. 2008c. "Public Sector Reform: What Works and Why?" World Bank, Washington, D.C.

———. 2009a. "Improving Effectiveness and Outcomes for the Poor in Health, Nutrition, and Population." World Bank, Washington, D.C.

———. 2009b. "The World Bank's Country Policy and Institutional Assessment." Draft, June. World Bank, Washington, D.C.

———. 2009c. "How Effective Have Poverty and Social Impact Analyses Been?: An IEG Study of World Bank Support to PSIAs." World Bank. Washington, D.C.

IMF (International Monetary Fund). 1998 (revised 2001). "Code of Good Practices on Fiscal Transparency." International Monetary Fund, Washington, D.C. http://www.imf.org/external/np/fad/trans/code.htm.

Iyer, Param, Barbara Evans, Jason Cardosi, and Norman Hicks. 2005. "Operational Guidance for World Bank Group Staff in Rural Water Supply, Sanitation and Budget Support—Guidelines for Task Teams." Water Supply and Sanitation Sector Board, World Bank, Washington, D.C.

Jayarajah, Carl, William Branson, and Binayak Sen. 1996. "Social Dimensions of Adjustment: World Bank Experience, 1980–93." World Bank, Washington, D.C.

Kharas, Homi. 2007. "The New Reality of Aid." Presented at the 2007 Brookings Blum Roundtable, Session I: Fighting Global Poverty: Who'll Be Relevant in 2020? Wolfensohn Center for Development, Brookings Institution, Washington, D.C.

Killick, Tony. 1996. "Principals, Agents and the Limitations of BWI Conditionality." *World Economy* 19 (2): 211–29.

———. 1999. "Making Adjustment Work for the Poor." ODI Poverty Briefing 5. Overseas Development Institute, London.

———. 2005. "Did Conditionality Streamlining Succeed?" In Stefan Koeberle, Harold Bedoya, Peter Silarsky, and Gero Verheyen, eds., *Conditionality Revisited: Concepts, Experiences, and Lessons*. Washington, D.C.: World Bank.

Killick, Tony, Ramani Gunatilaka, and Ana Marr. 1998. "Aid and the Political Economy of Policy Change." ODI Report, Joint Library Catalogue. Overseas Development Institute, London.

Klugman, Jeni. 2008. "Poverty Reduction Support Credit Results Frameworks: A Partial Review of Practices and Constraints in the Africa Region." World Bank, Washington, D.C.

Knack, Stephen, and Philip Keefer. 1995. "Institutions and Economic Performance: Cross-Country Tests Using Alternative Institutional Measures." *Economics & Politics* 7 (3): 207–27.

Knack, Stephen, Mark Kugler, and Nick Manning. 2003. "'Second Generation' Governance Indicators." Global Corruption Report 2003. Transparency International, Berlin.

Knoll, Martin. 2008. "Budget Support: A Reformed Approach or Old Wine in New Skins?" Discussion Paper No. 190. United Nations Conference on Trade and Development, Geneva, Switzerland.

Koeberle, Stefan. 2003. "Should Policy-Based Lending Still Involve Conditionality?" *World Bank Research Observer* 18 (2): 249.

———. 2005. "World Bank Conditionality—Issues, Trends and Perspectives." Presentation at Development Policy Forum, Berlin.

Koeberle, Stefan, and Zoran Stavreski. 2005. "Budget Support: Concept and Issues." Practioners' forum on Budget Support, May 5–6, Cape Town, South Africa.

Kraay, Aart. 2004. "When Is Growth Pro-Poor? Cross-Country Evidence." IMF Working Paper 04/47, International Monetary Fund, Washington, D.C.

Lawson, Andrew, and David Booth. 2004. "Evaluation Framework for General Budget Support, Evaluation Framework, Report to Management Group for the Joint Evaluation of General Budget Support." Overseas Development Institute, London.

Lawson, Andrew, David Booth, Meleki Msuya, Samuel Wangwe and Tim Williamson. 2005a. "Does General Budget Support Work?: Evidence from Tanzania." Overseas Development Institute, London, and Daima Associates, Dar es Salaam.

Lawson, Andrew, Richard Gerster, and David Hoole. 2005b. "Learning from Experience with Performance Assessment Frameworks for General Budget Support: Synthesis Report." Swiss State Secretariat for Economic Affairs.

Lawson, Andrew, Gyimah Boadi, Ato Ghartey, Adom Ghartey, Tony Killick, Zainab Kizilbash Agha, and Tim Williamson. 2007. "Ghana 2007 Joint Evaluation of Multi-Donor Budget Support to Ghana: Report to the Government of Ghana and to the MDBS Partners." ODI-CDD, London.

Lensink, R., and O. Morrissey. 2000. "Aid Instability as a Measure of Uncertainty and the Positive Impact of Aid on Growth." *Journal of Development Studies* 36 (3): 31–49.

Mallaby, Sebastian. 2004. *The World's Banker: A Story of Failed States, Financial Crises, and the Wealth and Poverty of Nations*. London: Penguin Press.

Managing for Development Results. 2008. "Emerging Good Practice for Managing Development Results, Third Edition." MfDR Secretariat, World Bank, Washington, D.C.

Mauro, Paolo. 1995. "Corruption and Growth." *Quarterly Journal of Economics*. 110:3.

Miovic, Peter. 2004. "Poverty Reduction Support Credits: Results of a Stocktaking Study." Africa Region, World Bank, Washington, D.C.

Morrissey, Oliver. 2004. "Alternatives to Conditionality in Policy-Based Lending." Discussion Paper, University of Nottingham Credit and School of Economics, UK.

———. 2005. "Fungibility, Prior Actions and Eligibility for Budget Support." Abstract. University of Nottingham Credit and School of Economics, UK.

Mosely, Paul, Jabe Harrigan, and John Toye. 1991. *Aid and Power: The World Bank and Policy-based Lending*. London: Routledge.

Moyo, Dambisa. 2009. *Dead Aid: Why Aid Is Not Working and How There Is Another Way for Africa.* New York: Farrar, Straus, and Giroux.

Nilsson, Maria. 2004. "Effects of Budget Support: A Discussion of Early Evidence." Department of Evaluation and Internal Audit, Working Paper 2004:4, Swedish International Development Cooperation Agency, Stockholm.

NORAD (North American Aerospace Defense Command). 2007. *Norway's Provision of Budget Support to Developing Countries: Guidelines.* On behalf of the Norwegian Ministry of Foreign Affairs, NORAD, Oslo.

OECD. 1995. "Budgeting for Results: Perspectives on Public Expenditure Management." OECD, Paris.

———. 2006. "Survey on Monitoring the Paris Declaration: Overview of the Results." OECD, Paris.

———. 2008. "Survey on Monitoring the Paris Declaration: Making Aid More Effective by 2010." OECD, Paris.

———. 2009. Aid Aggregates Statistics Database. http://stats.oecd.org/qwids.

OECD-DAC. 1996. "Shaping the 21st Century: The Contribution of Development." OECD, Paris.

OECD. 2003. OECD International Database of Budget Practices and Procedures. http://www.oecd.org/gov/budget/database.

Paris Declaration International Working Group. 2009. "Approach Paper for the Phase 2 Evaluation of the Paris Declaration." Unpublished.

Paris Declaration on Aid Effectiveness. "Ownership, Harmonization, Alignment, Results, and Mutual Accountability." High-Level Forum, Paris, February 28–March 2.

Perry, Guillermo, J. Humberto Lopez, and William F. Maloney. 2006. *Poverty Reduction and Growth: Virtuous and Vicious Cycles*. World Bank: Washington, D.C.

Picciotto, Robert, and Eduardo Wiesner. 1998. *Evaluation and Development: The Institutional Development*. World Bank Series on Evaluation and Development. World Bank, Washington, D.C.

Political Risk Services Group. 2008. "International Country Risk Guide." PRS Group, East Syracuse, N.Y.

Premchand, A. 1990. "Management of Public Money: Issues on Government Financial Management." In A. Premchand, ed., *Government Financial Management: Issues and Country Studies*. International Monetary Fund, Washington, D.C.

Rajan, Raghuram, and Arvind Subramanian. 2006. "What Undermines Aid's Impact on Growth." NBER Working Paper No. 11657. National Bureau of Economic Research, Cambridge, MA.

———. 2008. "Aid and Growth: What Does the Cross-Country Evidence Really Show?" *Review of Economics and Statistics* 90 (4): 653–65.

Ravallion, Martin, and Shaohua Chen. 2003. "Measuring Pro-Poor Growth." *Economics Letters* 78 (1): 93–99.

Ravallion, Martin, and Gaurav Datt. 2002. "Why Has Economic Growth Been More Pro-Poor in Some States of India than Others?" *Journal of Development Economics* 68: 381–400.

Reichmann, T., and R. Stillson. 1978. "Experience with Programs of Balance of Payments Adjustment: Stand-by Arrangements in the Higher Credit Tranches, 1963–72." *IMF Staff Papers* 25 (June): 119– 39. International Monetary Fund, Washington, D.C.

Reinikka, Ritva, and Jakob Svensson. 2003. "The Power of Information: Evidence from a Newspaper Campaign to Reduce Capture." Policy Research Working Paper No. 3239. World Bank, Washington, D.C. http://go.worldbank.org/QY1IJKNM70.

———. 2005. "Fighting Corruption to Improve Schooling: Evidence from a newspaper campaign in Uganda." *Journal of the European Economic Association* 3 (2–3): 1–9.

Rice, Susan, and Stewart Patrick. 2008. "Index of State Weakness in the Developing World." Brookingss Institution, Washington, D.C. http://www.brookings.edu/~/media/Files/rc/reports/2008/02_weak_states_index/02_weak_states_index. pdf.

Robinson, M. 2006. "Budget Analysis and Policy Advocacy: The Role of Non-Governmental Public Action." IDS Working Paper 279. Institute of Development Studies.

Rodrik, Dani. 1997. *Has Globalization Gone Too Far?* Peterson Institute for International Economics, Washington, D.C.

———. 2005. "Why We Learn Nothing from Regressing Economic Growth on Policies." Unpublished, Kennedy School of Government, Harvard University, Cambridge, MA.

Rodrik, Dani, Arvind Subramanian, and Francesco Trebbi. 2004. "The Primacy of Institutions Over Geography and Integration in Economic Development." *Journal of Economic Growth* 9 (2): 131–65.

Ronsholt, Frans. 2008. "PEFA Assessments in PFM—Creating a Common Information Pool." Presented at DAC conference on *Whole of Government Approaches to PFM in Fragile States*, PEFA Secretariat, Paris, March 17–18.

Roodman, David. 2004. "The Anarchy of Numbers: Aid, Development, and Cross-Country Empirics." Center for Global Development, Washington, D.C.

Rubin, Irene S., and Joanne Kelly. 2005. "Budget and Accounting Reforms." In Ewan Ferlie, Laurence E. Lynn, Jr. and Christopher Pollitt, eds., *The Oxford Handbook of Public Management*. Oxford: Oxford University Press.

Sachs, Jeffrey. 1989. "Conditionality, Debt Relief and the Developing Country Debt Crisis." In J.D. Sachs (ed.) *Developing Country Debt and Economic Performance*. Chicago IL: University of Chicago Press.

Sala-i-Martin, Xavier, Gernot Doppelhofer, and Ronald Miller. 2004. "Determinants of Long-Term Growth: A Bayesian Averaging of Classical Estimates (BACE) Approach." *American Economic Review* 94 (4).

Santiso, Carlos. 2006. "Banking on Accountability?: Strengthening Budget Oversight and Public Sector Auditing in Emerging Economies." *Public Budgeting and Finance* 26 (2): 66–100.

Schiavo-Campo, S., and D. Tommasi. 1999. "Managing Government Expenditure." Asian Development Bank, Manila.

Sen, Amartya K. 1985. *Commodities and Capabilities*. Oxford: Oxford University Press.

———. 1999. *Development As Freedom*. New York: Knopf.

Shand, David. 2001. "Changing Perspectives in the World Bank on Asia and Other Regions." In Lawrence Jones, James Guthrie and Peter Steane, eds., *Learning from International Public Management Reform*. Oxford: Elsevier Science.

———. 2006. "Managing Fiduciary Issues in Budget Support Operations." In Stefan Koeberle, Zoran Stavreski, and Jan Walliser, eds., *Budget Support as More Effective Aid?: Recent Experiences and Emerging Lessons*. Washington, D.C.: World Bank

Stern, Elliot. 2008. "Thematic Study on the Paris Declaration, Aid Effectiveness and Development Effectiveness." Evaluation of the Paris Declaration, Phase I. Development Assistance Research Associates, Paris.

Stevens, Mike. 2004. "Institutional and Incentive Issues in Public Financial Management Reform In Poor Countries." PEFA, Washington, D.C.

Stewart, Frances. 1991. "The Many Faces of Adjustment." *World Development* 19 (12).

Stiglitz, Joseph. 1997. "An Agenda for Development for the Twenty-First Century." *Annual Conference on Development Economics*, Washington, D.C., April 30–May 1.

———. 1998. "Towards a New Paradigm for Development: Strategies, Policies, and Processes." Prebisch Lecture, UNCTAD, Geneva, October 19.

Strategic Partnership with Africa (SPA). 2004. "Survey of the Alignment of Budget Support and Balance of Payments Support with National PRS Processes for 2004." SPA-6 Budget Support Working Group (BSWG).

———. 2006. "Strategic Partnership with Africa: Survey of Budget Support, 2005." SPA-6 Budget Support Working Group (BSWG).

———. 2007. "Strategic Partnership with Africa: Survey of Budget Support, 2006." SPA-6 Budget Support Working Group (BSWG).

———. 2008. "Strategic Partnership with Africa: Survey of Budget Support, 2007." SPA-6 Budget Support Working Group (BSWG).

———. 2009. SPA Budget Support Alignment Survey: Results Database, http://www.spasurvey.info/. Last accessed June 2, 2009.

Svensson, Jakob. 2003. "Why Conditional Aid Doesn't Work and What Can Be Done About It?" *Journal of Development Economics* 70 (2): 381–402.

Tavares, Jóse. 2003. "Does Foreign Aid Corrupt?" *Economics Letters* 79 (1): 99–106.

Transparency International. 2008. *Corruption Perceptions Index*. Transparency International, Berlin.

United Kingdom National Audit Office. 2007. "Department for International Development: Providing Budget Support to Developing Countries." Report by the Comptroller and Auditor General.

United Nations. 2000. *Millennium Development Goals*.

Ware, G. T., S. Moss, J. Campos, and G. Noone. 2007. "Corruption in Public Procurement: a Perennial Challenge" in J. E. Campos and S. Pradhan, eds., *The Many Faces of Corruption*. Washington, D.C.: World Bank.

Wescott, Clay. 2008. "World Bank Support for Public Financial Management: Conceptual Roots and Evidence of Impact." IEG Working Paper. World Bank, Washington, D.C.

White, Howard. 2005. "Dollars, Dialogue, and Development: An Evaluation of Swedish Program Aid." SIDA Evaluation Report. SIDA, Stockholm.

White, Howard, and Geske Dijkstra. 2003. *Programme Aid and Development: Beyond Conditionality*. London: Routledge.

Williamson, John. 1990. "What Washington Means by Policy Reform." In John Williamson, ed., *Latin American Adjustment: How Much Has Happened?* Washington, D.C.: Peterson Institute for International Economics.

Williamson, Tim. 2005. "General Budget Support and Public Financial Management Reform." In Stefan Koeberle, Zoran Stavreski, and Jan Walliser, eds., *Budget Support as More Effective Aid?: Recent Experiences and Emerging Lessons*. Washington, D.C.: World Bank.

Wolfensohn, James. 1997. "The Challenge of Inclusion." World Bank Annual Meetings, Hong Kong.

———. 1998. "The Other Crisis." Address to Board of Governors, World Bank, Washington, D.C.

Wood, Angela. 2005. "World Bank's Poverty Reduction Support Credit—Continuity or Change?" Debt and Development Coalition, Dublin, Ireland.

Wood, Bernard, Dorte Kabell, Nansozi Muwanga, and Francisco Sagasti. 2008. "Evaluation of the Implementation of the Paris Declaration, Phase One." Kabell Konsulting ApS.

World Bank. 1967. Commission on International Development (Pearson Report). Washington, D.C.

———. 1970. "International Organizations and the Generation of the Will to Change." Report of the Commission on International Development (Pearson Report). UAI Study Papers INF/5. Washington, D.C.

———. 1981. "Accelerated Development in Sub-Saharan Africa: An Agenda for Action." (Elliot Berg Report). Washington, D.C.

———. 1988. "Adjustment Lending: An Evaluation of Ten Years of Experience." Country Economics Department, World Bank, Washington, D.C.

———. 1990. "Report on Adjustment Lending II: Policies for the Recovery of Growth." Country Economics Department, World Bank, Washington, D.C.

———. 1992a. "The Third Report on Adjustment Lending: Private and Public Resources for Growth." Report No. R92-47, IDA/R92-29. Washington, D.C.

———. 1992b. "Guidance to Bank Staff on Adjustment Lending." Washington, D.C.

———. 1994. "Adjustment in Africa: Reforms, Results, and the Road Ahead." World Bank Policy Research Report. New York: Oxford University Press.

———. 1997. *World Development Report: The State in a Changing World*. Washington, D.C.

———. 1998. *Public Expenditure Management Handbook*. Washington, D.C.

———. 1999. "HIPC Initiative: Strengthening the Link between Debt Relief and Poverty Reduction." Development Committee DC/99-24 (E). Washington, D.C.

———. 2000a. "Supporting Country Development: World Bank Role and Instruments in Low- and Middle-Income Countries." Discussion draft. OPCS. Washington, D.C.

———. 2000b. "Guidelines for Programmatic Adjustment Loans / Credits" Washington, D.C.

———. 2001a. "Adjustment Lending Retrospective." Operations Policy and Country Services, Washington, D.C.

———. 2001b. "Guidelines for the World Bank's Work on Public Expenditure Analysis and Support (including PERs)." Draft report. Public Sector Group, Poverty Reduction and Economic Management Network. Washington, D.C.

———. 2001c. *Aid and Reform in Africa. Lessons from Ten Case Studies*. Washington, DC: World Bank.

———. 2001d. "Interim Guidelines for Poverty Reduction Support Credits." OPCS. Washington, D.C.

———. 2002a. *World Development Report: Building Institutions for Markets*. Washington, D.C.

———. 2002b. *Better Measuring, Monitoring, and Managing for Development Results*. Washington, D.C.

———. 2003a. "Interim Guidelines for Poverty Reduction Support Credits." Washington, D.C.

———. 2003b. "Strategic Framework for IDA's Assistance to Africa: The Emerging Partnership Model." Africa Region, Washington, D.C.

———. 2003c. "Public Expenditure Management; Country Assessment and Action Plan for HIPCs Questionnaire: Benchmarks, Explanations, Standard Tables." Poverty Reduction and Economic Management (PREM) Public Sector Group, World Bank, and Fiscal Affairs Department, International Monetary Fund, Washington, D.C.

———. 2004a. "OP/BP 8.60 Development Policy Lending." Washington, D.C.

———. 2004b. "Good Practice Notes for Development Policy Lending." Operations Policy and Country Services (OPCS) Report, Washington, D.C.

———. 2004c. "Coordinating with the IMF on Development Policy Lending (DPL)—Guidance for Bank Staff." Washington, D.C.

———. 2004d. "Public Expenditure Management Country Assessment and Action Plan (AAP) Ghana." World Bank and IMF, Washington, D.C.

———. 2004e. "Evaluating Financial Management Risk in the Country Financial Accountability Assessments." Operations Policy and Country Services, Washington, D.C.

———. 2004f. "Conditionality Note." Electronic transmission to staff from James W. Adams. September 14. World Bank: Washington, D.C.

———. 2004g. "From Adjustment Lending to Development Policy Lending: An Update of World Bank Policy." Washington, D.C.